Religion in Higher Education

The politics of the multi-faith campus

SOPHIE GILLIAT-RAY

Department of Religious and Theological Studies
Cardiff University

Ashgate

Aldershot • Burlington USA • Singapore • Sydney

© Sophie Gilliat-Ray 2000

Published by
Ashgate Publishing Ltd
Gower House
Croft Road
Aldershot
Hants GU11 3HR
England

Ashgate Publishing Company
131 Main Street
Burlington, VT 05401-5600 USA

Ashgate website: http://www.ashgate.com

British Library Cataloguing in Publication Data
Gilliat-Ray, Sophie, 1969-
    Religion in higher education : the politics of the
    multi-faith campus. - (Ashgate new critical thinking in
    religious studies)
    1. College students - Religious life - Great Britain
    2. Education, Higher - Religious aspects 3. Religious
    pluralism - Great Britain
    I. Title
    378.1'9'041

Library of Congress Control Number: 00-134434

ISBN 0 7546 1562 6

Printed in Great Britain by
Antony Rowe, Chippenham, Wiltshire.

RELIGION IN HIGHER EDUCATION

'The multi-faith campus becomes a prism through which to view religion in modern British society: all the strains and stresses of a supposedly multi-faith society are present on campus in a generation which will be in positions of leadership as the 21st century gets underway.'

–Grace Davie, University of Exeter, UK

The place of religion in universities and institutes of higher education has become increasingly topical and contested in recent years, largely due to the growth of religious diversity on campus. Issues such as shared worship spaces, equal opportunities, and the management of inter-religious conflict, concern university administrators and students alike. Based on primary empirical research, this book indicates the need for clear guidelines on these issues and provides the data to inform policy-making.

Offering the first study of the practical and sociological implications of the multi-faith campus, this book provides a context for examining some of the dynamics of religious diversity in Britain more generally as well as providing a useful analysis for the wider international context. Key themes covered include: religion in institutions; inter-faith relations; the changing roles of religious professionals; secularisation and resacralisation; and religion, youth and identity. Exploring questions about why claims for the recognition of different religious identities are becoming so contested, to what extent religious activity should be regulated and monitored on campus, and how institutions are challenged in different ways by diversity, this book contributes both in method and conclusions to the debate about the provision of religious and spiritual care in public institutions in a multicultural society.

Religion in Higher Education will be essential reading for all those responsible for the practical management of campus life, as well as those interested in the sociology of religion and, more broadly, in contemporary religion in Britain.

ASHGATE NEW CRITICAL THINKING
IN RELIGIOUS STUDIES

The *Ashgate New Critical Thinking in Religious Studies* series aims to bring high quality research monograph publishing back into focus for authors, the international library market, and student, academic and research readers. Headed by an international editorial advisory board of acclaimed scholars spanning the breadth of religious studies, this new, open-ended monograph series presents cutting-edge, international research from established as well as exciting new authors in the field. With specialist focus, yet clear contextual presentation of contemporary research, this series aims to take research into important new directions and open the field to new critical debate within the discipline, into areas of related study, and in key topics for contemporary society.

Series Editorial Board:

Contents

List of Tables

List of Appendices

List of Abbreviations

BOSS	British Organisation of Sikh Students
CU	Christian Union
CVCP	Committee of Vice-Chancellors and Principals
FOSIS	Federation of Students Islamic Societies
HEFCE	Higher Education Funding Council for England
IUJF	Inter-University Jewish Federation
NHSF	National Hindu Students Forum
NJC	National Jewish Chaplaincy Board
NRM	New Religious Movement
NUS	National Union of Students
SCM	Student Christian Movement
UCCF	Universities and Colleges Christian Fellowship
UJS	Union of Jewish Students

Preface

Since the 1960s there has been a steady growth in the religious diversity of the United Kingdom. Christians remain the most significant community numerically and in terms of the history of Britain. But alongside them, and the long established Jewish community, there are now significant communities of other world faiths: Baha'is, Buddhists, Hindus, Jains, Muslims, Sikhs, Zoroastrians, as well as other smaller or less formal groupings.

Institutions of higher education reflect this increasing religious diversity in their student population and are perhaps even more diverse than the UK generally because of the large number of students of different faiths from overseas. This has prompted reflection by some institutions on the best ways to ensure good relationships between the faiths on campus. Staff working in these institutions have sought to address specific issues such as worship space, dietary needs, and timetabling which takes account of religious festivals. This book is based in part upon research carried out in 1998 that gathered information about how institutions are responding to these aspects of university life and provision. The aim was to facilitate sharing of good practice and to provide an opportunity to reflect on the implications of the multi-faith campus. However, I have also been concerned in this book to explore wider questions about religion in Britain's universities and the way in which a wide variety of institutions of higher education have responded to different religious identities over time. This study of religion in universities also enables readers to draw conclusions and make comparisons (and there are many) with other types of public institution, such as prisons or hospitals.

Accommodation to change is not a one-way process. While I explore how institutions of higher education have responded to religious diversity, I also consider the impact that universities and colleges of higher education – as one type of public institution – have on religious groups themselves. For example, there is evidence that the involvement of religious professionals from the other faith communities in public institutions, such as universities, is beginning to expand and shape their traditional roles and functions. Similarly, I argue that the identity of students from minority faith traditions becomes more strongly defined in relation to religion within the context of a university institution. This research also shows that the traditional roles of Christian chaplains serving in public institutions are beginning to change as a result of religious diversity (see also Furniss 1995; Beckford and Gilliat 1996).

This study of religion in higher education highlights some important questions and paradoxes about processes of secularisation, the meaning of the term 'secular' in public institutions, and how this concept relates to societies characterised by religious diversity. I discovered that there is a distinctive pattern of *de-secularisation* taking place on many university campuses, largely reflecting the prominence of religious identity in the lives of many young Muslims, Sikhs, Jews, and others. Similarly, the avowedly 'secular' principles that underpin many universities in fact conceal a multiplicity of different responses to religion *per se*, with attitudes ranging from the determinedly anti-religious to the distinctively 'multi-faith'. Some 'secular' institutions have actively sought to capitalise on the opportunities that stem from religious diversity, particularly with regard to the recruitment of students from overseas and from ethnic minority backgrounds. I found that the terms 'secular', 'secularist', 'secularism', and 'secularisation' need to be understood as terms encompassing a range of nuances and interpretations.

This book is based in part upon research that was commissioned by a small charitable organisation seeking to further good relations between different religious communities in Britain, the Inter Faith Network for the United Kingdom. During the 1990s, its staff noticed a rise in the number of enquiries coming from personnel (usually chaplains) in higher education. These questions often centred on the practicalities of belief and worship for students belonging to faiths other than the Christian. The Inter Faith Network responded as well as its limited resources permitted, especially in terms of practical advice. There was, however, one frequent question that it could not answer. Chaplains and other enquirers wanted to know how *other* institutions were meeting the religious and spiritual needs of staff and students of other faiths. At the time, there was simply no data available to answer this question.

I was first asked by the Inter Faith Network to undertake research towards the end of 1997, and by March 1998 the funding was in place for an intensive national study involving questionnaires, fieldwork, and interviews. Two project reports emerged from the study. The first was a very detailed and lengthy unpublished account of the practicalities of provision for the religious needs of students in higher education, while the second summarised the key findings of the longer report. The summary was published by the Department of Sociology at the University of Exeter, in association with the Inter Faith Network, in January 1999. Some of the material from the lengthier unpublished report is reflected here. However, this book makes a significant departure from the earlier reports in offering a much wider theoretical and historical discussion about religion in higher education, and by particularly considering the issues raised by the growing number of Muslims in British universities.

A successful research project often reflects the input and support of many different people and organisations. This study was no different, and it is only fitting that this much appreciated assistance and encouragement is acknowledged at the outset.

Thanks must firstly go to the funders of the research: to the Inter Faith Network, directly and through generous grants from the Spalding Trust, St Luke's College Foundation, Exeter, an individual donor, and the University of Exeter Research Committee. Without their generous sponsorship, this project would never have been undertaken. The support, advice, and involvement of Dr Harriet Crabtree, Deputy Director of the Inter Faith Network were especially appreciated.

Her subsequent comments on the first draft of this book were also most helpful. Thanks are also extended to Dr Grace Davie and Dr John Vincent, both from the Department of Sociology at the University of Exeter. They helped to facilitate the location of the project at Exeter, and to secure some internal funding for the research.

In the early stages of the project, valuable guidance was given from the project's Steering Group who offered regular and constructive feedback. They also gave comments on the final report. Members of the Steering Group, in alphabetical order, included: Revd Paul Brice (Chaplaincy/Higher Education, Board of Education, Church of England), Dr Harriet Crabtree (Deputy Director, Inter Faith Network), Dr Grace Davie (Senior Lecturer in Sociology, University of Exeter), Mr Rashid Siddiqui (Trustee of the Islamic Foundation, Leicester, and member of the chaplaincy at Leicester University), and Mr Indarjit Singh OBE (editor of the *Sikh Messenger*). I would particularly like to thank Dr Grace Davie for her assistance and support not only during the original research project, but also subsequently. Her helpful comments on the first draft of this book were much appreciated. Colleagues in the sociology of religion and those involved and interested in higher education and religious diversity also contributed by providing comments on the project questionnaire. Particular thanks go to Revd Gillian Cooke, Revd Giles Legood, Revd Alan Walker, and Professor Paul Weller. I have also benefited from on-going contact with Ms Helen Thorne, the Multicultural Awareness Project Development Officer at Kingston University. I am grateful to her for sharing her research findings about religious facilities and chaplaincies with me. Similarly, special thanks must also go to Professor James Beckford, not only for his helpful comments on the project's original questionnaire, but also on the first draft of the manuscript for this book. Thank you to you all.

An essential aspect of the project was the piloting of the questionnaire; a number of chaplains in higher education assisted in this. Thanks are therefore extended to Revd Dr Martin Eggleton from the University of Middlesex, Revd Karl Freeman from the University College of St Mark and St John in Plymouth, Revd Andrew Gorham from the University of Birmingham and Revd Jeremy Law from the University of Exeter.

Towards the end of the project, follow-up site visits were made to a number of different higher education institutions. Thanks are due to all those who made these visits so worthwhile, informative, interesting, and enjoyable. To protect the identity of the institutions surveyed, they are referred to anonymously in this book.

A number of national student organisations participated in the project; telephone interviews were conducted with representatives from the Student Christian Movement (SCM), the Universities and Colleges Christian Fellowship (UCCF), the National Hindu Students Forum (NHSF), the Union of Jewish Students (UJS), the Federation of Students Islamic Societies in the UK and Eire (FOSIS), and the British Organisation of Sikh Students (BOSS). The time and reflections of all those who were willing to be interviewed is much appreciated, as is their willingness to allow the material to be drawn upon in this book.

Similarly, thanks are due to representatives of other national and regional organisations who generously shared their time and experience during interview. It is a pleasure to record the contributions of Mr David Tupman, Policy Adviser from the Committee of Vice Chancellors and Principals, Rabbi Jonathan Dove from the National Jewish Chaplaincy Board, and Rabbi Deborah Myers-Weinstein from the Youth and Students Division of the Reform Synagogues of Great Britain.

The short report arising out of the research was the basis for the Archbishop of Canterbury's annual inter faith meeting at Lambeth Palace in April 1999. Thanks are extended not only to Dr Carey for his interest in the research, but also to the faith community leaders and representatives who offered many useful comments and reflections both on the day, and afterwards.

The project would not have been so successful had it not been for the many higher education chaplains across the UK who completed the project questionnaire. Sincere appreciation is extended to all those who shared their experiences, hopes, struggles and successes. Thank you. I am particularly grateful to those chaplains who later sought permission from their institutions for the reproduction of codes of practice and policies covering religion, found in the appendices.

I remain profoundly grateful to the Inter Faith Network for initiating the project upon which this book is based, although, as I have made clear, this text covers territory beyond that of the initial research. I alone take responsibility for any deficiencies, shortcomings, or lapses from the high standards set by the Network.

Finally, my greatest thanks are reserved for my husband, Dr Keith Ray, who has provided continual support, inspiration, advice and encouragement throughout the preparation of the book.

Sophie Gilliat-Ray
Cardiff University

In memory

of my Grandmother
Diana Mary Gilliat (1912-1999)

With much love and thanks for all the support of my own higher education

and

my Father-in-Law
William John Ray (1921-1994)

Whom I sadly never knew

Chapter 1

Introduction

Contemporary issues in religion and higher education

It is rare for higher education *and* religion in Britain's universities to constitute the leading items on Radio 4's prime time evening news on the same day. But on the 12th May 1999, the determination of the non-Labour parties to abolish tuition fees in Scottish Universities was being hotly debated on the first day of the new Scottish Parliament in Edinburgh. Further south, a chaplain from Cambridge University was being criticised by some and applauded by others for using 'God' as part of his e-mail address, in an effort to make the chaplaincy more accessible to students.[1]

Issues of religion in higher education hit the headlines in this way very rarely: more usually the religious and spiritual lives of academic staff and students go unnoticed, even within the universities themselves. The outbreak of disturbances between different religious groups on campuses does occasionally, however, subvert the normal lack of interest. There are two extremes here: on the one hand, a generalised apathy towards the religious identities contained within universities, and on the other, individual attempts by chaplains, and a determination by extremists from some religious groups, to become more visible. Between these extremes, there lies a more serious debate about the way in which institutions of higher education have responded to the increasing religious diversity of their populations. This is an issue that a variety of academic and student organisations have recently begun to take up, continuing a longer-standing debate within Church circles about the place of religion in universities. This debate is by no means confined to British universities either, and the question of how universities and chaplaincies in higher education can meet the religious and spiritual needs of students from different faith backgrounds is now high on the agenda in a number of other countries (Blundell 1999).

This book addresses a variety of issues, such as how institutional policies that have been adopted or are in development relate to student religious identity and cover such matters as respectful interaction between religious groups. Others include the provision of worship facilities, how religious dietary needs are accommodated, and timetabling which takes account of religious festivals. An important question that this book considers is the way in which chaplaincy arrangements have been developed in multi-faith contexts, and how pastoral care has been provided for students of different faiths. An additional area for exploration is how faith communities have developed national structures to meet the religious needs of their student members.

The information gathered about these practical issues not only enables patterns of provision to be identifiable, but also provides the basis for a much wider questioning of the place of religion in higher education, and religious diversity and institutional change more generally.[2] For example, to what extent do universities and colleges have a responsibility for the spiritual and religious welfare of students and staff, and how far should they go, if at all, to meet the needs of different groups? Does the responsibility for the religious welfare of students lie solely with religious communities? The importance of spiritual beliefs and practices to religious groups often contests the 'secular' foundations and assumptions of many institutions, while the specifically Christian foundations of some universities (particularly 'Church colleges') in Britain are challenged by the growth of religious diversity. An examination of religious issues in higher education also serves as a context for exploring questions about the religious identity of a new generation of young people in Britain today from a diversity of traditions. For instance, I have been especially interested in how young British Muslims have structured their participation in higher education.[3]

In recent decades, and particularly in the past ten years, religion in universities has only tended to capture public attention when it has been regarded as problematic. Some new religious movements have from time to time caused public consternation through their capacity to prey on more vulnerable students. Heated and occasionally violent confrontation between extremists from different religious groups has more than once led to the temporary and often media-saturated closure of institutions (Bora 1994:7). All this points to a serious question about the extent to which universities in Britain should regulate and control the religious activity of students and of outside religious organisations that recruit on campuses. Where does the responsibility of institutions begin and end?

In many ways, the issues and trends surrounding religion in universities mirror in microcosm similar questions about religion in Britain more generally. For example, as membership of and frequent attendance at many traditional Christian places of worship has declined in Britain, there has been a steady increase in religious activity in other places of worship, such as mosques, temples, and some charismatic churches.

> In the briefest of summaries, I would describe the major trends of the religious life of the British in the post-war period as a decline in popular involvement in the main Christian churches, a corresponding and related decline in the popularity of religious beliefs outside the churches, a small shift to the "right" in Protestantism, an increase in the popularity of non-Christian religions (explained largely by the arrival of significant bodies of immigrants), and a small but very interesting increase in the popularity and respectability of what were once deviant supernatural beliefs and practices (Bruce 1995:30).[4]

I would also add that members of many of Britain's other faith communities have become more articulate about their wish to participate in public life on their own terms – as religious minorities – and to have their interests adequately represented. A good example of this is to be found in recent and on-going campaigns by faith communities for the inclusion of a religious question in the 2001 Census, in order that the religious variable in discrimination and inequalities may be more clearly identifiable (Kundnani 1999).[5] Religion in public life generally, and, I would argue, in many universities more particularly, is 'leaving its assigned place in the private sphere [and has] thrust itself into the public arena of moral and political contestation' (Casanova 1994:3).

As we shall see, many of the wider patterns of religious change and activity in Britain are mirrored by a trend in higher education. The growth of religious activity among students of other faiths and the wish for a range of religious identities to be recognised by the institution is evident nationally and on a number of campuses.[6] So too is the decline in the number of students claiming a mainstream 'traditional' Christian affiliation (Kingston 1994; Worrall 1988), while the popularity of evangelical and Christian Union (CU) activities remains strong in many universities[7] (Worrall 1988). Religious life within universities is subject to the same patterns of change and increasing personal 'consumer' choice that are evident outside the boundaries of the institution.

Many of the issues surrounding religion in higher education also parallel current debates about religion in other public institutions, such as prisons and hospitals. For example, to what extent can (or should) institutional chaplaincies founded upon Christian principles accommodate religious professionals and advisers from other religious traditions (Forest Health 1993:3)? How are the roles of religious leaders, regardless of faith or denomination, changing in the face of increasing religious diversity? These questions are particularly pertinent in the case of universities (as well as hospitals) as institutions historically founded upon the traditions of the Christian church.

Research has already been carried out to examine how some public institutions in Britain have adapted to the new plurality of faiths in their midst. Examples of such research are examinations of the way local authorities have responded to Muslim needs (Nielsen 1992; Joly 1995), and the extent of religious provision for members of other faiths in prisons (Beckford and Gilliat 1998). This book takes particular account of the perspectives of chaplains in higher education, as the individuals to whom institutions and students tend to turn regarding religious issues. It also considers the perspectives of the organisations – religious, student-run, and academic – that are concerned with religion in universities. In describing how educational institutions are 'managing' religious diversity and responding to change, the study points to insights which have relevance to other kinds of public institution, both in terms of challenges and good practice. There are many manual-like books that offer prescriptions for how the practical needs of different faith groups should ideally be met in public institutions (see for example Sampson 1982). But few studies exist which explore in detail the wider consequences of, and implications posed by the multi-faith nature of public institutions, especially in a so-called 'secular' society.

All this amounts to an argument that religion in higher education throws up a number of wider practical and theoretical issues of interest to those with an interest in religion in contemporary Britain. A study of religion in a specific context, namely universities, and an examination of the way in which religion 'fits' into the life of British universities casts a new light on matters of secularisation, religious diversity, and religion in the public sphere.[8]

Over recent decades, there has been a tendency to approach the question of religion in higher education from the perspective of race and ethnicity (e.g. Acland and Modood 1998). However, the case for exploring the issues squarely from a religious dimension is particularly valid in the light of the fact that ethnic and religious minorities themselves often regard their religious identity as one of the most significant markers of self-definition. Reflecting on the strength of feeling in the Muslim community after the Rushdie affair, Paul Weller noted that

> by insisting that they do not want to be dealt with as an *"ethnic minority group"* or in terms of *"race relations"* considerations, and in demanding recognition primarily as a faith community, Muslims are posing fundamental questions to British society. In a cultural milieu where ethnicity, nationality, class, and fashion have been seen as the major determining factors of individual and corporate identity, for a group to define itself primarily in terms of religious identity represents a major break with the prevailing social ethos (Weller 1990:4).

There is evidence among the other religious communities in Britain, such as Hindus and Sikhs, that religion is similarly important for them as the basis of identity (Gerd Baumann 1996; Nesbitt 1998).

Martin Baumann's general observation of the way religion is sidelined in most policy and academic discussions is as applicable to higher education, as to many other arenas of debate.

> Most discussions about multiculturalism focus on "ethnicity". As a side effect, the recognition of religion and religious identity is marginalized or not considered, yet research shows that religion "still" plays a significant role in groups' relations among each other and the society at large (Baumann 1999:1).

There is some evidence that the significance of religious identity is starting to be recognised, generally, as well as specifically in relation to British universities. In *Race and Higher Education* (Acland and Modood 1998), it was clear that the debate is beginning to take a new direction. Whilst issues of access to higher education for ethnic minority groups remain important, several contributors to that volume pointed out that more attention now needs to be paid to the *quality of experience* that members of ethnic minority groups have whilst at university.

> We need to know people's expectations of [higher education]...and the appropriateness of support services, counselling, careers guidance, *religious provision....* (Acland and Azmi 1998:75, emphasis added).

The discussion can be taken further forward by beginning to answer such questions specifically in relation to religion and religious identity, and this is what I have set out to do in this book. I am especially mindful of the very real differences in the quality of student experience reported by graduates of different backgrounds. 'White students report having enjoyed their time at university and having received much easier access to academic and *pastoral* support compared to the experiences of ethnic minority students' (Acland and Modood 1998:169, emphasis added). My research uncovered numerous examples of structural discrimination against students from other faiths in some universities, limiting their access to pastoral and religious support.

One of the issues that is highlighted by this investigation of the willingness and the ability of universities to recognise the religious diversity of the student population is their capacity to manage change, and especially change wrought by religious diversity. My research has shown that

- Some universities have seen their changing constituency as a business opportunity, and diversity has provided scope for an expanded vision of their purpose and ability to recruit students.
- Discord is often expensive, directly (in terms of time and personnel needed to solve conflict) and indirectly, through the implications of a damaged reputation. Inter-religious conflict, and the regulation of religion on university campuses, has put some institutions' mechanisms of conflict and risk-management in the spotlight.
- The changing religious composition of universities has provided a challenge to the institutional identity of many universities. Some have deliberately marked themselves out as 'modern' in terms of their willingness to accommodate different religious groups and they have deliberately cultivated a new self-definition of themselves as part of a multicultural, multi-faith society.
- Conversely, some traditional universities have shown a marked complacency about provision for different faiths, and an unwillingness to break from the institutional traditions that characterised their foundation in the 19th century, or earlier.
- Finally, increasing numbers of students have led to a corresponding increase in the number of administrative staff required to manage the corporate life of institutions. The discussion of equal opportunities policies in Chapter 6 therefore becomes also an investigation of institutional efficiency. For some universities, comprehensive policies about religious issues embracing staff and students are regarded as part of a constellation of policies governing institutional life where up-to-date and ordered systems of management are perceived to be *de rigueur*.

This book is therefore not only a study of religious dynamics in universities, but it is also an examination of the relationship *between* religion and higher education.

The permutations of the relationship are varied; hostile, accommodating, indifferent, or embracing. But one of the conclusions that becomes evident is that most universities are far from being wholly 'secular' institutions. Even those founded without any reference to religion and which clearly and explicitly emphasise a 'secular' approach to university matters, still do so from a standpoint that is far from neutral on the place of religion in the institution.

To evaluate much of the data presented in this book about religion and higher education, a few basic points about the sociology of organisations and institutions in general may be helpful. To begin with, universities can be regarded as organisations in that they bring people together for the same shared purpose and objective: in this case, for academic scholarship and instruction. As institutions they involve more than just the people within them, but also the taken-for-granted and accepted procedures and norms that govern social life in a university. They are social entities, with distinct (though permeable) boundaries between who is 'in' and who is 'out'; there are distinctive criteria for identifying and recruiting members. Despite many shared objectives and the unifying *raison d'etre* of teaching and research, as organisations they require management, and a range of individuals to co-ordinate, control and structure roles and activities. Hence, universities as institutions involve a division of labour and the allocation of tasks and functions for different members. Finally, as organisations, universities have recognised patterns of decision-making and process (Jenkins 1996).

The corporate life of institutions of higher education is both formal and informal. It is formal in the sense that there exist established management, strategies, structures, and goals. At the same time corporate life is also informal in as much as there are norms and practices which define their habitual character, or 'how things are done round here'. Across the spectrum of different types of university, each one embodies a more or less shared 'institutional culture', distinguished in higher education (as opposed to other kinds of organisations) by a concern with issues such as learning methods, standards of assessment, funding, and so on. Each particular university will also have its own particular 'culture', and its own 'history, tradition, mission, momentum [and] inertia' (Brummett 1990:xvii). The way that universities in Britain respond to religious diversity will often be a reflection of these 'traditions' and 'inertias'. Certain stories, myths, rituals, celebrations, values, assumptions and codes will be distinctive to each particular institution. The institutional culture of each university will shape the way in which conflicts are managed, successes rewarded, and risks are managed.

Organisational theorists sometimes use the metaphor of an iceberg to understand the particular logic of how institutions 'tick' (Senior 1997:99). Above the surface of the water a relatively small mass of the total volume of ice will be identifiable procedures, management structures, documented goals, and visible strategies and services. Below the water, a much larger mass of the institutional 'iceberg' will be informal groupings, power politics and conflicts, distinctive and usually unwritten organisational and leadership systems, corporate values and attitudes, and so on. It is within these more covert aspects of institutional life that decisions are effectively made and values shaped, sometimes quite unconsciously.

Universities, like other institutions and organisations, are changing due to internal forces within higher education itself, and in response to external, socio-cultural changes in the wider society. However, the stability and maintenance of existing practices and norms needs to be carefully balanced with the need for change. When it comes to recognition of religious diversity, especially vis-à-vis other policy issues, some universities are charting a careful and strategic course. For example, the discussion of equal opportunities policies in Chapter 6 observes that some universities are cautious about including clauses on sexuality in their policies, for fear that their institutions might become off-putting to high fee-paying overseas students with conservative religious beliefs, particularly from Muslim countries (Neal 1998).

This book attempts to examine how the higher education sector in Britain has responded to change due to religious diversity by identifying some distinctive patterns of response. The main focus has necessarily been upon the visible, the documented, and the 'official', such as in equal opportunities policies covering religious identity and material provision or allowance for religion. However, from interview data, in some questionnaire responses, and from institutional policy documents sent to me by chaplains, it has been possible to deduce some of the unwritten, unspoken, assumptions that are powerful indicators of how universities view religion *per se* and have responded to changing religious trends. Hidden agendas are by definition difficult, if not impossible to research, but their more obvious outcomes and resulting patterns of inclusion or exclusion can be exposed. I have tried to explore these as much as the data gathered will allow.

Specialists in the sociology of organisations have pinpointed some distinctive indicators of the capacity of an organisation to accommodate change (Senior 1997). I have tried to apply these to my data, by looking, for example, at the ease with which structures facilitate change; the willingness of the organisation to give people autonomy and support them in their actions; the institution's view of experimentation in processes and practices; views of conflict; and the degree to which senior members of the organisation are open to change and/or new ideas coming from those beneath them in the hierarchy (Senior 1997:133). I will try to consider the way that universities as a generic group of institutions, or as representatives of particular 'types' (such as 'new' or Oxbridge), or individually, have been more or less willing to accommodate religious diversity. This consideration is largely practical, by examining such things as worship provision, but also ideological in terms of their ability to engage with and to embrace diversity in their corporate identity.

As well as stating what is within the remit of the book, it is important to be clear about what lies outside its scope. The discussion here does not consider in any depth wider debates about multiculturalism, ethnicity and ethnic minorities, the ideology of pluralism, or organisational theory. Readers with expertise in these fields will be able to apply their own insights to the data presented, and make their own connections and criticisms. I have however tried to use some of the analytical tools and concepts from these disciplines to describe and explain changing trends in the relationship between religion and universities.

Methodology of the study

There are a range of ways in which one might set about finding out how institutions of higher education have managed the changing religious diversity of the student population.   Within each institution, there are a variety of administrative officers, student union representatives, student service officers, as well as religious professionals who may all be able to supply valuable information about religious facilities and provision. In addition, there are a number of national organisations concerned with the religious welfare of students.

I employed a number of different strategies in order to gather data from as wide a range of sources as possible within the confines of a short five-month research project. Firstly, chaplains in higher education[9] were identified as the individuals who could best supply information – via a questionnaire – about their institution with regard to religious facilities and provisions. The organisation of religious facilities and provisions varies considerably across institutions but one key religious professional/chaplain was sought as a respondent for each institution. In particular, chaplains appointed as *chaplains to the institution* were sought; those who had official university or Church/denomination recognition or accreditation and who had the fullest pastoral role. The project was not primarily concerned with how *chaplaincies* were responding to the religious diversity of the student population, but how *institutions* were responding to the make-up of the student body in their recognition of religious issues and provision of religious facilities. Chaplains were simply identified as the best individuals to make a response, on behalf of their institutions, about the way in which provision was being made for students of different religious traditions.[10]

At the time of the research, there were 176 publicly funded higher education institutions in the UK, serving a student population of about 1.7 million (HEFCE 1997:v). On the basis of this information, one might expect there to have been 176 questionnaire recipients. However, many smaller institutions do not have a chaplaincy, and religious provision for students may amount to little more than publication of information about local places of worship. In other words, in such institutions there is no formally recognised serving 'chaplain'.

In contrast, the collegiate universities such as London, Oxford, Cambridge, and Durham, typically have a full-time chaplain assigned to each college or 'school'. For the purposes of my research each collegiate university college chaplain that could be formally identified received a questionnaire, swelling the number of recipients beyond 176, to 186. Questionnaire respondents were identified using a number of sources of information: *Crockford's Clerical Dictionary 1998/9*, *The Church of England Yearbook 1998*, university web sites, and the assistance of individuals from ecumenical chaplaincy networks such as the Churches Higher Education Liaison Group (CHELG). By the middle of June 1998, after a follow up reminder in May, a final response rate of 52 per cent had been achieved. This can be regarded as an acceptable response rate from which to draw valid conclusions, though it is nevertheless towards the lower end of average response rates for a postal questionnaire. The degree to which the different types of institution were represented in the database of recipients as a whole and the extent to which they were represented in the overall response rate is summarised in the table below.

Table 1.1 Response rates to questionnaire

Type of institution	Representation in database	% of overall responses
Collegiate university colleges	33%	30%
Church colleges	7%	7%
'New' universities	22%	29%
University of London colleges	4%	4%
'Old' universities	22%	26%
'Other' institutions (e.g. drama schools)	8%	3%
Total in database	186	Responses 97

The large majority of questions in the questionnaire were open-ended, and thus well-suited for analysis using the data analysis software package 'Idealist'.[11] Analysis of questions took very specific account of the different types of institution, such as 'new' universities, or 'Church colleges'. The responses to most questions were analysed by grouping together the answers from the different kinds of institution.

Though all higher education chaplaincies are likely to offer a wide range of ecumenical activities and contact with clergy and ministers from other Christian denominations, the large majority of senior chaplaincy posts in England and Wales are held by members of the Anglican Church. In Scotland most full-time senior chaplaincy posts are held by members of the Church of Scotland. Among the respondents to the questionnaire, there were five Methodists, one Baptist, two United Reformed Church ministers, and two Roman Catholics. In Wales and Scotland, responses from members of the Church in Wales (Anglican), the Scottish Episcopal Church (Anglican) and the Church of Scotland (Presbyterian) figured strongly. Overall however, responses from members of Churches other than the Church of England accounted for only 19 per cent of respondents.

From the outset of the research, the importance of making visits to particular institutions was clear. Fieldwork helps to contextualise data gathered from questionnaires and provides opportunities to explore issues in more depth. With limited funding and a tight schedule there was scope to do four case-study fieldwork visits. There were a number of different approaches that could have been used when it came to deciding which institutions would be selected for more detailed fieldwork study. One option would have been to choose sites with very different histories, such as a Church college, a new university, a university in Scotland, Wales or Northern Ireland, or universities founded upon explicitly and strictly interpreted 'secular' principles. Alternatively, I could have chosen to concentrate on institutions with very different kinds of student bodies across a diverse geographical area, perhaps combining a veterinary college, an Oxbridge college, or an institute of higher education. The decision about which institutions to visit could also have been determined by the extent to which particular religious issues figured in the life of the university/college, and hence the provision of facilities for students of different religious backgrounds. To some extent, the sites that were chosen combined each of these different approaches, and the resulting sites included two new universities in England, a new Scottish university, and an old pre-1992 university in England. The different institutions were located across a wide geographical area, and each, in different ways, was responding to, or being challenged by, the increasing religious diversity among their student bodies.

Each of the institutions approached with a view to a fieldwork visit agreed to co-operate with the research, and interviews were arranged with relevant personnel on site. There were a number of aims during each visit. The chaplain at each institution was interviewed about issues of particular concern at his or her university, and about more general issues of higher education and religious diversity. Wherever possible, other relevant university officers were also interviewed, such as Equal Opportunities officers, Student Services officers, and other religious advisers. The data gathered from these sites amplified questionnaire responses, and helped to illustrate in more detail particular issues of concern to the research.

As a way of further supplementing the information gathered from questionnaires, interviews were conducted with representatives of a number of student religious organisations. The interviews with the national umbrella organisations representing students of different faiths enabled important information to be channelled into the project's findings. Representatives of the Student Christian Movement, the Universities and Colleges Christian Fellowship, the National Hindu Students Forum, the Union of Jewish Students, the Federation of Students Islamic Societies, and the British Organisation of Sikh Students could offer an informed assessment about how the 'consumers' of higher education from different religious backgrounds perceived the adequacy with which institutions were responding to their needs.[12] Some of the data gathered from these interviews is reflected in Chapter 7.

To ensure that all faith groups with organisations concerned about students and higher education were given the opportunity to contribute to the project, the Inter Faith Network wrote to its extensive network of member organisations around the country at the start of the research. They were asked to supply information about relevant groups or individuals concerned with higher education within their faith community, particularly those that had not already been identified. Very few responses were received, but on the basis of this mailing, it was possible to be reasonably confident that all faith groups with organisations or individuals concerned for students, such as those listed above, had already been accurately detected.

It became clear at an early stage in the research that chaplaincy provision for Jewish students in Britain is very different from an organisational and structural point of view compared to the other main faith traditions. For this reason, it was necessary to make contact with, and interview representatives from a number of Jewish organisations. Approaches were thus made to the National Jewish Chaplaincy Board and the National Student Chaplain for the Reform Synagogues of Great Britain.[13]

As a further source of data, where chaplaincies had pages on their institution's web sites, these were accessed and examined.

Some readers will no doubt regard the overall reliance upon questionnaires and interviews as the sources of data for the research as methodologically suspect. There is some justification for arguing that important perspectives about the way institutions have responded to religious diversity will be missing in a study that does not include a more anthropological approach and greater reliance upon fieldwork. It could also be argued that students themselves should have been extensively surveyed. To these critics there are a number of responses. The primary aim of the research was the gathering of large amounts of factual data from which *overall patterns* of religious provision could be assessed. The nature of the information required from this study largely dictated the methods used, and as with most sociological research, budgetary and time considerations were also not insignificant. Furthermore, the focus of the research was very much upon the relationship between institutions and changing religious trends rather than upon student perceptions of religious provision in universities. This would be another, quite separate investigation. Necessary limitations aside however, this study is the first sociological examination of religious diversity in higher education in Britain, and it does not make any claims to be definitive. It is the first exploration of a subject that scholars from other academic backgrounds using different research techniques will no doubt undertake at some stage. Their work will hopefully develop the findings of this present study and compensate for its limitations.

A note about terminology

Frequent reference is made in the book to 'faith communities' or 'other faiths'. These terms are employed as a means of referring to members of the following religious faiths in Britain, namely: Baha'is, Buddhists, Hindus, Jains, Jews,

Muslims, Sikhs, and Zoroastrians.[14] The use of the term 'other faith' is contentious, but is perhaps the lesser of two unsatisfactory options compared to the notion 'non-Christian'. Both imply that 'other' faith traditions are a departure from a Christian 'norm' and suggest a default value to Christianity. The term 'ethnic religions' is also unsatisfactory since it allies ethnicity and religion too closely, making the term unsuitable for Muslims, or Buddhists, for example. My use of the phrase 'other faiths' is thus employed for want of a more appropriate term, and in no sense is my use underpinned by a normative assumption about the truth of Christianity. Deficiencies of language aside, it is important to be aware that while reference is made to various religious groups and communities, they are not monolithic entities. All major religious traditions are characterised by an internal diversity of language, regional origins and contexts, ethnicity, race, gender, age, class, and membership of different philosophical schools of thought. This makes the term 'faith community' difficult and often imprecise, in so far as it suggests a static and unified group of people sharing a common background.[15] However, for the purposes of this discussion, the term 'faith community' is used to describe a collection of individuals who share a common religious heritage and identity, though with different degrees of individual attachment and practice, and undercut by a range of sociological variables.

Those surveyed for the research were asked to comment upon the involvement of 'religious professionals and advisers' in higher education chaplaincies. This phrase, sometimes shortened to simply 'religious professionals', refers to members of other faith communities who are attached to institutional chaplaincies in higher education, either as full-time religious professionals in their own right (e.g. Rabbis, or Imams) or as knowledgeable volunteers or 'community leaders'. This latter phrase 'community leaders' describes individuals who, often for a variety of reasons, such as a distinguished education or extensive professional ties, have become 'representatives' for their faith community on a local or national level. They may not necessarily be *religious* professionals (i.e. salaried and trained to undertake specific duties), and their claims to 'represent' the community may be ill-founded. They are often men, belonging to the 'elder' generation, and they are often unaware of issues facing, for example, youth or women (see for example Reid and Burlet 1998).

It should not be implied from the use of the word 'campus' that I was only interested in single-site campus institutions. Underlying the study there was a keen awareness of the very different geographical layouts of each institution, and the fact that as institutions have grown, they have sometimes evolved onto numerous different sites. The word campus thus refers to the whole geographical estate of an institution.

Throughout the book, the terms 'secular', 'secularism', 'secularist', and 'secularisation' are employed, and it is the first and last of these words that are of particular significance here. They are multidimensional, and carry a range of interpretations: 'at the entrance to the field of secularization, there should always hang the sign "proceed at your own risk"' (Casanova 1994:12). There has been extensive discussion within the sociology of religion about the precise definitions of these words and the various meanings of the concepts associated with them. This is especially the case when it comes to the degree and the forms in which the 'process' of secularisation is said to have occurred. I do not engage with these debates in any depth here.[16] However, a brief explanation of how the terms have been used in this book may be helpful.

The original meaning of the Latin word secular was 'that which belongs to its own time', but later, 'secular' came to mean 'that which is concerned with the affairs of this world' (Russell 1998). The word is rarely used in neutral, descriptive way, since it is often used 'as a term of approval indicating that modern society has loosed itself from the thraldom of antiquated and irrational belief' (Russell 1998:12). Others regard the word 'secular' as capturing and describing all that is wrong with the world, caused by a perceived lack of moral standards or a dwindling sense of community. Mindful that the word is rarely used in a value-free sense, I use the word 'secular' to mean the absence of things 'religious' or pertaining to religion. Many universities, for example, describe themselves as 'secular'. As we shall see, the way this is interpreted differs enormously between institutions, but in a strict sense, it implies that the academic assumptions, business, and life-world of the university are conducted without reference, reliance, or favour upon religion or religious matters. It suggests that employees will be appointed to, or paid for by the institution, without reference to their religious identity or role. That is to say, no chaplain or other religious professional will be appointed because of their religious affiliation, or in order to fulfil a specific religious function. It might also be assumed that a 'secular' university would not allocate *any* part of its finances to religious provision or the spiritual or religious support of students or staff, though it may officially tolerate a Church (or other faith community) presence. Equally, a 'secular' university would, presumably, be unlikely to provide or maintain, from its own funds, a purpose-built place of worship, chaplaincy, or chapel, on land owned by the institution. The ritual or ceremonial life of a 'secular' university could be assumed never to feature any explicitly religious ceremonies, nor would there be any religious presence or input to academic congregations.

The term 'secularism' quite simply refers to the ideological perspective and normative assumption that matters of state, education, morals, or politics should be independent of religion, and an individual who subscribed to this stance could be described as a 'secularist'. In so far as most universities in Britain have, for example, more or less abolished religious tests for academic appointments,[17] and Christianity and the established Churches have been gradually 'eased out' of many aspects of academic life, so it is possible to assert that higher education in Britain has been subject to the ideological forces of 'secularism'. I would add that a secularist perspective that is also demonstrably or explicitly *hostile* to religion, and goes beyond simply the separation of religion from worldly or 'profane' matters, should be more accurately regarded as *anti-religious,* or even perhaps a form of secular 'fundamentalism'.

The meaning of the word 'secularisation' – the process whereby religion is regarded as having gradually less social significance for individuals and collectivities – is more contentious and a lengthy discussion of the on-going debates surrounding this topic would be an unnecessary distraction at this point. I agree with Casanova that

> what passes for a single theory of secularization is actually made up of three very different, uneven, and unintegrated propositions: secularization as differentiation of the secular spheres from religious institutions or norms, secularization as decline of religious beliefs and practices, and secularization as marginalization of religion to a privatised sphere (Casanova 1994:211).

The following chapter outlines the way in which Christianity and the established Churches have had less and less influence upon academic assumptions and lifestyles. Though some of the 'Church' colleges retain close connections, the university system in Britain has largely developed its own autonomy from religious institutions. As a result it is possible to claim 'the secularisation of the academy'.[18] Higher education is no longer legitimated by the traditions of Christianity or the established Churches, and universities that have 'secularised' or undergone a process of 'secularisation' have been gradually less influenced by the authority or worldview of religious organisations.

However, in the following chapters of this book I will be suggesting that although higher education in Britain has been subject to 'secularisation' as described by Casanova above, this has not led to the creation of entirely secular universities. The collegiate university colleges and Church institutions are explicit about their on-going religious connections and histories (if occasionally, only 'symbolic'), but a thorough scrutiny of the so-called 'secular' universities uncovers a wide range of different responses to, and involvement with, religion. Few can be accurately described as *wholly* secular, according to the definition I have offered above.

I investigated a wide spectrum of higher education institutions: Oxbridge/collegiate university colleges,[19] new universities,[20] 'old universities',[21] Church colleges,[22] and other degree-awarding institutes of higher education.[23] In most instances, the collective term 'institutions of higher education' has been used to cover this wide variety in the different types of institution. Occasionally, and purely on the grounds of stylistic preference, the word 'university' has been employed as a generic term to describe and encompass all higher education institutions. The sheer diversity between institutions – in terms of departments, styles, norms, and modes of thinking – in some senses makes it difficult even to group together the various types of institution into generic categories, such as 'old' or 'new' universities. However, these categories have the virtue of bringing together, if only for the sake of analysis, institutions with broadly similar origins. The future diversity cross-cutting these categories remains as yet unknown.

Towards the end of this book, I suggest how the different types of universities have responded to religious diversity, as generic groups. For example,

I outline how the collegiate universities tend to represent an explicit, establishment Christianity and its privileges. Civic universities as a generic group tend to represent the secular hegemony, though with some concessions to religion on their own terms. The new universities have often (but not in all cases) been more willing to engage with the multi-faith society and student body in their midst, through an inclusive 'secular' approach where religious and non-religious voices can be heard. There are, however, important divergences from the general patterns I have identified, and some institutions do not conform to any distinctive typology. In this situation, their deviations from normative patterns become interesting in themselves, and where possible I have tried to discuss interesting examples. Readers familiar with patterns of religious provision or policy at a particular type of university should not be dismissive of my findings if their institution happens to represent the interesting departure from the norm! As Philip Hammond notes in his study of campus ministry in the United States, any sociological study which endeavours to describe and evaluate generic patterns, particularly in a study of religion on campus rather than campus ministers themselves, will not capture the experience of each and every chaplain or institution in higher education (Hammond 1966:xiv).

The scope of the research was institutional with the staff working in universities also being an important part of the study. Issues of equal opportunity, worship facilities, and dietary requirements can be as pertinent for staff, as for the more transient population of students. This is especially so in view of the increasing management of universities and the growing numbers of administrative staff that have necessarily paralleled the rise in student numbers. Matters relating to religious discrimination and equal opportunities are perhaps particularly pressing for staff. At one Midlands university, for example, a Jewish applicant for a part-time academic post was forced to withdraw his application when the institution refused to re-schedule an interview due to be held on Yom Kippur, the Day of Atonement.[24] Examples of such insensitivity and lack of accommodation to religious diversity and sensitivities continue to occur, despite the existence of overt policies to combat them.

Structure of the book

This chapter has outlined the context and methods of the research, and the range of questions that emerge from a study of religion in higher education. The following chapter traces the way in which religion has hitherto figured in the life of UK universities, from 1945 until the present day. This is the first comprehensive published survey of such a history to date. Inevitably, the chapter is largely an account of Christian activity, and of the emergence of chaplaincies. However, I also chart the way in which the issues of religious diversity have become more pertinent, not only for faith communities, but also for institutions of higher education and national academic bodies themselves. The chapter further indicates that questions related to universities and religious identity are becoming increasingly prominent.

Chapter 3, 'University Faith Communities: Diversity, Identity and Rights' explores in more depth the growth in the number of students from different faiths, and the particular role that religion plays in shaping the identifications of a new generation of young British Hindus, Muslims, Sikhs, and others in higher education. I explore the way in which the assumptions of some sociologists of religion, especially in relation to secularisation, are challenged by the religious trends observable in universities. The chapter also explores the particular dynamics of religion in institutions, rather than in localised communities. For example, the recognition of religious identity within universities has become a contentious issue, especially where students have demanded certain rights based on religious claims. The very fact that the issues are so contested makes them interesting subjects for academic discussion. These expectations of recognition and religious provision are part of much wider sociological processes, such as the increasing politicisation of lifestyle politics and identity assertion.

Chapter 4, 'Chaplaincies: Organisation, Funding and Staffing' examines issues such as the staffing of chaplaincies, the accreditation and recognition of religion on campus, and the 'mechanics' of the organisation of religion in universities. A central concern is the organisational and political question of where financial resources for religious activity come from, and how these resources are utilised. Some structural and financial inequalities surrounding religion in higher education become strikingly apparent. The chapter also explores the participation of religious professionals and volunteers from other faith communities. It makes the case that, as they have come into increasing contact with Christian chaplains and public institutions, the roles of some religious professionals are beginning to adapt and change. In particular, I identify a process that I term 'approximation' as central to the accommodation of change. Christian chaplains have likewise not been immune to change, and I also consider how chaplaincy roles are being re-shaped in modern institutions.

Chapter 5, 'Meeting Student Needs' examines a range of examples of how institutions are taking account of religious diversity, such as meeting different religious dietary needs, and accommodating the need for students who wish to be housed in single-sex halls of residence on religious grounds. Those with a practical interest in these issues will find many examples of good practice. The chapter also explores some of the ways in which institutions 'make space' for religion by providing chaplaincy centres and prayer rooms, and also considers some of the thorny issues surrounding the sharing of worship areas by different faith groups. Many of the questions explored in this chapter are relevant to other public institutions where members of different faith communities may necessarily need to share the same facilities.

Chapter 6 addresses issues related to the corporate life and the 'public face' of institutions, such as academic and religious ceremonies, and equal opportunities policies. The explicit privilege accorded to Christianity, based on historical traditions, becomes clearly evident in the ceremonial life of many ancient universities, whilst at the other extreme, some secular universities celebrate their diversity through religious ceremonies at key moments in institutional history. The chapter also surveys the extent to which institutions have included a religious dimension to their institutional equal opportunities policies. This survey shows that there is a huge variety in the degree to which universities 'recognise' the religious identities of staff and students. The inclusion (or not) of policies covering religion masks a range of interest group power struggles and public relations exercises.

Chapter 7, 'Student Voices' examines questions of religion in higher education from the perspective of the national student religious organisations, and the main Jewish student chaplaincy bodies. This not only provides a student/consumer perspective on the extent to which institutions are meeting the religious needs of students, but also identifies some of the organisations that are emerging within the different traditions in Britain concerned with youth and student issues. The chapter closes with a critical evaluation of these organisations, comparing and contrasting their aims and objectives, and locating them within a wider discussion of youth and religious movements.

The final chapter, 'Religion in Higher Education and Public Life: Some Conclusions' reflects more generally on the research findings by highlighting the way in which religious matters have become more pertinent to many universities. I trace the patterns of secularisation and de-secularisation, and argue that the impact of the latter is in certain aspects outweighing the influence of the former. Based upon discussions in organisational studies and theory, the chapter also points to the various levels at which change is necessary for universities to effectively respond to diversity. This discussion is equally applicable to other types of public institution. The chapter closes by exploring how the traditions and underpinning principles of many British universities can be reconciled with the needs of, and the issues raised by students of different faiths. I argue that universities should become more responsive to the religious diversity of the student population.

Notes

1   This story also appeared the same day as 'God's e-mail address lands chaplain in row', in the *Guardian,* 12/5/99.

2   Some of these issues have been discussed by Paul Weller (1992a; 1992b) and his work was significant in helping to shape the direction of the research upon which this book is based.

3   My particular interest in the participation of Muslims in British universities was not a feature of the original research for the Inter Faith Network. It is an area I have developed in a number of places for this book as part of a longer academic interest in Islam in Britain.

4   Jenkins (1999) is highly critical of Bruce and other sociologists of religion who
        use statistics derived from Gallup, British Social Attitude etc. to measure religious
        change. Among other things, he suggests that their approach leaves unexamined
        'points of possible interest that do not fit in' (p.30), fails to define what
        'belonging' to a religion/church might mean, and ignores the 'complex self-
        definition of each institution (p.30). While I have much sympathy for Jenkins'
        more anthropological approach, nevertheless, statistics and survey findings about
        religious practice or belief can be regarded as just one dimension of a much wider
        'toolkit' for discerning patterns of change.

5   The recognition (or not) of community and religious identities by public
        authorities is nevertheless highly political. Readers are directed to Modood and
        Werbner (1997) for a more detailed discussion of this matter.

6   Evidence for the growth in the number of students active in Jewish student
        religious organisations is given by Webber (1993). He refers to an article in the
        Jewish Chronicle (21st March 1952) which gives a figure of 1500 Jewish student
        members of the IUJF (the predecessor of the UJS). He then refers to a UJS
        reported membership of approximately 4500 in 1993; my interviewee from the
        UJS in July 1998 gave a figure of approximately 12,000 members. Jacobson
        (1998) refers to the fact that 'Islamic societies are highly active in many colleges
        and universities' (p.54). An interviewee from the National Hindu Students Forum
        reported two local campus societies ('chapters') in existence in 1991, but over 45
        by 1998. From just a 'handful' of Sikh organisations on campuses in the early
        1990s, BOSS now reports over 50 (1998).

7   In her special report on religion in the UK for the *Guardian* (28th September 1999,
        'God: the remix') by Charlotte Raven, she writes of 'reading the news last week
        that student Christian unions are the fastest growing societies in colleges across
        the country...', but unfortunately fails to cite the precise source for her claim.

8   The provision of higher education for Roman Catholics formed the basis of
        McClelland's study of Catholics in England between 1830-1903. The problem of
        their full involvement in public life at that time 'can be seen in microcosm in the
        fight for the provision of higher education and in the internal tensions and turmoil
        to which it gave rise' (McClelland 1973:preface). My purpose in drawing
        attention to this fact is so readers might be aware that in some senses, Roman
        Catholics might be considered the first religious 'minority' group to contest
        established structures and fight for recognition in higher education.

9   Defined as those serving in institutions receiving funding from the HEFCE
        (Higher Education Funding Council for England), the HEFCW (Higher Education
        Funding Council for Wales) and the SHEFC (Scottish Higher Education Funding
        Council). The HEFCE advises the Department of Education, Northern Ireland
        on the two universities in Northern Ireland.

10   Questionnaire recipients were strongly encouraged to consult with all the religious
        professionals and volunteers associated with the chaplaincy in order to complete
        the questionnaire. Ideally, a longer study employing methodological triangulation
        would have surveyed each member of the chaplaincy individually to ascertain
        different perspectives on religious provision.

11   'Idealist' (produced by Bekon) allows an unlimited amount of textual data to be
        entered into each field. The programme facilitates analysis by making it possible

to examine all the responses to a particular question, and comparing answers to different questions.

12   The Student Christian Movement and the Universities and Colleges Christian Fellowship are the only non-denominational national student bodies representing Christians, and both serve as an 'umbrella' group in much the same way as the other student religious organisations. It was methodologically difficult to justify interviewing only one of these organisations, hence the inclusion of both in the study.

13   See Appendix 7 for more information about the work of these organisations.

14   Since the publication of *Religions in the UK: a Multi-Faith Directory*, (University of Derby and the Inter Faith Network for the UK, second edition, 1997), these faiths have come to be widely regarded as the main religious communities in Britain, along with the Christian community.

15   For an excellent discussion of this term 'community' (and other concepts) in relation to different faith traditions in Britain, see Gerd Baumann (1996).

16   For a useful short overview of the discussion and theorising about the term 'secularisation', see Dobbelaere, K. (1998). For a longer explanation see Casanova (1994), part 1, chapter 1.

17   The exception being Church colleges which normally state that senior appointments should reflect the religious identity of the institution.

18   This is the title of a book edited by two American scholars. See Marsden G.M. and Longfield B.J. (1992).

19   This category included the universities of Oxford, Cambridge and Durham. The constituent institutions that comprise London University were analysed as a separate category.

20   Those that gained university status in 1992 or since.

21   This category includes all those universities (sometimes also known as the civic or 'redbrick' universities) founded before 1992. There were, however, two distinctive phases of development of the so-called 'old' universities; around the late 19th century and early 20th century, and then much later in the 1960s and early 1970s. See chapter 2 for a brief description of the history of higher education in the UK.

22   Those which were founded by a Church or denomination and have retained their religious identity.

23   This includes institutions such as veterinary colleges, and institutions awarding degrees in performing or visual arts.

24   This information was supplied to me after the initial research project was completed. It was documented by a chaplain at a university in the Midlands as part of his efforts to see religious needs and issues incorporated into the institution's equal opportunities policy.

Chapter 2

Religion in Higher Education in Britain Since 1945

Higher education institutions – past and present

Universities have not only had to contend with growing religious diversity among their members, but they have also witnessed an unprecedented overall growth in numbers. All public institutions go through phases of intense and often cyclical political and media debate; as hospital waiting lists leave the news agenda, overcrowding in penal establishments replaces it. As noted in Chapter 1, university tuition fees, and their potential abolition in Scottish institutions, was headline news in 1999. All public institutions that have grown up around the welfare state have been subject to scrutiny of their performance, efficiency, and value. Universities have not escaped this new culture of assessment, accountability and auditing. The overall consequences for higher education have been massive upheavals in the internal processes of institutions themselves, and a massive upward leap in the numbers of students. The increasing numbers of students from different faith communities is just one dimension of a changing sociological base.

The origins of today's institutions of higher education are varied. Some of the earliest universities were founded upon monastic traditions where education took place in a tight-knit community setting (Legood 1999:132). The origins of today's university system can be traced back to the medieval Christian Church (University of Oxford, 1264; University of Cambridge 1284); and, later, St Andrews (1411); Glasgow (1451); Aberdeen (1495); Edinburgh (1583) and, Trinity College Dublin (1591).[1] What might be called the 'classical' or 'ancient' universities grew up around the patronage of the Church, and all activities could be subsumed beneath a 'sacred canopy' of taken-for-granted belief in God and a sense of common community and worship (Jenkins 1988:242). The extent to which the Established Church formed the basis of academic and community life in higher education is evident from the fact that, for example, at Oxford in 1850, all

> heads of house except one were in the Anglican ministry; virtually all tutors were clergymen; and about 80 per cent of undergraduates were intending to pursue a clerical career. Students had to subscribe to the Thirty-Nine Articles of the Church of England on admission to the university; they took an obligatory test in Greek New Testament and attended compulsory college chapel (Bebbington 1992:259).

The Established Church dominance by definition excluded Dissenters, Jews, Roman Catholics, and those unable to subscribe to the Thirty-Nine Articles, and throughout the first half of the 19th century there was considerable criticism of the religious exclusiveness of Oxford and Cambridge in both the popular press, and Parliament (Garland 1996). It was partly for this reason that the Catholic University was formed in Dublin in 1851, by John Henry Newman. Public pressure eventually led to the passing of two bills in 1852 and 1854 requiring reforms at Oxford and Cambridge, and these included access to students who were not members of the Established Church. But it was not until 1871 that religious tests were finally abolished at Oxbridge.

During the Victorian period there was an expansion in the university system with the founding of the civic and federal universities, such as Durham (1832), Aberystwyth (1872), Cardiff (1883), University College, London (1827)[2] and Liverpool (1881). Many of these civic, redbrick universities were founded on private, locally based sources of finance generated by industry, some being especially associated with food (Cadbury in Birmingham, Tate & Lyle in Liverpool, etc.) and tobacco (Bristol)![3] Several represented non-Conformist challenge to the existing order and were 'founded in opposition to the control exercised by the Established Church over higher education in the early nineteenth century' (Thom 1987:8). None came under any general ecclesiastical censure.

The religious exclusiveness of higher education began to wither further in the mid-nineteenth century due to a rising tide of Nonconformist pressure, activity by the Liberation Society (a pressure group aiming for the disestablishment of the Church of England[4]), and a liberal tradition within Anglicanism. This was furthered by W.E. Gladstone, Member of Parliament for the University of Oxford from 1847-1865, and later Prime Minister from 1868. He steered a bill through the House of Commons making religious testing at Oxford optional, and by 1871, all university tests were abolished except those relating to clerical fellowships in colleges (Bebbington 1992). The state was a 'powerful engine of secularization' (Bebbington 1992:265) when religious testing was later abolished at the Scottish universities, and at Durham. Roman Catholic responses to the abolition of testing were, however, mixed. The editor of *The Month* wrote in July 1885 that 'the abolition of tests, the admission of all forms of Dissent, Judaism, Paganism, tend to establish that sort of truce which men are almost compelled to make who differ in first principles...there is a common consent to exclude religion from their life more and more' (Fr Richard Clarke, *The Month,* July 1885, cited in McClelland 1973:355). He warned that a decline in morals was the inevitable outcome. It was not until 1895 that Pope Leo XIII permitted Catholic students to attend Oxbridge, and then only so long as there was a resident Catholic Chaplain who would give compulsory teaching in Catholic philosophy and Church history (Committee for Higher Education of the Catholic Bishops' Conference of England and Wales 1997).

Gradually, with the professionalisation of the clerical profession and the emergence of theological colleges for ministerial training (Russell 1980), university degrees were less interwoven with Christian values, and the staff, students and curriculum in the ancient universities displayed fewer Church or Christian connections. By the close of the 19th century, as now, the sustained strength of religion lay outside formal structures and statutes, and more within student-run associations and groups.

Since the early 1900s, wider social forces have largely determined the fate of religion in the universities. For example, as the state became the paymaster of higher education through the Universities Grants Committee, the Churches became gradually more irrelevant and marginalised in the structures of university life and administration. Advances in science and technology overshadowed the teaching of academic theology which itself became less concerned with ministerial formation for ordination. Religious practice by students gradually declined.[5]

Following the growth of higher education institutions in the Victorian period, the next most significant expansion of the university system came following the publication of the Robbins Report in 1963. The report recommended that not only should the number of university places be increased, but that new institutions should also be founded to accommodate the planned increase in the number of students. This led to the establishment of 18 new 'green field' universities, such as York (1963), Kent (1964), and Lancaster (1964). Around the same period, a number of Colleges of Technology were upgraded to university status and these included institutions such as Aston (1966), Salford (1967) and Surrey (1966). It was during this period of the 1960s that higher education ceased to be an experience for a privileged minority, and assumptions about entrants to university as being white, middle class, 18-20 years old, began to be questioned. The number of university students grew from 200,000 in 1968, to 360,000 in 1991 (HEFCE 1994:1).

The 1960s saw the establishment of what were known as 'polytechnics'. From their foundation in the mid-1960s up until 1991, there was an exceptional growth in the number of students attending the 'polys'. In 1969 there were 60,000 polytechnic students, but by 1991 the number had risen to 370,000 (HEFCE 1994:2). The polytechnics provided an alternative to the universities, attracting students wishing to pursue more vocational degree courses. Polytechnics offered diversity of access, flexible learning, strong links to local industry and business, and they were intended to complement existing university provision. However, the separate funding and administration of universities and polytechnics came to an end with the passing of the Further and Higher Education Act in 1992. This Act abolished the 'binary-line' separating the two different types of institution, and brought about a unitary system for higher education based on the creation of Higher Education Funding Councils for England, Scotland and Wales and the Northern Ireland Higher Education Council. All the former polytechnics are now universities.

Universities are self-governing institutions, and in most cases are established by Act of Parliament or Royal Charter. As autonomous institutions with academic freedom, they are responsible for their own curricula, student admissions, academic appointments, and the awarding of their own degrees. In England, ultimate responsibility for higher education rests with the Secretary of State for Education and Employment, and with the Secretaries of State in Wales, Scotland and Ireland. The Government is advised about higher education policy by the Higher Education Funding Councils for England, Wales and Scotland, and by the Northern Ireland Higher Education Council.

Some universities and colleges were founded with a link to the Church, others on a 'secular' basis. A number were developed as institutions for specific education in a particular discipline, such as teacher training, or agriculture. Many institutions can trace their roots back to religious origins, but the mergers and amalgamations that have taken place during their history have weakened the Church connections, and in some cases these are all but forgotten (Turner 1996b). On the other hand, some of the colleges and universities from which information was sought for this book have maintained their identity as distinctively Christian places of learning with an ethos based upon Church traditions.

The history of many institutions of higher education is often long and complex.[6] For example, the religious origins of King's College, London, contrast with the explicitly secular, non-denominational foundations of University College, London (Turner 1996b). King's appointed a chaplain and built a chapel as a direct response to what it perceived as 'the godless institution of Gower Street' (Legood 1999:133). The University of Wales, Lampeter, was originally founded in the early nineteenth century as a theological college for Welsh ordinands, only becoming part of the University of Wales in 1971. Religion, and more precisely Christian theology, is at the core of Lampeter's history and traditions, but it is no longer an explicitly religious foundation. I found that different institutional histories to some degree influence the way in which individual institutions respond to increasing religious diversity.

A thorough reading of any current issue of the *Times Higher Education Supplement* will point to a number of current debates in universities and colleges of higher education. This book is not the place for any detailed discussion of the major changes that have taken place in government policy over the past decade, nor is it the place to provide a detailed analysis of how these have affected institutions themselves. However, the significance of the findings and discussion in this book will perhaps be a little clearer following a brief overview of some of the key issues within the world of higher education today.

Under both the previous and present Governments, there has been a strong concern to avoid youth unemployment and the depressing image created by young people out of work. One consequence of this debate has been a recent and dramatic expansion of higher and further education. This expansion has created many more university places, and institutions have been rewarded for filling those places and meeting targets. The process has not always been adequately resourced, and rapid expansion has also led to concerns about 'dumbing down', and a sacrifice of quality for quantity. In many ways the issues today are not new. Instead of allowing higher education to expand organically in the 1960s, the post-Robbins era led to a similar rapid expansion. There was as much a concern *then* about the creation of new 'green field' universities such as Warwick, as there is *now* about the proliferation of some courses offered in today's 'new' universities.

During 1997/8, many debates in higher education circles centred on the report of the National Committee of Inquiry into Higher Education, chaired by Sir Ron Dearing. This report outlined some of the major priorities and challenges in higher education for the next two decades. Combined with new Government policy, some of the changes and challenges include wider participation in higher education by under-represented groups, lifelong approaches to learning, better institutional response to student needs, the introduction of tuition fees and the scrapping of maintenance grants, and funding of continued higher education expansion. Whatever the impact of the finer details of the Dearing Report, or Government policy about higher education, Britain's institutions of higher education are facing an on-going period of upheaval in the face of limited funding and scarce resources. Universities are characterised by an 'audit' mentality as a result of pressure from numerous quarters to justify and account for every facet of their expenditure and activity.

Students today

The experience of being a student in higher education has changed in recent years. Fear of debt, for example, means that it is increasingly normal for full-time students to be in part-time employment during the course of their studies.[7] One consequence is that fewer students now have much time for extra-curricular sporting, religious, cultural, and even academic activities. A former chaplain at Manchester University commented, 'it all went wrong during the '80s. Education is no longer about developing the individual or building a person, it's about finding a job, it's become part of the economic machine' (Fern 1997). His view might be contested, but it is not unusual.

University life-styles have also changed over the course of time. Newman's 'idea of the university' in which shared cultural, social, religious, and sporting exchanges were an integral part of community life, has given way to new forms of campus interaction.[8] Many larger institutions now operate on multi-site campuses, and there may be limited contact between students on different parts of the site. Limited accommodation in the face of growing student numbers means that fewer students can choose to live in institutional accommodation. The idea of residence and study going hand in hand has given way to new student lifestyles, with increasing pressure upon students to take up paid employment during their higher education careers. The sense of community within institutions is breaking down as student numbers continue to rise under the pressure of market-driven learning. Religious activity and chaplaincy is perhaps one of the few areas of student life that can stem the tide of an increasingly fragmented campus. Chaplaincies are frequently one of the most sensitive parts of institutions, alert to some of the consequences of the sense of fragmentation and the decline of collegiality (Riem 1998).

Today's students are in institutions under many pressures, and where the growth of communications has enlarged the confines of the campus (e.g. through distance learning and Internet-based courses). Winning resources and surviving in the marketplace have become paramount, and the connection between students and staff more distant. Universities are becoming increasingly fragmented, fractured, and differentiated; more aspects of university life are measured and audited, leaving little time for discussion about the *raison d'etre* of the institution as a whole.

From time to time, serious engagement and reflection about the nature and purpose of universities occurs. At a colloquium held in Oxford in 1996, academics such as Zygmunt Bauman and Peter Scott, met with other scholars who shared their concern for the wider purpose of higher education.[9] Among the various perspectives to emerge was a concern that universities should return to a more holistic and broader based approach to their function.

> The university's role in the transmission of up-to-date knowledge is no longer an exclusive one and in the era of advanced communication technologies there are plenty of other ways readily available in which people learn 'how' to do things; but there is a powerful case opening up for universities to concentrate upon the entire life course and to act as a resource for facilitating personal and social development, the exploration of ways of living (Smith and Webster 1997:9).

Other contributors to the colloquium emphasised the plurality of backgrounds – class, religious, ethnic, life experience, family – that students bring with them, and the opportunities to learn from different talents and experiences outside the formal curriculum. 'What is now spoken and often thought of as "extra-curricular" must come to be seen and attended to as the real heart of university life and the main justification of the university's existence' (Kumar 1997:29). Such calls clearly embrace religious activity, as well as sporting, social, or political involvement. Implicit are the opportunities for inter religious exploration.

The emergence of higher education chaplaincies

Religious diversity in British higher education on any significant scale did not occur until the late 1980s and 1990s. It is inevitable that an historical survey of religion in Britain's universities prior to these decades is predominately a history of the influence and involvement of the Christian Churches, and particularly a history of the emergence of higher education chaplaincies. Of course, both prior to, and after 1945, there was some religious diversity among the British student population, but most of the Muslims, Hindus, Sikhs or members of other faiths in higher education were predominantly from overseas and their numbers were relatively small. The Jewish community in Britain, from the middle part of the 20th century onwards, became increasingly active in establishing religious and educational welfare support for Jewish students, especially through the Hillel Foundation and the development of chaplaincy services. But the number of Jewish students in British universities during this time was still relatively small (Webber 1993).

The following account of religion in higher education will begin from the post World War II period. This of course ignores the traditions of chaplaincy prior to 1945, especially in Church colleges and the ancient universities, and readers are advised to consult other texts in the field of ecclesiastical and educational history for further information about this work (see Legood 1999:133). However, it was from 1945 onwards that the Churches began to make a significant investment in terms of resources and personnel into a much wider range of institutions, hence the utility of starting with this date.

Religion, and Christianity in particular, has been at the core of a number of Britain's universities from their earliest foundation. Higher education chaplaincy has evolved over the course of time in order to accommodate to changes in both society and the world of higher education itself. Though this book is not about chaplaincy *per se* any clear understanding of how institutions have responded to religious diversity must necessarily take into account the sociological and professional changes that have taken place in higher education ministry. A brief history and discussion of chaplaincy in universities is as good a place as any to begin a more general discussion about religion in higher education.

One of the most useful texts giving an insight into chaplaincy in higher education, despite its primary focus upon Anglican higher education ministry, is a doctoral thesis written by the present Bishop of Llandaff, Rt. Revd Barry Morgan.[10] His thesis, *Anglican University Chaplains: an Appraisal of the Understanding of Mission and Ministry in the work of Anglican University Chaplains in England and Wales 1950-1982,* was accepted by the University of Wales in 1986. This thesis was subsequently summarised by the then Anglican Secretary for Chaplaincies in Higher Education, Revd Kennedy Thom; the following paragraphs draw on this summarised version of the thesis.

Prior to 1945, the Church of England had a relatively confined interest in higher education, and its budget for this area was almost exclusively directed towards the provision of hostels and Church halls of residence for Christian students. With the establishment of the Council for Education of the Church of England in 1947, there was a forum for the Church to examine its role in higher education more carefully. In 1950, having taken advice from Diocesan Directors of Education, the new Council for Education presented a memorandum outlining the future priorities for financial provision. It reported that Church halls of residence were no longer an effective means for furthering the Church's work, and instead, 'special chaplaincies having pastoral responsibilities would secure the advantages now claimed for Church halls of residence' (Thom 1987:3). A later working party report affirmed the value of appointing chaplains, of providing chaplaincy centres instead of halls of residence as the physical base for Church work in universities.

By 1954, the Church Assembly (now the General Synod, the main governing body of the Church of England) passed a resolution that would set aside money for the work of Anglican chaplains in modern universities. Dioceses arranged and financed the appointment of new chaplains, while a Chaplaincies Advisory Group provided a mechanism for national co-ordination, training programmes, and communication. When the Council of Education was replaced by the Board of Education in 1958, the Chaplaincies Advisory Group continued, and by 1967 the Board was appointing a full time Secretary to administer the work of the Advisory Group. By creating this kind of national appointment, the Church of England was following the precedent set by the Methodist Church in the previous year and both the Roman Catholic Church and the Baptist Church made similar appointments soon afterwards.

In 1952, there were just eight university chaplains outside Oxford and Cambridge, of which only three were full time. By 1985 most universities, polytechnics and colleges of higher education had some kind of Anglican chaplaincy provision. This rapid growth suggests that dioceses were concerned to develop this aspect of the Church's work. Why?

The post-Robbins expansion of higher education in the 1960s led to an increase in student numbers, combined with a decreasing proportion of students living at home during the course of their studies. The then Bishop of London addressed the 1954 Church Assembly by noting that

> in modern universities there were thousands of young men and women who were almost unshepherded except for the work done by parish clergy who had a difficult task because they did not know where people were and could not get at them. It was necessary therefore to have someone who was detailed to give his whole time to this specific job (Thom 1987:7).

The experiences of having army chaplains during the war, plus the more general development of sector ministries, meant that the educational and pastoral circumstances for the emergence of a widespread ministry of university chaplains were ideal. Furthermore, wider social changes in British society, in particular the emergence of professions associated with counselling and social work, meant that there was an increasing expectation that chaplains could provide an equivalent emotional support.

The emergence of university chaplaincy posts developed alongside the already existing Student Christian Movement (see Chapter 7). This student-led society did not, however, have a pastoral or sacramental role, so there was a pastoral vacuum to be filled by ordained chaplains. However, as my interview with the present SCM indicated, the growth of chaplaincy appointments did leave the SCM somewhat sidelined from its previously prominent role in the life of

Christian students. In addition, the increasing number of specifically denominational chaplaincy posts failed to recognise the ecumenism that SCM had successfully fostered.

Early models of chaplaincy

Morgan's thesis identifies not only the key historical and social factors that led to the growth of higher education chaplaincy, but also some of the assumptions underlying this ministry during the three decades between 1950 and 1980. He suggests that between 1950 and 1960, there was a widespread view, certainly within the Church, that whilst chaplains would serve the whole institution, nevertheless, the primary reason for making chaplaincy appointments was to serve the interests of the Church. A full-time chaplain would serve the institution as a parish priest, meeting the needs of the regular churchgoers, but also the wider community. The chaplaincy centre was the base for this pastoral activity and the model of ministry was essentially 'parochial', and directed principally towards individuals. Most Church of England chaplaincy appointments were made at this time without reference to other Christian denominations – a situation that had begun to change by the time polytechnic chaplains were being recruited in the 1970s.

The 'parochial' model of chaplaincy that characterised the pre-1960 decade began to give way between 1960 and 1970 to a new understanding of the chaplain's role. The ministry of a chaplain was more clearly articulated as *enabling the Christian community* within the institution to serve the interests of the Church and the Gospel. More responsibility passed to lay members of the university community, with the chaplain as a specialist facilitator and figurehead for this now more mission-orientated approach to chaplaincy.[11]

Between 1970 and 1980, greater emphasis began to be placed on the chaplain's role across the whole institution, and the need for chaplains to have a deep understanding of the context in which they were ministering. In other words, the chaplain had a pastoral responsibility not only for individuals, but also for the institution as a whole. This was different from the 'parochial model' of ministry in the pre-1960s, since chaplains had the task of helping to understand the effects of the institution upon its members, and identifying where or how its structures might be more sensitive to individuals. The chaplain was called upon to relate the Gospel to the distinctive world of a university, and facilitate discussion between people and groups who might otherwise never meet, including different religious groups. Furthermore, the chaplain was in the best position to remind members of the institution of their responsibilities outside and beyond the confines of the 'ivory tower'.

In the penultimate section of Thom's summary of Morgan's thesis, there is some discussion of the tensions inherent in the chaplain's role. The treatment of these tensions reflects a time when the Churches almost exclusively funded chaplains, but the conclusions drawn are still relevant today. In the late 1990s, as the research for this book found, a substantial number of higher education chaplains are still paid by Churches, rather than by the institutions in which they serve, although the balance does appear to be changing.[12] Morgan and Thom point out that chaplains straddle two different institutions – the Church and the university. Both institutions are likely to regard the chaplain as on the fringe of their central concerns and activities. In the university the chaplain, 'has no ready-made niche since he is not employed by it and *his function cannot be defined by it*' (Thom 1987:28, emphasis added).

As a consequence, there may be conflicting expectations on the part of the university and the Church about the role of the chaplain, with his being regarded as no more than a useful addition to 'welfare' by the former, and a missionary by the latter. With the inevitable tensions that arise when a chaplain is paid by one institution to work in another, and when the chaplain may feel like an amateur in an environment surrounded by professionals, the calling to full-time ministry in higher education is not for the faint hearted. This is especially the case in those institutions of higher education where the chaplain has to struggle for recognition, status and inclusion, and for access to the essential informational and institutional tools to work effectively.

As a result of Morgan's thesis (and the summary report written by Kennedy Thom as a result), the emergence of higher education chaplaincy was carefully documented at the point when the most critical decades in the establishment and formation of this new ministry had only just passed. Theirs was not a retrospective glance at events that had taken place beyond the living memory of the key individuals involved. Their work provides insights into some of the social, pastoral, educational and historical conditions that created a context for the development of the Church's presence in higher education. They point to the link between the development of chaplaincy, and wider theological reflection taking place in the Church itself. Furthermore, they analysed the implications of this new area of Church activity for institutions of higher education, for the Church, for clergy, and for the chaplains themselves.

The insights provided by Morgan and Thom pave the way for discussion of another important document that emerged in the 1980s, this time on the experiences of the polytechnic chaplains. Where Thom and Morgan had provided important historical and ecclesiastical reflections, the report published by the polytechnic chaplains shortly afterwards examined more sociological concerns, especially those related to issues of professionalism and institutional structures (Wright 1985).

Insights from polytechnic chaplains

The 1985 report of the National Consultation of Polytechnic Chaplains contains one of the clearest accounts of the various traditions of chaplaincy in higher education. Though a little dated, the key points raised in the report about the structures, funding, and models of chaplaincy are extremely valuable, and to some extent, the findings of my research prove that they are as applicable to the current situation of higher education, as they were thirteen years ago. The *underlying* context of higher education chaplaincy has not changed dramatically, though there have been important developments. The Polytechnic Chaplaincy report is worth discussing in some detail since it provides a framework for understanding the different contexts and structures of chaplaincy in higher education.

A brief outline of the models of chaplaincy presented in the report is offered below.

- The Collegiate Model – refers to chaplaincy carried out in institutions usually with religious origins. It is essentially a community-based ministry, and the chaplain often lives alongside those he or she is serving. The chaplain's place in the life of the institution is integral, and he or she will have some role in many different aspects of community life, which will often including a teaching role. This 'collegiate' model of ministry is most clearly reflected in Church colleges, and in the ancient universities of Oxford, Cambridge, and Durham.

- The Congregational Model – is the most apt way of appreciating the distinctive traditions of chaplaincy in the larger civic, campus, or redbrick universities. These institutions include those universities founded during the Victorian period, up to the establishment of the new 'green field' universities in the late 1960s and early 1970s. In their constitutions, many of these institutions lacked any explicit religious dimension, but chaplaincy provision was nevertheless part of the life of the institution. The Polytechnic Chaplains' report provides a useful summary of how this 'congregational' model operates:

  > here the chaplaincy is identified as a gathered congregation of Christians meeting in a visible and often deliberately separate building. The chaplaincy is then seen as primarily a meeting place sponsored by the Church and representing a religious interest as one among many competing for attention on the campus. Because it is a place which people use in their spare time, it is not easily seen as centrally concerned with the life and educational purposes of the whole institution, whatever the aspirations of those who run it (Wright 1985:19).

- The Waterloo Model – was the image employed by the Polytechnic Chaplains to describe the secular context in which their ministry was largely carried out. They likened their ministry to working in a busy railway station, with people continually coming and going to a wide range of different destinations. In this context, the chaplain might choose to focus upon the whole station community, especially the permanent staff, and the chaplain will not be identified with a particular 'place' within the station community. Or, he or she might have a religious bookstall on the platform as a 'base' from which to meet people.

Having outlined how the Waterloo analogy applied to the context of polytechnic chaplaincy, the report explored the pros and cons of having a chapel or chaplaincy as a base for ministry. The arguments from those in favour centred around the value of the chaplain having an identifiable location and point of contact, providing a meeting space for individuals and groups. Those against the idea of a chaplaincy 'place' based their arguments on the restrictions that a chapel or chaplaincy imposed, firstly by tending to confine the chaplain to the place itself, and secondly, by inviting others to regard the chaplaincy as set apart from the broader life of the institution. The report called for the exploration of new approaches, and a move away from chaplaincy centres provided either entirely by the Church or entirely by the institution.

Similarly, the report suggested that chaplaincy appointments call for an exploration of innovative funding. A chaplain appointed and funded entirely by the Church would be in the valuable position of having an independent voice within the institution, but at times, it might be a lone voice. Students may regard chaplains who are funded solely by the university with suspicion. The Polytechnic Chaplains' report regarded the 'ideal' model as a collaborative and co-operative funding arrangement involving the institution and the Church, administered within the framework of an independent charitable trust. The chaplain thus becomes an employee of the trust, rather than either the Church or the institution, thereby allowing an equal investment by all parties and giving the chaplain some degree of independence.

The way in which chaplains are funded determines how they are likely to 'fit' within the life of the institution. The perspicacity of this observation in the Polytechnic chaplaincy report will become apparent in Chapter 4, since the way in which a chaplain 'fits' within the life of the institution is likely to have a bearing on his or her ability or motivation to work for a multi-faith approach to religious life in the institution. The Polytechnic Chaplains observed that:

> if a chaplain is appointed and paid by Church authorities, lives in a church house and works from a church-provided chaplaincy centre, the role is quite clearly that of a representative of the Church with permission to minister in the institution…

> …if a chaplain is appointed and paid for by the educational institution, works from an office provided by the polytechnic and is an owner-occupier of a house, like all other members of staff, again the expected role is clear – to be part of the "welfare" services of the institution (Wright 1985:26).

Many of the arguments about the pros and cons of chaplaincy premises, the way in which chaplaincy is funded, and the institutional structures into which the work of chaplains are accommodated, will resonate in later chapters. Some questionnaire respondents and interviewees during fieldwork had strong opinions about their place, for example, within or outside Student Services. Others regarded the sources of funding for their posts as critically affecting their scope for the development of greater institutional awareness about religious diversity. Premises, funding and structures were some of the key elements determining how institutions have responded, and there remained some truth to the maxim, 'he who pays the piper calls the tune'.

Over the course of time, higher education chaplains themselves have reflected on their own changing ministerial role, and the changing environment in which chaplaincy is exercised. Even in the early 1980s, the National Consultation of Polytechnic Chaplains report identified increasing religious diversity as one of the consequences of the widening access to higher education by non-traditional students, through the establishment of the polytechnics. They noted that 'the cultural, social and religious spectrum represented in the public sector...certainly by comparison with the religious foundations of the traditional ancient universities...is PLURALISTIC' (Wright 1985:6, emphasis original). Their report called for new styles of ministry appropriate to the secular and religiously diverse context of polytechnics, and recognition that pastoral care for individual students is now only one part of a chaplain's role. It identified some of the particularities of polytechnic chaplaincy thus: 'where the prevailing ethos is more akin to conditions of urban working life than to membership of an academic community, where the underlying assumptions are secular and rationalistic and where it is clearly inappropriate to reproduce "rural" church models' (Wright 1985:13). In view of the emergence of many 'new' universities out of the polytechnics and other higher education institutions, interesting questions are raised about models of ministry in these institutions. If there were distinctive models of polytechnic and university chaplaincy, has the creation of the new universities perpetuated these distinctions or blurred them?

Chaplaincy and higher education today

Turning away from some of the issues about how chaplaincy has evolved, what do chaplains actually do? The Christian Churches have a long history of involvement in higher education. It has been part of the ministry of the Churches to have a presence in universities and colleges, helping students to interpret their studies in the context of the world around them, and assisting in the process of spiritual and self-discovery. Chaplains have also had responsibility for rites of passage, pastoral care, and the organisation and leadership of corporate worship. In a *Church Times* article about higher education chaplaincy in the 1990s, a further role for chaplains was identified. Besides the well-known reasons why institutions might have a chaplain – tradition, moderation, kindness[13] – chaplains also have an important function as: 'people to think with; so that people can remind themselves of the central concerns of the university amid the material constraints that the world imposes' (Jenkins 1997). Debates about the role of chaplains have taken place almost exclusively within Christian circles, and have not, until more recently, been a concern to universities themselves.

Commenting on the world of higher education chaplaincy today, Father Fabian Radcliffe, national co-ordinator for Catholic Chaplaincies in higher education in England and Wales, reported that 'as the number of undergraduates has doubled, numbers active in chaplaincies have at best stayed the same. Nowadays, more than 50 per cent of students coming to the chaplaincies are from overseas' (Fern 1997).　Apart from these anecdotal observations, there is no evidence to prove conclusively who the 'consumers' of higher education chaplaincy are, and how patterns have changed over time.　Care of Christian groups remains an important aspect of much chaplaincy work, but it is clear that with more students in higher education from a wide variety of religious and ethnic backgrounds, one of the areas of chaplaincy growth is among those from faith traditions other than Christian.[14]　In an article in *The Guardian* about university chaplaincy, Richard Fern writes, 'Muslim adviser Dr Mohammed Naseem, who works from the Chaplaincy at Birmingham University, says his flock has grown. And Rabbi Fishel Cohen, Midlands regional Jewish chaplain, reports an increased level of student involvement' (Fern 1997).

Chaplaincy appears to be becoming less about spiritual direction and reflection, and more about co-ordination, counselling, and crisis management.[15]　It has a reactive dimension, but also an important and necessary proactive aspect in terms of the chaplain being known and being visible across the institution.　Each reinforces the other.　The work of a chaplain in higher education today is increasingly involving some kind of responsibility or facilitation on behalf of a wide variety of faiths.　But Father Radcliffe is concerned to know how much longer the Churches will continue to support this changing chaplaincy role in a system that appears to give little status or recognition for the work.　He fears that Churches see chaplaincy as having little priority: 'Chaplaincy is viewed as an optional extra, a luxury, like having a conservatory added to your house.　It's not essential, but a nice thing to have if you can afford it, and anyway, it's only for lounging around in (Fern 1997).[16]

In recent years, there has been clear evidence that the world of higher education chaplaincy has begun to engage seriously with issues of religious diversity and its implications for ministry.　At conferences, in newsletters and in journals, multi-faith issues are increasingly on the agenda, in an attempt to educate and inform chaplains about other faiths.[17]　At a conference for newly appointed chaplains organised by the Chaplains Higher Education Liaison Group in 1996, Canon Ipgrave, the Bishop's Adviser for Interfaith Relations from Leicester was invited to address the conference about 'The Inter-Faith Challenge' (Ipgrave 1996).[18]　This is a topic unlikely to have been a part of a similar conference a decade ago.　Early in his talk, he pointed to two key questions, or rather, two key relationships.　Firstly, there is the relationship between religious groups themselves on campus.　Secondly, there is the complex relationship between religious groups and the institutions in which they are based.　He identified four different attitudes to religions in universities.   Marginalisation has been the outcome in some universities of a sense of disdain and apathy from staff and students, often combined with religious illiteracy.   Religion might also be regarded as problematic in terms of providing for the needs of diverse groups, and managing conflicts between them.   Chaplaincy and religious activity in other institutions however may be viewed more positively, with an integral place in welfare provision.   At some universities, there is a more general interest in religion, from both pastoral and academic perspectives.   Canon Ipgrave pointed to the growth in the number of courses and departments concerned with religion.

Having a concern for inter-faith dialogue, Canon Ipgrave examined how chaplaincies might respond to the religious diversity of the student population.   He identified three areas for action:

- Pastorally – building relationships that meet the needs of staff and students, particularly with, and through the involvement of local faith communities.
- Theologically – through creating an environment for dialogue between faiths, and enabling the institution to understand the diversity of lived, faith traditions.
- Prophetically – 'to commend spiritual values and practices in the multi-faith and secular institution of the modern university'.

To some extent, the key issues and relationships identified above are recurrent themes in this book.   Chaplains' comments about their sense of isolation, or their difficulties in enabling greater institutional sensitivity to religious diversity, are all evident in the following pages.

A recent working party convened by the Board of National Mission for the Church of Scotland set out a policy for the Church of Scotland in higher education (Church of Scotland 1998).   Throughout the report, there is a clear recognition of religious diversity and the need for inter-faith awareness in higher education.   In outlining the aims and objectives of university chaplaincy in relation to spiritual and ethical awareness, the report identifies six key areas.   It should:

- Be a resource for the conscious broadening and developing of the spiritual insight and ethical awareness of those willing to be challenged by the broader implications of university life.
- Offer the opportunity to explore the theological and ethical implications of the kind of religious groups for whom a university setting provides a unique opportunity for such interaction.
- Provide a welcoming situation for overseas students.
- Reflect on university and academic life.
- Provide an opportunity for dialogue between those of different faiths.
- Be a reference point for those with particular faith needs.

In reviewing the current situation of Scottish higher education chaplaincy, the report points to the provision being made in most institutions for Jewish and Muslim students, and the necessary co-ordinating role of chaplains in facilitating this provision. Though the report is a summary of the current situation of Scottish higher education chaplaincy, the truths and challenges identified in many ways have national or even international application.

Religion on the university agenda

Outside the world of professional chaplaincy, the place of religion in universities has been debated within an academic context. In 1964 the Gerstein Lectures at York University were devoted to the subject of 'Religion and the University'.[19] The very fact that religion was the topic for the series of lectures caused some degree of surprise, if not consternation.

> There are some who assume that because a university by its very nature must consistently raise questions and search out new truths, it cannot deal with religion in which, it is suggested, truth is already presumed to be known (Ross 1964:v).

The contributors to the lecture series (and one subsequently commissioned chapter for the resulting book) sought to defend the scholarly study of religion in the university, and, to outline the extent to which religious identities might be appropriately expressed in, and supported by, the institution. Arguments in defence of academic study of religion broadly rested upon the fact that religion is a social reality which academics with an interest in human life and civilisation can not afford to ignore; hence the argument for its place in the university curriculum. However, when it came to the religious life of the university campus, contributors expressed firm convictions regarding appropriate arrangements. Charles Moeller suggested that if it was necessary to organise in some way the practice of religion on campus, this should be clearly distinguishable from the academic administration of the university (Moeller 1964:102). He also suggested (and in some ways ahead of his time) that the ecumenical spirit should govern the organisation and use of worship facilities, and that spaces for religious activity should be open to all denominations.[20] Liberty in religious matters, the avoidance of proselytism, and the linking of principle and action were central to Moeller's case *for* organised religion in the university. In many ways, the legitimacy of religion in the extracurricular life of the university was also defended by Alexander Wittenberg, but based on the premise that religion is a 'privileged private concern of the individual' (Wittenberg 1964:114).[21] His arguments become slightly more nuanced through examples about the circumstances in which universities may or may not act with regard to religion. For example, he suggests that,

> the university may *not* compel an orthodox Jew to write an examination on the Sabbath. It *may*, however, compel him to take lectures in which religions,

including his own, are examined from an objective standpoint – for instance the standpoint of a comparative study of religions, or that of sociology. Furthermore, I do not believe that the university should establish for that student an orthodox Jewish residence, which would shield its members from intellectual contact and debate with members of other faiths…
Religious observances of any kind have no business whatsoever in the official and ceremonial life of the university. The university is dedicated to the pursuit of truth [and] this dedication is clearly violated when the university as a corporate body performs religious exercises which are potentially meaningless…I might add that this matter is of particular significance in a new university. In very old institutions, the patina of the centuries sometimes endows traditional ceremonies with a meaning of their own which is different from their manifest meaning (Wittenberg 1964:114-5).

There are a number of issues raised by Wittenberg that we might evaluate, but underpinning his standpoint is a particular vision of the role of the university, especially what he identifies as 'the pursuit of truth'. While this may no doubt remain part of the vision of today's universities other functions also play a significant role, such as serving local communities, linking to local industry, commerce and enterprise, and providing a wide range of different forms of learning to a broader range of the population. Academic excellence is less explicitly connected to the 'pursuit of truth' in today's universities, in part reflecting the expansion of higher education and the shift of academic life from the hands of an elite and exclusive minority. The mission statements of many of today's universities rarely refer to matters of truth, and tend to emphasise instead their aspirations in terms of creativity, opportunity, accessibility, flexibility, innovation, professional and personal development, and contribution to the social, cultural and economic life of the region in which they are based.

This evolution in the character of universities, reflecting wider social change, has implications for matters of religious life on campus. For example, some British universities *have* made some institutional halls of residence, corridors, or other accommodation available to students with a particular religious identity. Rightly or wrongly, this is often closely connected with the recruitment strategies of universities. But it is also an acknowledgement of the right of students to maintain their particular religious observances whilst at university, to live as *they* wish, rather than in a way dictated by the institution, and sheer expediency for the institution in terms of social and religious support (especially for overseas students). Wittenberg's assumption about religious ceremonies, especially their place in old universities (as opposed to new institutions) also does not stand up to scrutiny in contemporary higher education. It can no longer be assumed that everyone in an ancient university will understand and appreciate the distinction between the various meanings that are implied by traditional ceremonies. To an overseas student perhaps, Oxbridge functions held in college chapels (or other venues) are likely to appear entirely Christian, rather than simply a matter of age-old tradition and anachronism that carries meaning based on historicity. Finally, corporate ceremonies reflecting different religious traditions can, with careful planning, be extremely meaningful for those involved, not least for the public acknowledgement and recognition of their inclusion as a part of campus life. In Chapter 6, I will be discussing multi-faith ceremonies in more detail, especially their prevalence in 'secular' universities. Meanwhile, Wittenberg and the other contributors to *Religion and the University* if nothing else provide a benchmark for evaluating the changing function of universities, especially in relation to the new realities of religion on campus.

More recently, individuals within higher education administration are beginning to take religion in higher education, and especially the implications of religious diversity, more seriously. Weller (1992b) identified some of the areas where institutions might evaluate, for example, their institutional policies. He noted that whilst institutions have developed equal opportunities policies to cover areas such as race or gender, there has so far been inadequate attention to *religious identity* as an equal opportunities question. He identified issues such as dietary provision, worship facilities, and institutional policies and attitudes towards different traditions as areas warranting examination. Within his own institution, Derby University, consideration and delivery of these aspects of provision has come about not through an extension of a Christian chaplaincy, but through the emergence of a 'Religious Resource and Research Centre' – a multi-faceted department combining academic, social, institutional, as well as pastoral functions.[22] Weller also undertook a small-scale survey of religious facilities and policies in higher education during 1995. Some of the (unpublished) findings of his survey are used comparatively in this book.[23]

The Inter Faith Network for the UK, a small charitable organisation, has also developed a concern for issues of religious diversity in higher education as part of its more general work on faith communities in British public life. As a result of on-going contact with the main student religious organisations, and through receiving regular enquiries from those professionally involved in higher education, the Network has identified key issues and questions. In July 1995, the Network circulated its code on 'Building Good Relations With People of Other Faiths and Beliefs' to Vice Chancellors and Principals of all the UK's institutions of higher education in response to growing concern about inter-religious difficulties on some campuses. As noted earlier, it was due to a growing awareness of the importance of inter-faith issues in higher education that the research upon which this book is based was initiated by the Network.

Within the world of inter-faith relations, two organisations have made particular efforts to work at a student and institutional level to further the cause of good relations between Christians and Jews, and Muslims and Jews respectively. The Council of Christians and Jews (CCJ) is an organisation particularly concerned to educate Jews and Christians about the beliefs and traditions shared by Judaism and Christianity, as well as their distinctive areas of difference and practice. As an extension of this work, CCJ works to combat all forms of religious intolerance between people of different faiths. This national organisation began work on university campuses some eight years ago, firstly in Cambridge. At the time, an evangelistic Christian group had decided to target its missionary activity towards Jews in particular. A Christian student who was especially concerned about this development, together with a young Jewish social worker who was a Theology graduate, called upon the University's Jewish Society to form 'Cambridge Jews and Christians'. This organisation operated separately from the local CCJ group, though with strong links. Since the early 1990s, five other university branches of CCJ have been founded, the most successful ones being initiated and led by students themselves.

More recently, the establishment of a new organisation, the 'Calamus Maimonides Student Forum' was publicly announced in the summer of 1998 after several years of careful planning by Muslim and Jewish students concerned for better relations between their respective faiths on campus. The organisation is co-ordinated by twelve Jewish and Muslim students, each working under the auspices of charitable inter-faith bodies linked to Jewish and Muslim communities respectively: the 'Maimonides Foundation' and the 'Calamus Foundation'. 'Its founders intend it to fill a vacuum, which extremists exploit for recruitment, by providing unprecedented opportunities for the many peace-seeking followers of both religions to get together and find out more about one another' (Kingston 1998). Speaking about the new organisation, Douglas Krikler, Executive Director of the Maimonides Foundation said, 'what's given a sense of urgency to the student initiative has been an atmosphere on campuses for the past few years of hostility between Muslim and Jewish Students...our aim is a more long-term solution and to provide alternative points of contact for Jewish and Muslim students to allow them to break away from this divisive posturing and sloganising' (Kingston 1998). In a press release issued by the new organisation, the explicit aims of the new Muslim-Jewish society were stated:

- To foster and encourage links between Muslim and Jewish students.
- To unite Muslim and Jewish students through educational, cultural and social activities.
- To provide a safe environment within which Muslim and Jewish students can explore and expand upon both their similarities and their differences.
- To embrace the diversity held within both communities.

The new organisation was formally launched at the beginning of the new academic year 1998/9 focusing its activities on a limited number of campuses with large intakes of Jewish and Muslim students. It aims to become a nationwide student body in the future. Sadly, its launch was blighted by disruption by members of the radical extremist group 'Al-Muhajiroun'. Muslim students involved with the Calamus-Maimonides Foundation were particularly vocal in declaring the behaviour of the militants as 'un-Islamic' (Schogger 1998).[24]

Religious life in institutions of higher education has *always* been contentious, sensitive, diverse, and exciting in one way or another. But over the course of history, the nature of these sensitivities and issues has changed, often as a reflection of wider social changes. During the 1970s for example, anti-Semitism and anti-Zionism were highly emotive issues. The NUS came under considerable pressure to pass anti-Zionist resolutions, equating Zionism with racism, and to ban Jewish and Israeli Societies from campuses. At a number of universities, the NUS passed such a resolution (Webber 1993). Today, the increasing religious diversity of society in general is now reflected in the student body, and multi-faith issues, and tension between different faith groups as they compete for limited resources, are now on the agenda for those with a concern and responsibility for religion in higher education. Similarly, the proliferation and confidence of a number of new religious movements, especially over the past decade, has led to concerns about proselytism and aggressive evangelistic activity directed towards students. This is one of the reasons for greater security on many university campuses, particularly in halls of residence.

It was partly as a response to some of these newly emerging issues that the Committee of Vice-Chancellors and Principals (CVCP) set up a working group to explore some of their *legal and disciplinary* implications. In many ways, this was something of a departure from the CVCP's normal remit. But within its Student and Staff Sector Group, the CVCP has a concern for student welfare issues and there was an increasing awareness of a need to examine public order issues on campus. Professor Graham Zellick, Vice-Chancellor of the University of London chaired the working party, and the resulting report, *Extremism and Intolerance on Campus,* was published in July 1998 (CVCP 1998). The report made clear that its remit was limited, and that important questions of inter-religious, multicultural and inter-racial harmony were outside the scope of the working party's terms of reference. However, these questions were highlighted as issues that others might consider, and this book begins the process of exploration.[25]

Whilst the CVCP has to chart a careful course between prescription and direction while also respecting the autonomy of institutions of higher education, the *Extremism and Intolerance on Campus* report is an attempt to address the legal obligations of institutions, for example under the 1986 Public Order Act. It aims to 'offer practical advice to university authorities so that they have in place appropriate rules, regulations, codes and machinery to enable them to respond lawfully, fairly and effectively to these situations, howsoever they arise – whether in political, religious or other contexts' (CVCP 1998:6). The report begins by outlining the general principles that govern university life, such as the necessary and intrinsic place of vigorous debate in academic enquiry. This is followed by an outline of various legal perspectives on fear or provocation of violence, harassment, alarm or distress, and racial hatred. Thereafter, the report addresses the implications of the Education (No.2) Act 1986, and issues of freedom of speech, unlawful speech, public notices and the distribution of literature, codes of discipline, the banning of meetings and the activities of individuals/groups from outside the institution.

Responses to the interim version of *Extremism and intolerance on campus* were received from numerous institutions, and there was consultation with a number of organisations concerned with issues in higher education. Some national religious organisations are however conspicuous by their absence, and an article about the CVCP report in the Muslim monthly magazine *Q News* is critical of the lack of consultation with the Federation of Students Islamic Societies (FOSIS), or any other specifically Muslim organisation (Yaqub 1998:14).

In the light of a number of disturbances on campuses over the past five years or so, involving members of Islamic groups from both within and outside institutions, there is a widespread, but, according to the CVCP, unfounded assumption that the report was a direct result of these incidents alone. The CVCP has responded to these assumptions by pointing out that the activities of 'Christian Scientologists [sic] the British National Party, the Socialist Workers Party, and various other groups' (Yaqub 1998:14) had led to more recent concerns, rather than Islamic groups. However, some Muslim critics of the report nevertheless regard the document to have been framed 'exclusively with the Muslim student community in mind' (Yaqub 1998:14). It is still too early to assess other Muslim and non-Muslim responses to the CVCP report, or how its recommendations and advice might have an impact on religious and political life in institutions of higher education. However, the report perhaps marks the first attempt by a non-religious national higher education organisation to examine a number of aspects of student life, of which religion is one.

Religious diversity in higher education has already received some degree of academic attention. I have already referred to Paul Weller's survey of institutional policies and religious facilities, carried out in 1995. More recently, Kingston University has carried out a study of multicultural awareness and chaplaincy provision. The 'Multicultural Awareness Project' has tried to assess Kingston's own provision for other faiths and cultural groups vis-à-vis other higher education institutions. As part of this endeavour, a researcher was employed for 12 months, from July 1998-1999, to implement the findings of a six month research project undertaken during 1996 (Thorne 1998). As part of this work, a survey was carried out to assess staffing levels, space allocation and multicultural activity at a number of English University Chaplaincies. There were 75 institutions in the sample, of which 40 responded. This makes the response rate of 53 per cent comparable to my own, though my sample included *all* institutions of higher education, including of course Welsh, Scottish, and Northern Irish institutions. The Kingston survey uncovered similar patterns and much of the same factual data as my own research, but its primary focus upon facilities and staffing meant that wider questions about inter-faith relations were omitted. Furthermore, the scope of the research did not allow for a broader discussion of religion in higher education, or an assessment of how the different types of institution have responded to religious diversity. What is more significant is the fact that Kingston University itself funded a full-time researcher to undertake a study of religious provision with a view to improving and making best use of its own facilities. As such, it is perhaps the only institution of higher education that has made a serious commitment to serving its multi-faith student body through research.

As long ago as 1981, one possible consequence of discrimination or unfairness by institutions of higher education towards particular religious groups, especially Muslims, was identified.   Asking the question *Is Higher Education Fair?* (Warren-Piper 1981), in relation to religion, John Gay suggested that in Britain 'the founding of a Moslem institute of higher education could be justified in terms of fairness' (Gay 1981:158).   In the summer of 1999, this has indeed happened with the foundation of the 'Markfield Institute of Higher Education', a small centre based at the Islamic Foundation near Leicester, and affiliated to the University of Portsmouth.[26]   Being based within an existing Islamic centre, it is likely to be able to offer students the chance to study within a distinctively Islamic environment.   What, if any impact this institution has upon the recruitment of Muslim students into other institutions of higher education remains as yet unknown.

Over the past two decades some universities have made significant additions to their academic courses to reflect the changing make-up of the institution.   Several departments of Religious Studies now encompass specialist centres for the study of Islam, while at Birmingham University there is a Centre for the Study of Islam and Christian-Muslim relations, founded some 20 years ago. Reflecting the strength of the Jain community in Leicester, De Montfort University provided the base for a new Centre for Jain Studies.   It is now possible to undertake taught Masters degrees in Buddhist Studies in particular and Indian religions more generally at several universities, often taught by academic practitioners of these traditions.   Study of inter-faith relations at postgraduate level is now offered in a number of Religious Studies departments, while several Jewish colleges have their degrees validated by British universities.   Interestingly, the significant points of 'growth' in these newly emerging areas of study and new centres are undertaken from a scholarly but nevertheless 'confessional' perspective.   These emerging areas of study and new alliances between faith communities and universities also signify some of the ways institutions have accommodated to religious diversity in the curriculum.[27]   The question naturally arises as to how well they have addressed the needs of students of different faiths who are attracted to these courses.   This is one of the issues explored over the following chapters.

Conclusion

Higher education in Britain largely owes its origins to the traditions of the Christian church, but secular forces have made a dramatic impact on this legacy. Apart from some of the statues and traditions in the collegiate university colleges and Church institutions, there has been little to stem the tide of secularisation. Christianity has become a more marginal influence on the workings of university life in Britain, both in terms of academic assumptions and institutional rules and regulations.

However, one of the arguments that I shall be making in this book is that universities are far from being wholly secular institutions, even those founded upon the ideological principles of secularism in the Victorian period and in the post-Robbins era. 'If the substance of the establishment of religion in the ancient universities had been swept away in the nineteenth century, enough survived to bequeath a legacy to the whole university system in the twentieth' (Bebbington 1992:272). For example, many universities, even 'secular' ones, continue to hold religious ceremonies, such as carol services or 'start of year' ceremonies. An increasing number of institutions employ a chaplain from their own budget, and provide premises for religious practice; others are incorporating matters of religion into their institutional equal opportunities policies. Some 'secular' universities subsidise religious activity in largely 'hidden' ways, such as providing a budget to a chaplaincy. A thorough investigation of how these institutional funds are spent indicates the on-going privileging of Christianity, albeit in ecumenical forms. Behind the many assertions of being 'secular' (apart from Church institutions), universities in Britain display a wide range of responses to religion, from distinctly anti-religious, to a more embracing attitude and a willingness to recognise religious identities, sensitivities and needs. Religion may not underpin institutional life and assumptions in the way it once might have done, but the vestiges of Christianity remain, *even in many 'secular' universities*, largely due to the distinctive pattern that the established Churches placed upon the very character and shape of university life and norms (Aldridge 1993:110). Furthermore, as I suggested in Chapter 1 and in the earlier part of this chapter, historically and contemporarily the fate of religion in Britain's universities largely reflects religion in Britain more generally. Some scholars and observers assert that we live in a 'secular' society, but the legacy of the historical strength of the Established Church is evident in many arenas of contemporary public life, from the appointment of publicly funded prison chaplains, to the traditions of civic religion, locally and nationally. Religion may not be the 'sacred canopy' it once was, but the traditions of Christianity are deeply *embedded* in national life. Much the same can be said for religion in universities, even in the 'secular' institutions.

Against this background, we must now take account of the strength of religious belief and practice among other faith communities. The strongest force that might be considered as reversing the trend of secularisation has come through the increasing religious diversity of the student population over the past 20 years. For example, most universities, particularly the larger ones, have now had to consider and make provision for permanent or temporary Muslim prayer rooms, often on campus. Matters of religious practice reflecting a range of faith traditions have impinged on different areas of university life in many institutions, from equal opportunities policies to *kosher* fridges in halls of residence. The range of student religious organisations is diversifying, and most of the larger faith traditions in Britain now have a national student religious organisation. In turn, these are attracting growing support. As in the earlier part of the nineteenth century, the enduring strength of religion in higher education largely resides at what might be considered 'the margins', in voluntary activity and student-run organisations. The presence of other faiths on campus has significantly reversed declining trends in this area, and few universities have been untouched by the growth of students from different ethnic and religious backgrounds. Religion on campus is moving out of the strictly private realm, and challenging some of the norms and assumptions of 'secular' institutions as well as those with strong Christian histories.

The range of responses to the diversifying sociological base of university admissions has often been shaped by financial and political factors. The official designation 'secular' university can, with political will, be interpreted in a variety of pragmatic ways.[28]   The rhetoric of being 'secular' often, and perhaps unconsciously, collides with the reality of the need to attract and retain the growing ethnic minority population of students, many of whom regard religion as of central importance, not least for their identity.

Notes

1	For more information about university education in Ireland, see Garland (1996), pp.275ff.
2	There are conflicting dates given for the foundation of University College, London. McClelland gives the date 1825, when funds of £160,000 were raised for the foundation of premises in Gower Street, while HEFCE *Profiles of Higher Education Institutions* (1997) gives a date of 1827.
3	I am grateful to Dr Kieran Flanagan for this insightful observation!
4	For more information about the Liberation Society, see Nicholls (1967), p.111.
5	Evidence for the historical decline of student participation in religious activity can be drawn from a number of different sources (in the absence of accurate statistics). Anecdotes of chaplains, church reports, and some institutional histories often imply or refer to declining participation. See for example Fern (1997), Hey (1989), Ross *et al* (1964), and Worrall (1988).
6	The HEFCE document *Profiles of Higher Education Institutions*, (August 1997), gives a short history of each higher education institution in England. From this, one can discern some of the mergers, amalgamations, and origins of different universities and colleges. For example, University College, London was founded in 1826 specifically to make higher education more accessible: 'it was open to all who could profit by its teaching regardless of race, religion or class, and was the first university institution to admit Jews, Dissenters, and Roman Catholics to its courses' (p.170).
7	A report by the National Union of Students (NUS) in 1995 found that four out of every ten students are in employment during term time. *Times Higher Education Supplement,* 16th July 1999.
8	Newman advocated a university education which would result in an 'expansion of outlook, turn of mind, habit of thought, and capacity for social and civic interaction' (Turner 1966a:xv).

9   Oxford Brookes University and Magdalen College, Oxford, 19-21 July, 1996. The papers were subsequently edited and published in Smith, A. and Webster, F. (1997).

10   The thesis focuses exclusively upon chaplaincy in Wales and England. No sources were found documenting the history of higher education chaplaincy in Scotland. However, a recent Church of Scotland policy document (Board of Communication, Church of Scotland, 1998), does refer to the long and integral role of chaplains in many Scottish universities throughout their history.

11   The increasing involvement of laity was also occurring in many Churches as a declining number of clergy, priests and ministers were being called upon to serve more parishes.

12   Additionally, more institutions are now providing for the facilities and upkeep of chaplaincy centres.

13   Tradition might be understood as: 'we have always had a chaplain'; moderation could refer to the role of chaplains in tempering religious extremism. Chaplains are perhaps part of a shrinking minority within universities whose function extends to the simple and inexpensive role of providing kindness.

14   Another area of expansion is the emergence of pastoral care needs for specific overseas Christian groups, such as Chinese Christians and those belonging to the Greek Orthodox Church.

15   This was evident from the comments of a number of chaplains interviewed for the research.

16   Hammond (1966) observed that chaplains in American universities also suffered from limited acknowledgement by their churches and denominations, particularly those who were considered in some way 'deviant' from church expectations, or with a more innovative style of ministry.

17   See for example the bulletin 'Discourse' (for chaplains in higher education), no.13, which carried an article about Islam and Muslims in higher education, written by Umar Hegedus, March 1994. The article calls for a need to encourage Muslim students to learn more about their faith, understanding what they have in common with other traditions, and thereby working for a harmonious and respectful multi-faith society.

18   Michael Ipgrave has recently been appointed Secretary of the Inter Faith Consultative Group of the Church of England.

19   These were published in a book of the same title in 1964 in Canada by the University of Toronto Press.

20   The general line of his argument suggests that today he would make the case for multi-faith spaces, and not just inter-denominational worship facilities.

21   This assumption of course ignores the clear evidence for the 'deprivatisation' of religion in the modern world (Casanova 1994), and fails to recognise the importance of communal life in many of Britain's faith communities.

22   For more information about the history of chaplaincy at Derby, see May (1989), Hey (1989), and Weller (1992a).

23   I am extremely grateful to Paul Weller for making the data from his survey available for this book. In accordance with the assurances of confidentiality extended to Weller's respondents, none of the institutions that responded to his survey are named or in any way identified here. Use of his data is strictly for comparative purposes.

24   It is important to be aware that factionalism *within* religious groups, such as student religious organisations, often reflects wider tensions and divisions, in this case in the wider British Muslim community (see for example Zald and McCarthy 1998).

25   This book aims to take a much more positive view of some of the outcomes and challenges posed by diversity compared perhaps to the CVCP report. The latter, even by its title, seems to implicitly make the connection that extremism and intolerance have been a natural outcome of increasing diversity, and that diversity itself is thus somehow 'problematic' for universities.

26   New posts for the MIHE were advertised in the *Times Higher Education Supplement*, 9th July 1999.

27   For a more detailed discussion of the development of Religious Studies in Britain, see for example Ursula King (ed.) 1990, *Turning Points in Religious Studies*, Edinburgh: T&T Clark.

28   Some institutions of higher education actively define themselves as 'secular'. See for example, Appendix 2.

Chapter 3

University Faith Communities: Diversity, Identity and Rights

Religious and ethnic diversity in higher education

The only figures which at present indicate the growing religious diversity of the higher education population are those which deal with the ethnic background of students. Few universities require students to state their religious affiliation at admission or registration, but the ethnic monitoring of university entrants since 1990 has indicated the overall increasing number of ethnic minority students (Modood 1993). Whilst students from overseas have historically constituted the most significant population of students of other ethnicities and faiths, this predominance is being counterbalanced by the increasing numbers of young British-born members of different racial and faith communities now entering higher education. Ethnic minority groups are over-represented in UK higher education applications and entry statistics (Acland and Modood 1998:4).[1] Since few institutions currently gather information about the religious identity of their student populations it is difficult to assess precisely the changing balance between, for example, Muslim students from overseas, and Muslim students born and brought up in Britain. But to set in context the growth of religious diversity in higher education in particular, it would be helpful to chart briefly the increasing religious pluralism in Britain more generally.

There has always been some degree of religious diversity in Britain, but it was the rapid post-Second World War period increase in diversity that is the most significant for this book. As the table below indicates, there has been a steady increase over the past 20 years in the numbers of religious faith communities, smaller Christian groups, and sectarian movements. The table indicates the increase in other faith groups, as well as the decline in broadly Christian religious affiliation. Figures for the year 2000 are projected estimates. Whilst there is currently no census data on religious identity, it is worth noting that *any* figures about the size of different religious groups in Britain are only estimates.[2]

Table 3.1 UK religious community, 1975-2000

Millions

	1975	1980	1985	1990	1995	2000
Christian (Trinitarian)	40.2	39.8	39.1	38.6	38.1	37.8
Non-Trinitarian	0.7	0.8	1.0	1.1	1.3	1.4
Hindu	0.3	0.4	0.4	0.4	0.4	0.5
Jew	0.4	0.3	0.3	0.3	0.3	0.3
Muslim	0.4	0.6	0.9	1.0	1.2	1.4
Sikh	0.2	0.3	0.3	0.5	0.6	0.6
Other religions	0.1	0.2	0.3	0.3	0.3	0.3
TOTAL	42.3	42.4	42.3	42.2	42.2	42.2
Percentage of population						
Christian Trinitarian	72%	71%	69%	67%	65%	64%
Non-Trinitarian	1%	1%	2%	2%	2%	2%
Non-Christian religions	3%	3%	3%	4%	5%	6%
Total all religions	76%	75%	74%	73%	72%	71%

Source: (Brierley 1997:2.3)

The historical and sociological factors which led to the rapid post-World War II migration to Britain from former colonial countries, such as India, Pakistan, and Bangladesh, as well as from East Africa and the Caribbean, are well documented by scholars in the fields of ethnic relations, sociology and religious studies (e.g. Parsons 1993 or Ballard 1994). However, prior to this period a significant reason for migration to the UK was the opportunity to study in British universities. Higher education in Britain therefore has a history of religious diversity, though on a relatively small scale.

As migrant populations became permanently settled in Britain, so increasing religious diversity marked the religious and ethnic landscape of Britain. However, both now and in the 1960s and 1970s, there were significant regional differences in the extent of diversity. Job opportunities in centres of industry, such as Manchester and Leeds, major seaports, such as Cardiff and Liverpool, and the large cities of Birmingham, Glasgow, and London, meant that these places were the main destinations of many migrant communities. Today, these cities are more diverse than those in the West Country, East Anglia, or more rural parts of the country. However, regardless of the religious make-up of the local population, most institutions of higher education are marked by considerable religious diversity because of their wider catchment area and the presence of students from overseas.

For a variety of demographic reasons, there has been a steady increase of British students from other faiths entering university, particularly over the past decade. Furthermore, there is a particular 'push' factor behind the wish to acquire higher education qualifications by some of the newer communities. 'Asian parents stressed the importance of education for overcoming racial and socio-economic barriers' (Acland and Azmi 1998:78),[3] while ethnic minority 'parents who encourage their children to aspire to achieve the maximum level of education earn recognition, pride and status within their own community' (Singh 1990:349). Researchers in the field of ethnic relations have found differential but nevertheless increasing rates of entry to higher education by members of different ethnic groups.[4] From this it is possible to deduce a growth of students from other faiths in general, but particularly among those from faiths which predominate in the Indian sub-continent. Similarly, researchers have identified differential rates of entry to the various *types* of higher education institutions on the basis of ethnic background.[5] Neither these differences, nor the precise reasons behind them, are within the remit of discussion in this book. However, it will become clear in the findings presented in Chapters 4 to 6 that some 'new' universities appear to be more conscious of their ability to recruit non-traditional students through provision of religious facilities, despite their 'secular' foundations. This to some extent accounts for the fact that these newer institutions tend to have higher numbers of ethnic minorities, compared to Church institutions, and ancient or older 'civic' universities.

Religious and ethnic identity

A discussion of identity, and with it, rights and recognition forms part of much wider debates in political philosophy, social theory, and studies of multiculturalism and equality. I have deliberately not engaged with these in any detail here, largely due to the huge explosion of recent literature in these fields (for example, Bauböck and Rundell 1998; Baumann 1999; Modood 1998a and 1998b; Gutman 1994). I have, however, tried to map the terrain of some present realities and discussions, and I have tried to draw out their implications for an understanding of religious diversity and identity in higher education.

During the course of the past 30 to 40 years, the migrant faith communities that established themselves in Britain have undergone a process of internal maturation and development, and have begun to engage with British society in new ways. The 'new arrivals' to Britain in the post-war period did not plan to stay in the country on a permanent basis, but a number of political, social, and economic factors led to an almost unconscious revision of this intention. Following a wave of female migration in the wake of the 1962 Commonwealth Immigrants Act, faith communities began to establish more permanent religious, social, and cultural facilities in Britain. The psychological orientation of communities began to shift away from countries of origin towards a future in Britain. More and more resources were invested in the development of facilities to sustain and educate future generations living in this country. Naturally, faith communities have become active participants in Britain's political, economic, cultural, and religious life, and there is a new confidence built upon their increasingly successful participation in public affairs. Religious community newspapers and magazines, such as *Q News* or *Eastern Eye* regularly carry articles and features reporting on the activities of politicians, peers, religious leaders, and business people from different religious communities who are actively involved in national and community life. Likewise, faith communities have often used their major festivals as opportunities to court recognition from public figures. For example, the celebration of the tercentenary of the Sikh *Khalsa* in 1999 was marked by a gathering of over 5000 Sikhs at the Royal Albert Hall, addressed by HRH the Prince of Wales.

This sense of participation, and with it an increasing confidence, is part of the identity of the up and coming younger generations. For example, though speaking particularly in relation to the Muslim community, a previous President of the British organisation 'Young Muslims' described confidently the project ahead as he saw it: 'we want to create a British Islamic culture. It is our job to be innovative, creative, adventurous, bold, chivalrous and create a new British Islamic culture' (Mueen 1993:5). For many religious minority groups, religion is at the core of their self-definition, and religious identity has become one of the primary building blocks of personal identity (Jacobson 1998; Nesbitt 1998; Modood 1997; Anthias and Yuval-Davis 1992). The centrality of religious identity, combined a growing sense of participation, increasingly characterises the new generation of students from other faith communities now entering higher education. In many ways they can also be regarded as part of a whole new generation of youth in Britain experiencing radical change in attitudes and thinking. Contemporary theologians have observed an increase in what they call 'neo-tribalism' – the desire of young people to belong to a community with clear and pronounced beliefs and values (Williams 1999:19).

In many ways, the prominence and persistence of religious identity in general, and among youth in particular, is not surprising. A number of researchers have found not only that migration stimulates religious affiliation and practice rather than weakening it, but also that religious identity becomes more significant for succeeding generations (Martin Baumann 1999). Harold Abramson noted that the cultural diversity that arises due to migration leads to a recognition of ethnic differences

> and invariably, some further and more specific recognition of distinctions in presumed racial character, in tribal allegiance, in national origin, in regional background, and *particularly, in religious affiliation*, (Abramson 1979:6, emphasis added).

Additionally, other scholars have found that for the generations once and twice removed from the migration experience – the third generation in particular – religion is a highly significant dimension of identity. In his classic text *Protestant Catholic Jew*, Will Herberg (1960) noted what he called the 'third generation interest'.

...the third generation, coming into its own with the cessation of mass immigration, tries to recover its "heritage" so as to give itself some sort of "name" or context of self-identification and social location in the larger society. "What the son wishes to forget" so runs "Hansen's Law" – "the grandson wishes to remember". But what he can "remember" is obviously not his grandfather's foreign language, or even his grandfather's foreign culture; it is rather his grandfather's *religion* (Herberg 1960:257, emphasis original).

There are a number of specific reasons why religious identity has come to the fore amid a range of possible identifications over the past two decades. If the 1970s and 1980s can be considered as the period when faith communities were most actively establishing socio-religious infrastructures in terms of organisations and the ability to practise their traditions in Britain, the 1990s have been particularly characterised by the struggle for recognition and more effective representation in public life. Community leaders from many faith traditions have actively campaigned on a range of concerns, from the availability of *halal* meat in schools, to the Bhaktivedanta Manor campaign (Nye 1996) but also, increasingly, for recognition in the public sphere. Some community 'leaders' have also actively encouraged their followers to 'define themselves primarily in religious terms...this is one way they can retain their power base and attract money from British and international sources' (Parekh and Bhabha 1989:24). The promotion of an essentialist assertion of difference can therefore be highly strategic. Protest, campaigns, and resistance – whether or not spontaneous – can be 'a potent affirmation of group identity' (Jenkins 1996:175).

Out of a multiplicity of ethnic groups, languages, and religious schools of thought, a single unifying 'label' has often been needed in order to articulate community interests. As the 'myth of return' became more evident during the decades following migration, Shaw noticed in relation to Muslims in Oxford, for example, there has been a 'corresponding increase in settlers' perceptions of themselves as a *religious* minority, and thus a growing concern with the issue of Muslim identity' (Shaw 1994:36, emphasis original). Community leaders have thus been concerned to present a united front and a community identity centred upon religion, not only to articulate 'needs', but also to galvanise public and political recognition. Hence, the prominence and persistence of religious identity. Unfortunately, there are other, less positive reasons why religious identity has been so strongly forged, in this case among Muslims in Britain (see also Martin Baumann 1999 and Eade 1994).

To some extent, Muslim identity is made central for Muslim communities by the distinctive anti-Islamic racism currently prevalent in Britain and Europe. Thus Muslim unity and mobilisation is a necessary and legitimate strategy (Waqar and Husband 1993).

For a group which is defined as being both different and inferior and denied opportunities to assume identity and status relevant to the main stream of the metropolitan society, self-conception and self-esteem may increasingly focus on religious belief and practices (Barot 1993:8).

Whilst many of the young generations of Hindus, Muslims, Sikhs, and other faith groups share the claiming of religious heritage as the basis for identity, there are some specific characteristics and differences in the expression of religious identity between and within the main faith groups in Britain. Though running the risk of over-generalising the nature of different faith communities and glossing over individual and regional differences, for young Muslims, for example, theirs is often a positive identity based upon belonging to a worldwide multinational religious community, the *ummah,* as well as a perception of themselves as a minority group suffering from 'Islamophobia' in the wider society. Muslim identity is often clear-cut, and the boundaries well defined.[6] This of course does not preclude ambivalence in terms of other identifications, nor does it imply universal commitment, but Muslim identity often rests upon some non-negotiable central 'truths' and a distinctive way of life. The differences in the expression of religious identity between young Hindus and Sikhs are less distinctively nuanced, and both faith groups often express an overarching identity based upon a positive appreciation of Indian culture and an awareness of the threat of Muslim extremism. Indeed, in the early days of the formation of the National Hindu Students Forum (NHSF) in 1991, it took an especially 'prominent role in making [its] views known when there was a lot of *Hizb-ut-Tahrir* activities in university campuses such as SOAS, LSE and Sheffield Universities' (Chauhan 1997). They are likely to share a cultural identity based upon being 'Asian' but their core identities are shaped by their membership of their respective religions (Nesbitt 1998:197). Amid a range of various constituents and shifting, situational and often permeable boundaries (*caste,* language, region and so on), Hindu and Sikh identities are contextually-based, on-going processes of narrative construction, to some extent shaped by a clear sense of difference from Muslims. These differences are amplified all the more following inter-religious conflict in the Indian sub-continent itself (Kunda 1994). For young Jews, their identity is less distinctively shaped by recent migration, but nevertheless, preservation of an ethnic identity, in a context of diaspora, remains central. For some youth, regardless of their faith background, their religious identity is strongly allied to a political assertiveness, while for others, their religious identity is purely one of cultural association, without being underpinned by regular practice.[7] Any understanding of religious diversity among students not only has to take into account the persistence of religious identity shared across the major faith groups, but also the differences, distinctions, and similarities that cut across the traditions, between and within each, but also between individuals and groups within these collectivities.

Gerd Baumann has explored in detail the way in which 'all identities are identifications in context and that they are thus situational and flexible, imaginative and innovative – even when they do not intend to be' (Baumann 1999:138). He argues strongly that identity is formed in an environment characterised by a multitude of cleavages that cut across numerous ethnic, religious, linguistic, or regional categories. Baumann's understanding of identity has largely been shaped by ethnographic research in one location, Southall, a town between Heathrow airport and the Western suburbs of London. He has noticed what he calls 'double discursive competence', by which he means the ability of people living in multicultural milieu to know when to reify one of their identities, and when to question these reifications and give way to the 'everyday necessity of crosscutting identifications' (Baumann 1999:139). His observations of identity dynamics advance our understanding of multi-ethnic, multi-faith communities in general, and Southall in particular. However, identity dynamics within the confines of a university community are somewhat different from those in a community setting such as Southall.

The context of a university – or indeed many other large institutions – to some extent forces the reification of identity due to the relative transience of each student's time in the institution. Even prior to entry, students are required to complete application forms and tick boxes and define by pre-formulated categories where they 'belong'. Naturally, identity itself is far more complex than the labels institutions offer, and information is given that 'most nearly' describes the multiplicity of identifications, in terms of race or ethnicity, or other markers of identity. For hospital patients, prisoners, or students of other faiths,

> this encounter with rigid categories is their lived experience, and it probably influences their self-identity despite the fact that [they] may not be able to recognise or categorise themselves in such an unequivocal fashion. Although scepticism about the unitary character of cultures is justified…it is a mistake to ignore the fact that some institutions function *as if* the boundaries separating cultures were sharp and impermeable (Beckford and Gilliat 1998:6).

Universities, like prisons, exemplify the kind of institution that cannot easily accommodate ambiguity or multiplicity in 'official' categories. At present, only a small number of universities require students to state their religious affiliation on application forms, but the universal practice of ethnic monitoring nevertheless asks individuals to describe themselves in a way which leaves little room for the 'crosscutting identifications' observed by Baumann.

Identity dynamics in a multi-ethnic, multi-faith locality are different from those in multi-ethnic, multi-faith institutions. In a university, or a hospital, for instance, one may be required to ascribe a greater significance to some aspects of one's identity than to others, and to identify the most salient features of self-perception and 'modes' of being (as a Hindu, a Southallian, of East African origin, etc.). As yet, only a small number of universities recognise religion as a meaningful category of difference (as seen in equal opportunities policies covering religious identity), but the trend towards the recognition of religious diversity through such policies is growing, particularly in new universities.[8] I will be exploring these in more detail in Chapter 6, but for the time being, we need to be mindful of the distinctiveness of identity dynamics in settled localities and communities and in institutions with a continual turnover in population. In an institution, it is not so possible (or perhaps necessary) to interact with people in such a way that makes Baumann's 'crosscutting identifications' a meaningful strategy for daily life.

Two new student religious societies have emerged in the last decade – the National Hindu Students Forum and the British Organisation of Sikh Students, and both are becoming more active locally and nationally. This must surely tell us something about identity dynamics in institutional contexts, and the fact that identities are becoming more sharply delineated around religion. In the competitive environment of a university institution, identifications related to religious allegiances are becoming increasingly reified. Reflecting on identity in the wake of the Rushdie affair, Bhikhu Parekh notes

> All of us, in our traditional [or wherever we regard 'home' to be] settings, take lots of things about ourselves for granted. We are constantly growing and changing without being aware of it. The immigrant's predicament is different, especially for someone easily distinguishable by their colour or culture. Partly because of an inhospitable society, partly because of their own sense of unease, they feel forced to *define* themselves, to say to others and even to themselves, *who* they are, *what* constitutes their identity or claim to distinction. So to be a Hindu or a Muslim is to do *a, b and c,* and to reject *x, y, z.* And this self-definition then becomes a norm to which all members of a specific group are required to conform (Bhabha and Parekh 1989:25).

There is much that could be drawn out of this quotation. However, the salient point for this discussion is Parekh's observation of the fact that in some circumstances, particularly in unfamiliar, hostile, and I would add institutional contexts, identifications – in this case those relating to religion – become more sharply identifiable and defined, imposed to some extent by the nature of organisational structures and the social relations within them.

Evidence for this has been borne out of recent research on ethnic minorities in higher education by Adia *et al* (1996). In their survey of ethnic minority and white, full-time undergraduates, at 30 British universities in May 1995, respondents were asked to indicate whether or not they had become more aware of their colour and identity from their experience of higher education. Their findings were striking. Nearly 60 per cent of ethnic minority students agreed or strongly agreed with the statement ('from my experience of higher education I am very much more aware of my colour and identity'), compared with only 23 per cent of white respondents (Adia *et al* 1996:59). It was also evident from comments that some ethnic minority students were strongly aware of the importance, for them, of student religious societies, as well as the lack of university recognition of their religious identity.

> *All the different societies such as Sikh society, the Muslim society exist already and I feel are important.*

> *All of my religious holidays/festivals remain unrecognised in the university calendar* (cited in Adia *et al* 1996:64-65).

It seems possible that the *lack of recognition* of religious identity by the institution could be one reason for students becoming *more aware* of the aspects of their own identity that are significant to them. By virtue of the fact that their institutions fail to recognise different collective religious identities, identity becomes even more sharply defined.

If universities are one place where disadvantaged and traditionally excluded groups can construct alternative identities (Scott 1997:46), then for the younger members of Britain's faith communities, universities provide an important opportunity for the shaping of a new identity born out of participation and engagement with wider British society. Perhaps more than their parents and grandparents, young Hindus, Muslims, Sikhs, and others, are aware of the reality that their future lies in Britain, and not 'back home'. Jacobson's research among young Pakistanis in Waltham Forest found that there was 'an implicit or fairly explicit association of Britain with a real sense of home' (Jacobson 1998:69). While their sense of citizenship and belonging to Britain may in some cases be only official (i.e. in having a UK passport) rather than truly meaningful (in terms of regarding themselves as 'British'), youth of Asian origin are on the whole committed to future lives in Britain (Jacobson 1998:67). Universities provide a range of opportunities for furthering this commitment. For example, during my research interviews, a number of representatives from the national student religious organisations made the point that national (and local) leaders/presidents (and some members) of their societies are likely to contribute to the formation of a new generation of 'community leaders' and religious professionals in Britain. These individuals are likely to be significantly different from the previous (and to some extent present) generation of religious and community leaders. Many more are likely to have born in this country and they are likely to be highly educated, articulate, and with English either as their first language or as part of a bi-lingual identity. In only one respect is there likely to be continuity between the different generations of religious/community leaders. Most, if not all, are still men.[9]

There are some significant issues for sociologists of religion to consider arising from the wish of many young Hindus, Muslims, Sikhs, and other youth, for recognition of their *religious* identity in the public sphere and within public institutions. Their concern to engage as religious minority groups powerfully counteracts a dominant trend in the religious life of many British people. It is widely assumed that 'religion is a private affair only, not a driving force for entire groups or a significant symbol system of identification, demarcation and support' (Baumann 1999:2). It is a common presumption that religion and spirituality have largely become the preserve of the private, personal, individual domain. While this may indeed be true for many ordinary British people on a day to day basis, the persistence of religious identity among many of the young members of other faith communities challenges and goes some way towards reversing the trend towards the personalisation of religion, in Britain generally, and in universities particularly.

José Casanova describes this as 'deprivatisation' (Casanova 1994:5), and with it comes a challenge to 'secular' institutions as they are forced to reflect on their normative structures and assumptions. Religion, as it is explored, practised, and contested in universities is increasingly providing evidence for a deviation from the national, middle England norm of 'believing without belonging' (Davie 1994). 'The presence of the new ethnic minorities is not simply changing the character of religion in Britain by diversifying it, but [is] giving it an importance which is out of step with native trends' (Modood 1998:384). One of the challenges posed by the new faith communities is a critique of a definition of religion as a purely subjective, private matter, based upon a philosophy of religion which makes exclusive claims about the boundary and the distinctiveness between the private and the public realm. As a result of this contestation, religion is becoming increasingly politicised.

Religious affiliation and practice in public institutions, such as universities, therefore makes the widespread assumption that religion is simply a private matter unsatisfactory. It is often far from a private matter for many young Muslims, Sikhs, or others, even for those who claim a non-practising or 'associational' identity (Modood 1998:385). Universities bring together, often within a confined geographical space, individuals for whom religious identity, among many other identifications, is at the core of their self-definition. Institutions of higher education are a marketplace of religious ideas and beliefs, in microcosm, and the religious activity that takes place within them provide a unique context for exploring some of the collective dimensions of religion, such as membership and organisation.[10]   Furthermore, public institutions are important 'locations' for religious life and religious exploration, and studies of religious activity in prisons, universities, hospitals, schools, and even (more recently) shopping centres, all point to vigorous activity (Beckford and Gilliat 1996; Jamieson 1994) and debate. They provide a rich context for the ethnographic study of religion, made all the more exciting by the fact that universities are a 'charmed space in which young people are given opportunities to act as autonomous individuals' (Bruce 1995:30).

The vocal claims of religious identity among students can also be regarded as a rejection of the postmodern, and 'the universal melting of identities, dispersal of authorities, and growing fragmentariness of life' (Bauman, 1997:21). In a society where everything is open to question, the absolutes of religion can appear all the more appealing, particularly when the tradition has not been subject to liberal inquiry and attack (Jacobson 1998). The unchanging quality of religious doctrines can provide a foothold along the slippery 'postmodern' path. But the search for, and claiming of an identity, religious or otherwise, is not only confined to young people of migrant origins, but is part of a much wider search for new self-definitions. John Eade writes

> the politics of cultural difference and the process of identity construction are not confined to Britain's ethnic minorities, however. As national belongings in the West are challenged by local and more global imaginings of community, the assertions of a "British", "English", "French", or "Belgian" cultural hegemony

become more tenuous – the rhetoric of national unity notwithstanding (Eade 1994:378).

Young Hindus, Muslims, Christian, Buddhists, and others, are not immune from wider social trends and they are as implicated in the postmodern 'dynamic tension between excitement and terror' (Frosh 1991:cover) as the rest of us. But the so-called postmodern society in which this searching for, and assertion of, identity takes place, has perhaps affected universities even more than the rest of society, and it is within this context that the consequences are perhaps even more visible. This is evident in, argues Krishnan Kumar,

> the criticisms by different racial, ethnic and gender groups of the orthodox curriculum, and their demands for their 'own' studies and departments; the assault by non-Christian religious groups on the predominantly Christian culture of most universities in the West, and their call for the recognition of the distinctive ways of their own cultures (Kumar 1997:30).

Sociologists of religion who maintain that religion is in decline in terms of significance and in terms of numerical trends (see for example Bruce 1995) will find from this book that most universities are far from being wholly 'secular' institutions, regardless of their history or foundations. Some may be anti-religious, but that is not the same thing. Furthermore, there are values in the 'secular' stance promoted by some institutions that can be profoundly helpful for the management of religious diversity, as we shall see. The religious dynamics contained within universities and indeed their responses to religion belie any justifiable claim to be secular. The very nature of institutions themselves – universities included – makes them prime sites for engagement with religious practice, and the testing of religious identities: 'in an increasingly home-based, privatised society, universities are among the few surviving institutions that draw people out of their private spaces and, for a brief but crucial time, encourage them to engage in shared public activity' (Kumar 1997:34). The religious trends in contemporary Britain are ignored by universities at their peril, while sociologists of religion have much to learn about contemporary religion by its practice and politics in universities. For example, the closing chapters of this book explore the distinctive processes of *deprivatisation* and *desecularisation* that are taking place in many universities, and consider what this might mean for our understanding of religion in contemporary society. While there is certainly no evidence for a wholesale 'return to religion' on the campus, nevertheless, the increasing membership and activity of student religious organisations, is to some extent counterbalancing the evident and more general decline in Christian activity.[11] There is evidence for simultaneous but differential patterns of growth and dissolution.

Some universities in large cities, especially those already characterised by ethnic, cultural, racial and religious diversity, provide the potential context for a new (and sometimes explosive) religious and cultural dynamic where the diversity of identity claims meet head-on. Cohen (1995) also predicts from his perspective at the University of East London that

> global geopolitical issues will become increasingly mapped onto the local terrain of campus politics and may lead to the staging of culture wars around issues of race, ethnicity and Eurocentrism....In many of the newer universities, we have seen a change in the student culture away from the socialist agendas of the "broad Left", and also away from "alternative" green or feminist concerns towards a narrowly based and highly sectarian identity politics.   The emergence of Afrocentric ideologies preaching a form of ethnic absolutism as well as growth in support for Islamic fundamentalism amongst some Moslem students, point to one possible direction for the future, in which anti-semitism, anti-feminism and homophobia mesh in with anti-capitalist and anti-European rhetorics to create a "backlash" (Cohen 1995:5).

The situation does not have to be as confrontational as Cohen suggests, especially if universities foster an environment to creatively manage, nurture, and embrace the diversity within them. But it would not be surprising to find university administrators who wish that religion *would* remain in the private sphere, rather than contend with the difficulties and complications that a diversity of contested religious identities can pose on the doorstep of the institution. It is not for nothing that some feel that 'religion is one of the biggest issues on the campus' (Walker 1994).

Religious rights and recognition

The claims that different religious groups in Britain have made for public recognition are often mirrored in the interaction between students of different faiths and their universities. These claims are often a combination of practical concerns, such as the right to observe religious dietary requirements or worship obligations, as well as political aspirations, such as protection from discrimination and the right to recognition as distinctive religious (rather than, or as well as ethnic) minority groups. Both national religious community leaders and student religious society presidents are expressing a wish for inclusion and recognition, and the ability to shape their own destinies, on their own terms. Religious values are often the central organising principle for life in minority traditions, individually and collectively, and they underpin a wide range of activities. This radically contrasts with the more privatised, individually-orientated spirituality of many British people. For some faith communities, particularly Islam, it is impossible to make a distinction between sacred/private and secular/public spheres. Minority faith groups are therefore expressing a general desire not only for public recognition, but they are also making the claim that their *religious needs, life-worlds, and values must shape their interaction with public institutions*. In the case of Muslims, this amounts to the demand for 'some degree of Islamicisation of the civic' (Modood 1998:387).

The assertion of 'rights' is strongly connected to the creation of strong, politicised identities. When the characteristics of identity and difference are subject to discrimination, or are under threat, it is not surprising that dormant or latent identities come to the fore, and that collective identities become galvanised and politicised in the processes of community action and mobilisation. This was particularly evident among British Muslims in the wake of the Rushdie affair. Not only was Islamic identity strengthened, but Muslims became aware of a very particular way in which they were vulnerable as a religious minority group. One of the consequences has been concerted action for the right to protection from religious discrimination and recognition as an oppressed religious group[12] (UKACIA:1993).

Despite the changing sociological make-up of universities, not least the growth in mature students, most students are still predominantly in their late teens and early twenties, encountering perhaps for the first time a sense of adulthood, choice, and freedom away from the family environment. The years spent at university are part of an on-going project of personal formation and identity-development. The way that universities respond to students of different faiths, and especially their calls for religious 'rights' and representation, is likely to set the stamp upon their future perceptions of other public institutions and their place in public life. Universities are also sites of cultural engagement and exploration, and if issues of religious diversity, rights and representation cannot be debated and explored in this context, then where else?

'The belief in innate human rights has achieved quasi-religious status in the late-modern world' and belief in human rights now has 'considerable ideological force' (Spickard 1999:1). James Spickard traces this back to the European Enlightenment and the West's struggle against monarchy. He regards the high point of this venture as the adoption of the Universal Declaration of Human Rights by the United Nations in 1948. Since then, the vocabulary of human rights has been exported, developed, and has gained recognition in many parts of the world. Spickard identifies four key 'themes' or principles underpinning 'rights': moral individualism, human equality, social interconnectedness, and universalism. We read and hear about a wide range of groups campaigning for their individual 'rights' or the collective rights of others as part of a new wave of lifestyle politics: the right to privacy, animal rights, gay rights, environmental rights, the rights of minorities. 'People now use the idiom of rights to support anything that they think necessary for dignity and freedom, however defined' (Spickard 1999:4). I do not want to pursue here Spickard's argument that rights have become quasi-religious and sacrosanct, but rather highlight the fact that issues of religious rights and recognition played out in universities are part and parcel of a more general concern with 'rights' in many other social spheres.

Young Hindus, Muslims, Sikhs, and others from minority traditions, are part of a society where the vocabulary of 'rights' is prominent. However, while many of the UN or other declarations of rights are framed in terms of the rights of the individual, many of the concerns of student religious groups are conceived as 'a category of rights more collective in conception than the traditionally individualist Civil Rights, but far more exclusive in character than generally Human Rights' (Baumann 1996:13).   As succeeding chapters will make clear, demands for worship space, for example, are fought on the basis of a collective right of a distinctive group to observe the requirements of a religious tradition.   The Western vocabulary of 'rights' is used to campaign for provisions that may go against the principles that underpin 'rights' themselves.   The basis of 'rights' identified by Spickard, namely, moral individualism, human equality, social interconnections, and universalism, may in addition be used to assert collective rights *against* other groups and against individuals.   This reflects an

> exploring again whether some rights do not properly adhere to groups...and the perception that minority rights may need to be more broadly fashioned than is possible so long as they remain rights of individuals. The question of group rights has also become relevant in the context of new "third and fourth generation" rights now being proposed, such as the rights of indigenous peoples, and others. With regard to these "new generation" rights, there is still considerable debate as to their status as human rights, not only because of the novelty of groups or peoples as the beneficiary, but also because of the uncertainty of the content of the right or the obligations imposed thereby and on whom (Higgins 1996:387).

The way in which some young people are making collective claims on the basis of their religious identity can be regarded as part of a wider process of assessing and renegotiating the scope of rights, from the individual to the collective.   As the above quotation makes clear much uncertainty remains as to how this extension of rights might work in practice, especially in a context where different groups are making claims which may impact on other groups.   When the principles of religious freedom and equality are harnessed to the aspirations of different religious groups for recognition of their collective rights within the confines of a university campus, it is no wonder that clashes occasionally occur.

An earlier part of this chapter identified a 'push' factor behind the growth in the number of students of British-Asian backgrounds in higher education, namely family honour and reputation.   A son or daughter who enters a prestigious professional occupation following a successful university career significantly enhances the standing of his or her family among their local (and often international) network of kin.   But there is another significant 'push' factor.   Many parents of young Hindus, Muslims, and Sikhs, and other minority faith groups, wish upon their children better prospects and opportunities than they themselves experienced.   Acland and Azmi found that Asian parents stress the value of higher education for overcoming racial and socio-economic barriers.   One of their interviewees reported 'my parents don't want us to have the same struggle they had' (Acland and Azmi 1998:78).   Higher education is regarded as one avenue towards compensating and making-up for past discrimination and exclusion.   Young people from ethnic minority backgrounds are claiming their 'right' to higher education as an avenue towards better prospects.[13]

Some deeply embedded and entrenched values and assumptions in British society, and in universities, are challenged by the newly emerging collective religious identities on campus, especially when these are harnessed with assertive demands for certain facilities and rights in order to observe particular religious lifestyles. Universities are institutions where ideas of liberalism (and with it individual autonomy), and rationalism, are woven into the corporate fabric, and these ideas exert an enormous influence on *their* identity. Older universities represent continuity, stability, prestige, longevity, traditions, and 'reputation'. However, the ethos that results from these assumptions and ideas are implicitly (and sometimes even explicitly) hostile to the recognition of differences of race, ethnicity, religion, politics and culture. Many contemporary universities foster a worldview based upon a specific view of the individual, the institution, and of reciprocal rights and obligations, and the virtues of assimilation into the corporate liberal, individualist ethos. Parekh asserts that 'liberalism has always remained assimilationist: others must become like us, my present is your future' (Parekh and Bhabha 1989:27). It is a worldview that leaves little scope for the multiplicity of cross-cutting, contextual, collective identities emerging among religious and ethnic minority youth.

My research has examined the extent to which universities have responded to religious diversity and demands for recognition in a wide variety of practical ways. Yet underneath these responses to diversity and claims for recognition (or the ignoring of them), is a fundamental question of whether institutions have been able to recognise the significance of new religious collectivities. Through the provision of worship facilities, or a timetabling of examinations that takes the religious calendar into account, we are able to assess how universities have begun to engage with new social realities and the significance of group differences.

Universities often promote an institutional ethos of corporate belonging and identification with the ideals of the institution. Different religious affiliation, ethnicity, or sexuality are in this way regarded as private individual choices that should be confined to non-political social contexts. Yet this has a consequence for the overall character of the social environment of the university, in that such confinement automatically results in the exclusion of *groups* from engagement with corporate life. It is not surprising that lack of access to the public fora of an institution then results in some degree of assertiveness. 'It is a politics of projecting identities in order to challenge existing power relations; of seeking not just toleration for ethnic difference but also public acknowledgement, resources and representation' (Modood 1997:290). Campaigns for Muslim prayer facilities on campus are one expression of this politics. Furthermore, the relegation of religious perspectives to the private realm has the effect of defining 'each religion as a peculiar deviation, something to be measured against a more privileged secular norm...this hardly opens up the space for dialogue between different positions' (Philips 1997:26). One new university in the north east of England has taken the innovative step in establishing regular meetings between particular faith groups, senior officers and chaplains within the institution. In this way, students from different faiths have the opportunity to speak for themselves 'to the institution' in the knowledge that their voices will be heard. As well as furthering better mutual understanding, these 'Liaison Group' meetings can diffuse potentially difficult situations. This kind of innovation in a multi-faith, 'secular' university, indicates that formal recognition of collective religious identities can be an important mechanism for promoting good relations between students and institutions.

Compared to their counterparts 20 or 30 years ago, students themselves now have new expectations of higher education. In some senses they now regard themselves as 'consumers' in negotiation with 'providers', and going to university is now often perceived as a stage in everyone's life, and not an experience for an elite minority (Scott 1997:46).

> The university has become a crucial *rite de passage* in the development of citizens. It provides a transformative experience in people's lives when identities may be decisively shaped and lasting friendships and associations contracted (Smith and Webster 1997:8).

But the new perception of students as consumers (particularly since the introduction of tuition fees) while on the one hand empowering, is on the other hand diminishing. 'Their immediate demands are likely to be satisfied [while] their longer-term needs may be ignored and their participation in a symbolic, transcendental, and even magical, experience will be denied' (Scott 1997:46). Whatever the long-term implications of this more consumerist attitude to higher education, students now have a much stronger sense of their 'rights', as consumers of a 'product'. Where institutions once thrived on the intimacy of the learning experience between students and lecturers, the learning environment has been transformed into a rigorously assessed, evaluated, and negotiated sphere of expectations and demands. Students' anticipation of certain standards and provisions has extended beyond the strictly academic, and they now regard the provision of certain opportunities and facilities as a legitimate 'right'. A new poster campaign launched by the National Union of Students in August 1999 encouraged students to 'SPEAK OUT' and to 'name and shame' institutions that fail to listen and respond to complaints, whether about teaching quality or facilities (Pakes 1999). It is likely that continued demands for religious provision, for example, will be one consequence of this new expression of consumer rights.

In the Introduction I showed how, over the past decade, academic attention has begun to shift away from issues of *access* to higher education, to the *quality of experience* that students of different ethnic (and religious) backgrounds enjoy whilst at university. This shift marks an important change of focus, since 'the quality dimension requires addressing institutional behaviour and practices that affect the psychosocial environment and making explicit the impact of the environment on academic success' (Smith 1995:224). In other words, the focus comes to settle on institutional practices and climates, and on the way institutions respond to difference and/or intolerance. The structural and social inequalities – both implicit and explicit – begin to come into view. In the next three chapters, the ways in which universities have responded to religious diversity reveal the extent of some of these inequalities, as well as some examples of good practice and innovation in the face of change.

Notes

1	Latest figures from the Higher Education Statistics Agency (reported in the *Times Higher Education Supplement* 16th July 1999) show that students from ethnic minority backgrounds accounted for 14 per cent of the total home-domiciled first year undergraduates of known ethnicity in the academic year 1997/8. This represents a 13 per cent increase compared to 1996/7 figures. The rise in numbers is particularly due to the admission of students of Bangladeshi, Pakistani, and Indian background.
2	For a more detailed discussion of the issues involved in compiling statistics about the size of religious groups in Britain readers are directed to Weller. P. (1997), p.29. This volume also gives alternative statistical data about the size of religious faith communities in Britain and the figures offered by the *Directory* are, as follows, in alphabetical order: Bahai's – 6,000; Buddhists – 30,000-130,000; Christians – 40,000,000; Hindus – 400,000-500,000; Jains – 25,000-30,000; Jews – 300,000; Muslims – 1,000,000-1,500,000; Sikhs – 350,000-500,000; Zoroastrians – 5,000-10,000.
3	They also cite the findings of other research that suggests that many South Asian parents are keen for their offspring to use higher education to secure a better place for themselves in society. Females who are permitted to study away from home are particularly under pressure to succeed, as failure often brings shame upon the family.
4	See the section on 'accommodation' in Chapter 5 for a discussion of gender and recruitment to universities, particularly among some ethnic minority faith groups.
5	For example, in a press release issued by the Policy Studies Institute, prior to the publication of Modood, T. and Shiner, M. (1994), one of the main findings highlighted in the statement was that many British students with Caribbean and Pakistani origins were more likely to be entering the 'new' universities compared to, say, Chinese students.
6	In using the word 'boundary', I am mindful of Richard Jenkins' cautionary note that 'it is far from clear where or what the boundary of any particular identity "is"…[and that] identity is about boundary *processes* rather than boundaries' (Jenkins 1996:98).
7	The distinctiveness and overlaps between cultural, ethnic and national identity are very clearly discussed in Jackson (1997), pp.83-88.
8	Most hospitals and prisons require patients or prisoners to state their religion, or to identify themselves as having 'no religion'.
9	A recent exception to this is the election of a female president of UJS.
10	Peter Berger describes the pluralistic situation as 'above all, a market situation' where religious institutions become marketing agencies and the religious traditions become consumer commodities (Berger 1969:138). Certainly, the religious societies actively promote and 'sell' membership along with other student associations at Freshers' Fairs etc.

11   There are no statistics to provide conclusive evidence for the decline of Christian activity in higher education over time, or likewise, the increasing activity among students of other faiths more recently. However, the emergence and local and national support for student religious organisations is a good indicator. Similarly, evidence about a *local* situation can sometimes point to wider trends. For example, a chaplain at a Church college noted that by the 1970s, 'worshipping numbers were small' in the College chapel (Ridley 1989:45), and this observation is likely to be applicable nationwide, in other Church Colleges.

12   The Home Office has commissioned research on the nature and extent of religious discrimination in Britain. This work has recently begun at the University of Derby, under the directorship of Professor Paul Weller (*Q News,* no. 308, July 1999). Also see the Internet site http://www.multifaithnet.org/.

13   This 'push' factor finds a parallel in the early history of Roman Catholics in higher education: 'when most doors to professional advancement had been closed, they had not felt a pressing need for university education' (McClelland 1973:5). Likewise, the early migrants to Britain post 1945 were mainly employed in unskilled or semi-skilled work, and there were few opportunities in skilled professional work open to them. As for Catholics in the 19th century, the children and grandchildren of minority faith groups are using universities as an avenue towards better employment prospects.

Chapter 4

Chaplaincies: Organisation, Funding and Staffing

Chaplains in higher education

Most religious activity in universities is organised and managed through chaplaincies. To understand how universities have responded to religious diversity, it is useful to begin the investigation by considering the activities that take place in chaplaincies. This section begins by looking at the background, funding, and identity of chaplains themselves.

The range of higher education chaplaincies and the experiences of chaplains are as diverse as the institutions in which they are based. Some chaplains work as part of ecumenical chaplaincy 'teams', while others work alone. Some are on single site campuses, while others find themselves on several sites dispersed over a wide geographical area. In some universities, chaplains are paid employees of the institution, while others are more appropriately regarded as 'guests'. Some universities do not even tolerate a church/denominational presence or association. It would be difficult to draw any conclusions about how institutions of higher education have responded to increasing religious diversity without presenting as accurately as possible the range of financial and staffing profiles.

My research was more concerned with the institutions in which chaplains work rather than with chaplains themselves. In order to profile chaplains, much more data would have been needed about their background and training prior to their appointment.[1] For the purposes of the study, it was sufficient to know that the majority of chaplains were male, and at the time of the research, most had not been in their current posts for long. While higher education chaplaincy is a lifelong career for some, for the majority it appears to be a stage in their overall clerical or ministerial career, or an interruption from other types of sector ministry or parish work. It is clear that professional higher education chaplaincy experiences a relatively high turnover in personnel.[2] The consequences of this for the accumulation of wisdom about the politics of religion in universities are self-evident; chaplains who move on to other kinds of ministry are likely to leave the normative structures governing religious life on campus unchanged. But it is hard to reconcile the fact that there is not only a high turnover of chaplains, but apparently also no shortage of candidates for chaplaincy posts. Working among bright people engaged in interesting activities, while not having to cope with cubs, the Mother's Union and the steeple restoration fund has its attractions (Kingston 1994).

It would be interesting to identify precisely what appears to drive chaplains out of higher education ministry and back into parishes, or other sector ministries, though this would constitute a separate investigation.[3]

The title 'chaplain' is the most common label by which personnel in question are identified by their institutions, with the exception of some of the collegiate university colleges where the title 'Dean of Chapel' is more common. This question of titles is significant, especially given the explicit Christian connotations and origins of the word 'chaplain'.[4] If the sole religious professional employed by a university is titled 'chaplain', this can send a powerful message about the remit of his or her work, and the religious identity of the students and staff that the chaplain is assumed to work with. Furthermore, in a multi-faith institution, it cannot be assumed that everyone will know what a 'chaplain' is, or does. This was a concern for the chaplain at a large, new university in the north of England. During interview, she was at pains to point out that familiarity with religious terminology and vocabulary has declined, both within the institution and in society more generally. As a consequence, she had suggested adoption of an alternative label of 'Senior Pastoral Adviser'. This, she considered, would make clearer her multi-faith, ecumenical remit, and would indicate a general pastoral/advisory role, rather than a narrowly religious/Christian one. It is also significant to note that a title such as 'Senior Pastoral Adviser' does not imply that its holder belongs to any specific religious tradition, and this opens up the possibility that full time chaplains of other faiths might increasingly participate in professional chaplaincy.

The presence of a chaplain on a university campus inevitably leads to questions about precisely where he or she belongs. Are chaplains institutional employees, paid for by the university, or simply 'visiting' clergy? Questions about money, and particularly about its sources, are crucial. The findings that emerge about the source of chaplains' salaries indicate considerable diversity in sources, with the nature of the institution being a significant determinant of the source and level of funding. My research was concerned principally with how those individuals who are regarded by their institutions or their churches/denominations as 'the' chaplain are funded.

Table 4.1 Funding of institutional chaplaincy posts

Source of funding

	University	Church or denomination	Trust Fund	'Other'
Collegiate university colleges	23	1	1	1
Church colleges	3	1	0	2
New universities	3	12	1	10
University of London colleges	1	1	0	2
Old universities	2	22	1	2
'Other' institutions (e.g. music/art schools)	0	1	0	1
TOTALS	32	38	3	18

Before discussing some of the figures in this table, the funding category 'Other' warrants a little further explanation. This category reflects all those responses that suggest more complex funding arrangements, but at least three chaplains in this group are funded by a straightforward 'half and half' matched funding arrangement between the institution and the church or denomination. Among the remainder, some chaplaincy work is voluntary (especially where non-stipendiary clergy act as chaplains to smaller institutions on an occasional basis). In other cases, their salaries or stipends come from a collaborative funding arrangement between different denominations. Some chaplaincy posts are funded by a tripartite combination of institutional, denominational, and trust fund sources.

The integral role of chaplains in the history and foundation of collegiate university colleges is clearly reflected in current funding for chaplains in these institutions. Their colleges almost entirely and exclusively fund them. Funding patterns for Welsh and Scottish chaplains are diametric opposites. Most of the Scottish chaplains are paid by their institutions. In contrast, no chaplains in Welsh universities receive institutional support for their work, relying almost exclusively upon the Anglican Church (Church in Wales) for their salaries/stipends. Equally striking is the contrast between 'new' and 'old' universities in the UK in terms of funding chaplaincy posts. Chaplains in older universities appear to be supported very clearly either by their institution (rarely) or by their Church/denomination. This is a much more clear cut division than in the new universities where fewer chaplains are reliant upon their Church or denomination for their salary. Quite a number of institutions that gained the status of universities in 1992 appear to rely upon collaborative funding arrangements. This points to the forging of agreements between institutions, religious trust funds, and Churches, and suggests that some effort and thought lie behind the funding of a number of chaplaincy posts in new universities. Overall, it remains the case that the majority of chaplains outside collegiate universities are still funded by their Churches or denominations, rather than by the institutions in which they work. It is important to note however, that as the number of higher education chaplaincy posts has grown universities rather than Churches/denominations have increasingly assumed responsibility for the entire or partial cost of each post.

Chaplains occupy a unique position in the institutional hierarchy, being 'in' the institution, but not 'of' it. Serving two 'masters', the Church and the university, there can of course be tensions, but chaplains can use their ambiguous structural situation to good effect. Regardless of the benefit the Churches perceive in the presence of chaplains in universities, there is much for universities to gain by having chaplains. Academics are often unable or unwilling to engage with student support to any significant degree (it is not in their contracts) while counselling services generally operate a timetabled booking system. The presence of chaplains provides an important avenue for immediate student support, and relieves the pressure upon institutions in times of crisis. For example, during the meningitis outbreak in South Wales in 1997 that claimed the lives of two Cardiff University students, the chaplain was one of the only individuals 'free' to talk to and reassure anxious students queuing for vaccinations.

The overwhelming majority of chaplains are emphatic about an inclusive approach to chaplaincy work, and their availability for, and responsibility to, the whole institution regardless of the range of religious identities contained within it.[5] Despite this perception, some find that in reality they work primarily with Christians. The structured way in which some of them regard their ministry is interesting, one noting that he works with the 'whole institution (pastorally and structurally) but primarily with Christians (liturgically)'. Nearly half of the chaplains surveyed also went on to give examples of situations where they help students from the other faith communities. The kind of instances are both personal (family problems, bereavement, homesickness) as well as more practical, such as providing information about local faith communities, and helping students to establish their own religious societies. In reality, it appears that for many of the non-liturgical tasks chaplains perform, a religious professional of *any* faith could undertake the role just as adequately. Quite possibly, it is also increasingly difficult for chaplains to justify their position if they do not (at least in terms of rhetoric) aim to provide pastoral oversight for the whole institution, particularly if they are funded from the university budget. The question of how to justify this theologically is an issue for chaplains themselves, rather than a sociological matter.

Many institutions in turn expect their chaplains to work with the entire university community. The mutual perception of roles appears to coincide. For example, among those chaplains with job descriptions, a third specifically explain that they are required to work in a multi-faith capacity. New universities are more likely than any other kind of institution to make reference to the inclusive character of the chaplain's task.

The pastoral identity of chaplains

From these findings, we can identify a cluster of interesting paradoxes, some of which are paralleled in other institutional chaplaincy settings. In 1998 all chaplains surveyed were Christian and over half had their salaries met by their Churches or denominations. But many chaplains report working with students (and staff) of all faiths and taking responsibility, if only notionally, for the religious welfare of the entire institution. Their liturgical function is now one element of a wide range of religious 'management' tasks. This constellation of findings, combined with evidence from chaplaincy work in other public institutions, suggests that the title 'chaplain' (where it remains in common parlance) is likely to begin carrying a more generic (and professional) connotation, especially if other traditions adopt this title for some of their religious professionals. Though the context is clearly very different, a hospital chaplain from the United States has identified the kind of trend that we are beginning to see in Britain: 'although Presbyterian or Jewish or Catholic, the unit chaplain functions as a no-brand, "one-size-fits-all", generic pastor' (Furniss 1995:3). In a study of chaplaincy in English hospitals it was clear too that the 'management' element bound up with chaplaincy work is almost beginning to overshadow (but concomitantly professionalise?) other dimensions of the role. One chaplain commented, 'I sometimes wonder how long it will be before all the "managerial" responsibilities and expectations totally overwhelm my role as prophet/priest/pastor!' (Beckford and Gilliat 1996a:302). The result has been that chaplains on the whole tend to be regarded as the institutional 'experts' on religious and spiritual matters, and this role has apparently helped them to survive the contemporary culture of auditing, appraisal, assessment, and concern for efficiency. A direct consequence has been their scope to take up a more professional image and a greater degree of institutionalisation for chaplaincy *per se*, even if these transitions have not been subject to much theological scrutiny or reflection. As a hospital chaplain commented for 'The Church of England and Other Faiths Project',[6]

> as a full-time chaplain I was "made" a manager. This has increased my status in hospital. I have greater communication with the managerial staff in general and particularly with [the] Chief Executive and senior managers. I can exert greater influence on spiritual issues (Beckford and Gilliat 1996a:301).

The expectations that public institutions have of chaplains, when combined with the inclusive approach that chaplains themselves are more or less required to promote, suggests that chaplains are being increasingly pulled by the forces of diversity and secularisation towards the roles of 'humanistic professional' and/or religious counsellor (Furniss 1995:3). Some public institutions, and in this case, some new universities, are now requiring chaplains to take account of religious diversity by placing their own religious identity, in some senses, to one side. The centrality of the specific traditions of Anglican chaplaincy in collegiate university colleges would make such a move unthinkable. This discrepancy between two different types of higher education institution clearly locates new universities and Oxbridge colleges along very different courses in their response to religious diversity.

The previous chapter has already pointed to the growth in the number of chaplains being appointed by universities. Chaplaincy in other public institutions is also remarkably healthy (Fay 1994). Given that chaplaincy is one of the least 'measurable' aspects of institutional life, it is remarkable that this professional occupation has survived (numerically) rather than declined amid our contemporary culture of auditing and budgetary pressures. To some extent, the question of whether public institutions have a responsibility for the spiritual and religious welfare of their populations largely depends on the nature of the institution. Clearly, the Prison Service has a responsibility to enable prisoners to observe their religious traditions whilst incarcerated, and this is enshrined within various Prison Acts, Prison Rules, and Standing Orders (Beckford and Gilliat 1998:27-8). But in universities, and to some extent hospitals, it seems that institutional managers and decision-makers regard it as expedient to employ a religious professional. Chaplains will undertake tasks that other administrators or support staff may be unwilling to accept. The Head of Student Services at a new university in the north of England pointed out that only the chaplain was willing to be available 24 hours a day, and that this was in marked contrast to the scheduled hours of the counselling service staff. At the same institution, the chaplain regarded herself as the institution's 'ambulance service'. The move towards a role defined by increasing managerial responsibility and crisis management suggests a clear secularisation of the chaplaincy role, and a clearly pragmatic, utilitarian approach to the work of chaplains by institutions.

This utilitarian approach is most evident in the kinds of situations in which chaplains are consulted by their institutions. One chaplain commented: 'senior management is often dependent on us for on the spot information and support of staff in times of re-organisation'. The importance of chaplains to the institution – as they perceive it – is often sporadic, but in some situations they play a pivotal role in institutional responses to events such as the death or suicide of a student. However, the overwhelming evidence in the questionnaire responses and interviews with chaplains in 1998 suggests that many universities are attempting to engage with multi-faith issues, if only reactively, and chaplains have been important for the development of institutional responses.

Chaplains are consulted by their institutions about questions of religious diversity more than on any other single issue, regardless of the type of institution. Perhaps not surprisingly, the needs of Muslim students (particularly for prayer facilities) principally exercise institutions. This is because Muslim students often form one of the larger groups of students from a faith background outside the Christian Churches and also because of the particular requirements that they have for regular patterns of obligatory prayer and associated ablution facilities. The issues surrounding worship and prayer space are considered in more depth in the following chapter. Aside from responding to Muslim needs specifically, chaplains report a whole gamut of other institutional concerns. These include such things as the activities of new religious movements, institutional ceremonies, and rites of passage. Chaplains are being extensively consulted about ways in which their institutions might respond to the increasing religious diversity of the student population, and they are expected to be knowledgeable about the beliefs and practices of a range of religious traditions. The expanding role of 'chaplain-as-institutional religious-expert' is clear, and represents a significant departure from a historically narrower role of simply 'caring for souls' and leading corporate worship.

Expenditure of chaplaincy resources

Historically, most institutions have relied upon Churches and denominations when it comes to employing chaplains. Surrounded by general apathy about religious activity and assumptions of continuity, the gradual transition from Church/denominational funding of chaplaincy posts to entire or partial institutional support appears to have gone unnoticed in the world of higher education. Similarly, the sources and deployment of funds for religious activity more generally have not been subject to extensive scrutiny. This is one of the consequences of chaplaincy being widely regarded as marginal to the 'real' work of universities.

Many universities, in one way or another, fund religious activity. In institutions that perceive themselves as strictly secular this is an interesting situation, made all the more fascinating by rigorous investigation of how money is actually spent and the religious groups that benefit from it. Some universities, particularly those that claim to be secular, are decidedly embarrassed about institutional resources being spent on religion. For example, one chaplain at a civic 'secular' university founded at the end of the last century reported having had considerable difficulty in getting his institution to set an upper limit on chaplaincy spending for such things as printing and photocopying. He noted that the University authorities were uncomfortable and reluctant about specifying any figures, largely because this would amount to an open and documented authorisation and allocation of funds for religion.

Not surprisingly, there are some distinctive differences between the various types of institution when it comes to funding for chaplaincy and religious activities. But the differences are largely of degree, rather than of kind. Despite the fact that students of other faiths represent the growth area in religious activity on campuses, institutional resources channelled through chaplaincies continue to principally benefit Christian students. It appears that the inclusive, institutionally-focused pastoral identity of chaplains does not correspond with their deployment of resources.

Not surprisingly, collegiate university colleges support chaplaincy activities to the greatest extent. The comments of one chaplain at a Cambridge college capture the experiences of many others: 'finance is seldom an issue'. Money is freely available for such things as organ and choral scholarships; chapel clerk scholarships; heating, lighting and maintenance of the chapel and chaplaincy office; general expenses for the chaplain; chaplaincy trips and missions; expenses for high-profile visiting preachers; secretarial support, and, entertainment. Support for entertainment was specifically mentioned by eight different chaplains, but occurred in virtually no other responses from other types of institution. Clearly, Cambridge, Durham, and Oxford chaplains regard themselves as having a well-supported social life as part of their role! The fact that Anglican traditions lie at the very core of many collegiate university colleges appears to mean that scope for funding diverse religious groups is minimal. In keeping with the statutes and traditions of these colleges, funding is exclusively for Christian students and activities. The comments, 'totally', and 'a great deal' captured the extent to which funding is for the benefit of Christians only, whether practising or nominal. The implications of this are clear. Christian students who take an active part in the religious life of their colleges will have access to opportunities, scholarships, and a social life that will make their student experience distinctly more privileged than most other students in the UK, whether Christian or otherwise.

In other types of institution, whether explicitly secular or not, there is considerable diversity in the extent to which institutions support chaplaincy activities.[7] Some chaplains receive no support at all from their institutions, while others can boast the following: 'provision of centre (3 small, adjacent cottages); part-time secretary/receptionist; some expenses and staff development training; honorarium to team members; photocopier, post; phone; coffee; books; furniture'.[8] In between these extremes, most chaplains mention provision of premises, furniture, office support, and general expenses, ranging from the token (£250) to quite significant sums of money (£10,000). Provision of offices and office maintenance, largely 'hidden' support, can clearly be regarded as quite legitimate necessities for chaplains to function within the institution.

However, under a closer examination of how more 'visible' funds are spent which directly benefit one religious group rather than another, the lack of parity between faith groups becomes much more transparent. Where chaplains (regardless of the type of institution) make reference to one-off as opposed to regular religious provision financially supported by their institutions, these appear to be specifically for Christians. Students claiming a Christian religious identity are the principal beneficiaries of any money spent on hospitality, entertainment, chaplaincy outings, missions, retreats, or preachers.

If, in the future, institutional support is more evidently channelled via chaplaincies into one-off events such as Eid celebrations or expenses for visiting preachers from other faiths, then it might be possible to claim that funding of religious activity is beginning to reflect the religious diversity of the student body. But while most institutional support of religious activity – such as it is – remains the preserve of Christians, it is not surprising to find that students belonging to other faiths feel a sense of inequality and injustice.[9] There is some way to go before any claims to parity can be made. Of course, there are some notable exceptions, but often within institutions where the chaplain has been personally and very strongly committed to a multi-faith approach.

The involvement of other religious professionals

Chaplains are the personnel most concerned with religion at most universities and they take principal responsibility for managing budgets, and where necessary, recruiting volunteers or assistants onto the chaplaincy team. As individuals, they hold often hold little power within the institution, but within the remit of the chaplaincy, they can exert considerable and sometimes overriding influence. As a consequence, it is not surprising to find that the Anglican church and the other main Christian denominations often have two or three of their members associated with a particular chaplaincy, either on a voluntary basis or as part of their clerical/ministerial role. Provision for Christian students, in terms of personnel, is generally strong, particularly in large institutions operating ecumenical 'teams'. The denominational preferences of students can often be accommodated, and some universities even have Christian chaplains for students sharing a particular ethnic/racial background, such as Chinese Christians.

Given the gatekeeping role of most higher education chaplains, it is often they who decide who 'fits' within the definition of the chaplaincy team, and where the boundary of inclusion and exclusion lies. They can exert considerable influence in terms of who is 'in' and who is 'out' and ultimate responsibility for the composition of the team tends to rest with them. As a consequence, some chaplains will regard the Jewish Rabbi/chaplain as part of the team, but not the Imam or the Hindu priest.[10] The politics of 'recognition' vary from institution to institution, and depend on a wide range of variables: historical/institutional traditions, personal inclinations, the availability of religious advisers from other faiths, student demand, and so on. The extent to which Rabbis, Imams, or priests actively involve themselves in chaplaincy activities and conduct their work under the umbrella of the chaplaincy (as opposed to working solely with student religious organisations), also appears to be an important variable. However, some new universities have pro-actively sought to associate a wide range of religious advisers with the chaplaincy, in keeping with the promotion of a 'multi-faith' image in relation to religion on campus.

Mindful of the variables listed above, table 4.2 below gives a breakdown of the range and numbers of religious advisers of other faiths involved in higher education. The table measures both those who are 'included' members of a team, as well as more remote 'advisers' who are associated with the chaplaincy but who, for whatever reason are effectively 'excluded' from its corporate life.[11]

The table deliberately does not reflect the involvement of Rabbis/or Jewish chaplains, and responses from the collegiate university colleges. The exclusion of Jewish representatives is due to the fact that the Jewish community has a nation-wide structure whereby regional chaplains have responsibility for the institutions in their area. These structures and the work of Rabbis are discussed in Appendix 7. Full-time Rabbis or Jewish chaplains will be associated with a number of different institutions, so recording each occasion that chaplains mentioned the involvement of Jews would have given a misleading (over-inflated) impression of the numbers of Rabbis/chaplains professionally involved in higher education. The exclusion of data from the collegiate university colleges is a reflection of the fact that religious activity takes place not only within specific colleges but also at a university level. The provision for students of other faiths *at a college level* is virtually non-existent, but there are a number of religious professionals involved with these kinds of institution *at a university level.*

Table 4.2 Religious advisers of other faiths in higher education, excluding Rabbis/Jewish chaplains and responses from collegiate colleges[12]

	Full-time	Part-time	Volunteers	Totals
Baha'i	0	1	3	4
Buddhist	0	0	14	14
Hindu	0	0	5	5
Jain	0	0	0	0
Muslim	0	7	19	26
Sikh	0	1	5	6
Zoroastrian	0	0	0	0
'Other'	0	0	0	0
Total	0	Total 9	Total 46	Total 55

Representation from Muslim and Buddhist communities clearly figures strongly compared to other faith groups. There is little professional or volunteer religious support for Hindu and Sikh students, not to mention the other smaller faith communities. But to what extent do the figures in the table reflect a meaningful involvement of religious professionals in the life of universities?

Imams or Muslim advisers tend to have the greatest contact with institutions through student religious societies, and especially Friday prayers and other Islamic Society functions. The spectrum of contact varies from a daily or twice weekly commitment in some institutions (especially if the Muslim adviser is a member of academic staff), to attendance at occasional chaplaincy meetings when there are particular Islamic issues for discussion. Most advisers/Imams are regarded by chaplains as being available 'when necessary', but in some places this has not been tested. Other Muslims associated with an institution become more involved around the time of festivals and celebrations.

There was clear evidence of scope for much further research into the participation of Muslim advisers in universities (as well as other forms of chaplaincy and pastoral care). The background, suitability and training of religious or community leaders who become involved in chaplaincy work is of particular interest, not least to the Editor of the British Muslim publication *Q News*. The editorial marking the beginning of the 1994/5 academic year noted that the local Imams attached to chaplaincies 'are usually ill-equipped to deal with the problems facing students on campus'. The Editor stated that it was not possible to introduce 'Muslim counsellors' onto university campuses as 'their task would require both maturity and cultural compatibility, a combination which is at present nowhere to be found' (Nadhi 1994). This observation is in many ways parallel to a more widespread concern about the leadership of many local Muslim communities in Britain. An Indian Imam from the Barelwi 'school' who has been living in Britain for nearly 20 years pinpoints what he sees as the limitations of some Imams working in Britain:

> they lack a thorough knowledge of Islam [and] their knowledge is limited to the sectarian parameters of the sect they belong to…the leaders do not know anything about the context in which they are resident. Traditional leadership has no communication with the younger generation…British education opens the minds of the younger generation in its schools and universities but when the teenagers put questions to Imams they cannot get answers because the Imam is dogmatic or does not know how to reason (Raza 1991:33).

The way in which this might change in relation to higher education and chaplaincy is explored towards the end of this chapter.

Buddhist representatives attached to chaplaincies invariably come to lead meditation sessions, regularly on a weekly basis, or infrequently, or simply when asked. One Baha'i representative leads weekly meetings for students. Hindu and Sikh advisers do not tend to have close associations with their institutions, except of course where they are academic members of staff who are on site much of the time. Their involvement mirrors a similar trend in many hospital contexts. Doctors or nurses from these traditions sometimes find themselves acting as 'representatives' when patients request pastoral support, simply due to the fact that there is no other member of the tradition attached to the chaplaincy or the institution. Similarly, staff with particular religious commitments in universities can find themselves, by default, taking on an informal role as adviser to students belonging to their tradition.

Regardless of the level of contact, regular, occasional, or *ad hoc* it appears that faith communities have not actively nominated individuals to liaise with universities and work with students. Most religious advisers are recruited due to the initiative of chaplains and students, rather than through community-sponsored action.

There is further evidence to support the general finding that students are likely to take a particularly active role in securing the involvement of religious professionals from their own tradition where they feel the need. Students from the Leeds University Occult Society were behind the recruitment of the first Pagan university chaplain in 1994. She is said to hold the same responsibilities, religious influence and status as the university's 11 other chaplains, though the Senior Anglican Chaplain was at pains to point out that 'she is not, as is the case for all the chaplains, a university appointment' (*The Times* 12th December 1994). She helps students mark festivals, such as Halloween, solistices, and 'rituals to help the students' studies'. Her involvement, perhaps more than that of any other religious professional from another tradition, must surely place a tension between the institutional expectation that chaplaincies observe the norms of a pluralistic society (by showing tolerance of religious diversity), and the religious identity of Christian chaplains themselves. As in other spheres of public life, the boundaries between what is regarded as 'mainstream' religious activity and identity and what is not, and where the limits of tolerance and recognition lie, can be extremely blurred and highly variable between institutions. The scope of appropriate inclusion and the thorny question of where to draw the boundary of recognition in a situation of increasing religious diversity raises legal, financial, as well as pastoral issues that find no easy answers.[13]

Recognition and accreditation of religious personnel

This is, however, an issue that has begun to be tackled. As the membership of public institutions and particularly of universities has become more diverse, important questions have been asked about the recognition and accreditation of the different religious personnel on campus. Unlike prisons, for example, universities are easy places to 'infiltrate' and, paradoxically, security at a number of institutions has necessarily become much more rigorous, for all kinds of reasons; ID/swipe cards to enter buildings are not uncommon, particularly in halls of residence. Institutions no doubt ensure that members of the counselling service (or other student support personnel) are appropriately qualified to work with students, but the accreditation of chaplains or other religious professionals appears to be extremely haphazard. This is a reflection of the historically ambiguous position of chaplaincies in many universities. Institutions have largely left the question of who is 'in' and who is 'out' to chaplains themselves, and the processes have tended to be informal. In the light of the religious disturbances and activity of some new religious movements on campuses over the past decade, it is surely time for institutions to explore more carefully how members of different religions gain access to students, and the process whereby the names of religious personnel appear in institutional telephone directories, or on chaplaincy leaflets.

Referring to their own accreditation, many chaplains point to their ordination by their Church or denomination and/or their interview and appointment by their institutions and colleges (even if funded by their denomination). This in itself gives them licence to work with students, and oversee religious activity within the institution. When it comes to other chaplains and religious advisers, regardless of the extent of their involvement in the chaplaincy, it is similarly their ordination and/or nomination by their Churches or faith groups which is cited as giving them a legitimate and recognisable role in student activities. Chaplains appear to be reliant upon the reputation of nominees and their support from sending faith communities.

However, there is considerable diversity in terms of the formality or informality of the processes that lead to association with a chaplaincy. For example, at a college of higher education in the Midlands, 'it's all very informal, ad hoc and episodic' while at a new university in the Thames valley, 'they are nominated by their denomination, interviewed by the ecumenical chaplain, and then recognised in consultation with the Head of Student Services'. Between these two respectively informal and more formal processes there are many variations in how religious professionals come to be part of the chaplaincy, and the extent of their recognition. Some of the more radically secular universities make a determined effort not to acknowledge *any* religious professionals on the campus, including the chaplain. Undoubtedly this makes issues of security, management of inter-religious conflict, and protection of more vulnerable students all the more difficult to manage sensibly.

Where institutions do acknowledge the presence of chaplains and religious professionals, there is often a hierarchical process of accreditation at work. The full-time or senior chaplain is 'recognised' by the university, and he or she thereby carries the authority to 'vet' other religious professionals. In other instances, the existing members of the chaplaincy meet and interview potential new members together, and a decision is then made on a collective basis about whether applicants can participate in chaplaincy activities. At one institution, becoming a formal and recognised part of religious activity involves 'being signatories to the chaplaincy operational policy agreed between chaplains, the university, and the faith groups they represent'. For some chaplains issues of accreditation and recognition are only just being given serious consideration by their institution. One chaplain from an 'old' civic university near London commented:

> this is an on-going saga! We are recognised, but not formally. And we have no official authorisation or accreditation. A situation arose last year when someone arrived on campus purporting to be a part-time chaplain. We are working on improvements!

Though some institutions do undertake accreditation of religious personnel, many others do not. As things stand, in a number of institutions there is no recognition of any religious professional, including the chaplain.

> The university claims to be a secular institution. We are actively seeking recognition but the pace at which the university is moving has been slow and at times in the past, obstructive.

This comment from a chaplain at a Welsh university signifies a clear 'hands-off' approach to religion, pastoral care, and the presence of chaplains in the institution. This was by no means the only indication that some universities feel distinctly uneasy about religious activity and personnel on campus.

This was most evident in the comments of chaplains, both during interview and in questionnaire responses, about the levels of support they receive from their institutions. The affirmation of the work of chaplains is highly variable, but surprisingly, the *type* of institution appears to be insignificant in this regard, as well as the source of chaplains' funding. Even in collegiate university colleges where the appointment of a chaplain (and protection of the post) is covered by statute, this does not mean that chaplains can take support for granted. Most feel themselves to be dependent 'to a great extent' upon senior individuals in their institutions. They rely upon the university maintaining an attitude of goodwill. This is especially the case for some chaplains who work as part of a 'Student Services' team. Chaplaincy 'depends very heavily on support [from] the Head of Student Services (where chaplaincy is located – geographically and administratively)'. One chaplain supported his assessment of dependence on senior managers by saying:

> chaplaincies are in a very precarious position with cut backs always on the horizon. There is more pressure for chaplains to justify their existence and value for money. As universities become more secular places any form of religious presence may become a luxury of the past.

Leaving aside this perception of universities as 'secular places' for the time being, it is clear that many chaplains rely on institutional support. Ironically, one reflected, 'we are there with goodwill but the more multi-faith aware we are, the better we are received!'. The religious identity of senior managers and figures in the university also seems to have a bearing upon support for the chaplaincy. But the ambiguity of chaplaincy in the structure and organisation of institutions is clear in the comments of a chaplain at a Cambridge college.

> The chaplaincy is fully integrated into the administrative and pastoral structures of the university and is seen as part of the life of the community. The question [about support from senior staff/managers] could thus be answered "totally" (in that its present form presupposes this integration) or (confusingly) "not at all" (in that its existence is not dependent on any individual or group).

In this chapter so far, we have started to build up a general picture of some patterns and trends relating to religion and higher education. The focus has primarily been upon the people who provide pastoral services to students, Christian chaplains. The remainder of this chapter turns once again to the wider team of advisers from other faiths, and focuses especially upon their changing roles.

Approximation: consequences of an expanding 'ministry'?

Religious diversity is affecting British universities, and so far this has been evident in the expectation of many institutions that their chaplains will work with a wide range of religious identities, and act as institutional advisers on religious matters. But there is growing evidence of another interesting trend: namely, that the religious professionals and advisers from other faiths who engage in chaplaincy work in universities, and in other chaplaincy settings, are being shaped by the models of Christian pastoral care they encounter.

The traditional role of a chaplain is unique to the Christian church. It is a distinctive and specialised ministry, amid a range of other Christian professional/specialist roles (e.g. priest/clergy or monk/nun). In the other faiths, there is no direct equivalent religious role to that of a chaplain, and no formalised tradition of 'pastoral care' linked to clergy. For example, in Islam, an Imam may be regarded primarily and traditionally as a ritual specialist with particular responsibility for leading congregational prayers in a mosque. The title also has honorific connotations, perhaps in denoting the leader of a particular community or group. Among *Shi'ite* Muslims, the term Imam has yet another meaning as an intercessor between *Allah* and humanity. The framework for Islamic life and conduct, individually and communally, is shaped by the *Shari'ah*, or Islamic law. Scholars with a particular knowledge of Islamic law and teachings, known collectively as *ulema* (singular *alim)* assist with the development of Islamic thought, while *muftis* are legal functionaries empowered to make *fatwas* or legal rulings. In the Sufi or mystical tradition of Islam, the spiritual leader of a community is often known as a *sheikh.*

Indian religions, especially Hinduism and Sikhism, share the concept of a *guru* or teacher. Sikhism is founded upon the teachings of ten successive Punjabi *Gurus* during the 16th and 17th centuries, but for Sikhs, the term suggests more than just 'spiritual leader' or teacher. The Sikh *Gurus* are 'divine teachers and exemplars who conveyed God's word' (Weller 1997:606). Following the death of the tenth and final human *Guru,* Guru Gobind Singh (1666-1708), spiritual authority rested thereafter in the *Guru Granth Sahib*, the Sikh scriptures, and these underpin Sikh life and worship. Given the centrality of the scriptures, many *gurdwaras* (Sikh temples) employ a *granthi*, a professional reader of the *Guru Granth Sahib*, though any adult Sikh (male or female) may perform this recitation or conduct religious ceremonies.[14] However, Sikhism does not recognise a priesthood in the formal sense, and all Sikhs are regarded as sharing parity of religious status. In Hinduism, there are a range of different titles for religious professionals. The term *guru* (or *swami)* has a generic connotation as a religious teacher who gives personal instruction to devotees. *Gurus* or *swamis* are learned in the scriptures and the methods of worship, and have often renounced worldly attachments for a life of asceticism. The role of a Hindu priest, or *pandit* centres around the temple and the performance of rituals *(puja).* Traditionally, Hindu priests have been from the *Brahmin caste (varna)* at the top of the Hindu caste system, and as religious professionals their role principally involves the transmission of sacred Sanskrit texts and the performance of priestly sacrificial rituals.

The monastic life is perhaps the defining feature of religious specialists in the many traditions of Buddhism, whether Tibetan, Zen, Theravadin, or Japanese. Not surprisingly therefore, many of the titles associated with Buddhist religious functionaries relate to the hierarchy of the monastic order. With Buddhism becoming increasingly popular in the West, different titles such as *Ajahn*, *Bhikkhu*, *Roshi*, *Lama*, and *Rinpoche* are becoming more widely known and understood.

But none of these different religious specialists undertake roles that in any way correspond with the pastoral work carried out by Christian chaplains. For sure, a large hospital in the Muslim world is likely to employ an Imam, but his role will be generally confined to leading prayers in the hospital mosque, delivering a sermon on a Friday and, in some instances, distributing charitable income.[15] It would be quite beyond his remit to visit patients on the wards, or carry out any individualised pastoral care. The tradition for such work does not exist either in Islam or in any other faith tradition. It is generally the extended family system that provides emotional and spiritual support. However, the roles of some British Imams, for example, who find themselves associated with public institutions such as universities or prisons, are beginning to change.

Since other faith traditions do not traditionally have personnel who function as chaplains, it is becoming clear that if they are to engage with public institutions in Britain that *do* employ chaplains, it is necessary to promote some religious professionals into the proximal role of 'chaplain'. This has become such a feature of the development of modern chaplaincy that I shall refer to it by the term 'approximation'. The process of approximation refers to changing religious roles within a tradition engendered by contact with a dominant religious tradition. Professional roles that already exist in the 'host' context have a determining influence on how other faiths without such roles engage in public institutions. The 'traditional' role adapts to the 'host' role.

Some Imams and priests from different faiths in this country are in many ways becoming full-time chaplains to local public institutions, though with varying degrees of engagement with what might be regarded as 'pastoral' care or spiritual counselling. The Imam of a large mosque and Islamic Centre in the north of England interviewed for my research, was a good example of how this process of approximation had occurred. He was the Muslim adviser to a large new university, a local hospital, and he was a 'Visiting Minister' (to use Prison Service Chaplaincy terminology) to a Young Offenders' institution in the locality. He visited each of these institutions regularly, and when absent from his mosque, he delegated the responsibility of leading prayers to another member of the community. He said that his local worshipping community strongly supported his chaplaincy work.

He had received most of his religious training in Pakistan, as a student at the University of the Punjab in Lahore, and then at the Jamaat-i-Islami college 'Mansoorah', also near Lahore. He had all the requisite qualifications of a religious professional, and he was dependent for his livelihood upon this work. Ten years ago, speaking only limited English, he had come to Britain. Despite having trained in Pakistan, he felt confident that by now he understood the needs and problems of the local British Muslim community, especially the younger generations.

He could see clearly that the role of an Imam in Britain and in Pakistan was different. In this country, he explained that he took a more active public role in large institutions than a counterpart in most parts of the Muslim world. The Imam felt that it was not enough for him to simply give a religious lecture and then leave if real individual needs were to be met, whether in the prison, hospital or university context. The remit of his work and his focus was moving to encompass the individual, as well as the collective. He noted that this kind of extended pastoral role would be unlikely to occur in Pakistan, and it was his view that his country was 'not advanced' when it came to this kind of understanding about pastoral needs. His life and work in Britain over the past decade had brought an awareness of the need for Islamic religious professionals to have a deeper involvement in more general human needs, related to the wider society. He could envisage a time when more Imams in Britain would be devoting themselves to chaplaincy work, and delegating responsibility for leading prayers in their mosques to other members of the community. Looking back on his religious training, the Imam said that he had not been given any kind of professional pastoral education. It was, he noted, simply not part of Islamic religious training. Like his learning of English, the Imam had to learn pastoral skills in the course of his work.

The extent to which religious professionals find Western and Christian traditions of chaplaincy alien, and indeed whether it is appropriate to be (often unconsciously) influenced by them, is not the issue at this point. What is important to identify is the creation of a new kind of religious professional, evident in the Muslim community, but also within British Buddhism and Judaism, who is beginning to take on the proximal role of chaplain. These roles may be an extension of traditional religious professional roles, or they may be undertaken by lay members of the communities.

> Changes in the wider social structure [in this case, religious diversity] often have significant repercussions for the expectations surrounding the role of the clergy. For instance, Brotz in his study of suburban Jews points out that in a closed Jewish community the Rabbi was greatly esteemed for his scholarship. But with a greater degree of assimilation and acculturation within the wider society, new expectations have been created. There is a desire that the Rabbi should be able to develop satisfactory relationships outside his own community. These developing expectations place considerable strain upon the traditionally Talmudically trained scholar-Rabbi (Brothers, 1971:64).

This example, while also pointing to debates internal to the Jewish community about the relative weight to be accorded to pastoral and teaching roles, indicates that minority faith groups in diverse societies are subject to influences from wider social trends and dominant religious traditions. Members of these faith communities develop new expectations. I would also argue that the religious roles in the dominant faith, in this case Christian chaplains, provide the 'template' for the creation of new Jewish or Buddhist chaplains.

During the course of research for the 'Church of England and Other Faiths Project' (see note 6), some of the religious professionals interviewed noted that the traditional source of emotional and spiritual support for many minority religious traditions – the family – was now proving inadequate. They reported that the extended family system was beginning to fragment (due to wider social influences, such as mobility), leaving a need for the development of religious roles which accrue to the role of chaplain. Christian chaplains themselves, sometimes as a direct consequence of gender issues have stimulated the emergence of such roles in some instances. Relating specifically to the prison context,

> some faith traditions are not accustomed to regard women as appropriate suppliers of religious or pastoral care in the formal sense. In these circumstances, Church of England chaplains sometimes find themselves in the difficult position of trying to persuade the local leaders of a community to overcome their reluctance and nominate a female Visiting Minister for female prisoners. This is one of those areas where facilitation shades off into an activity more akin to inducement or pre-empting. *Chaplains in this position do far more than simply make it possible for Visiting Ministers to visit prisoners: they go one stage further and actually stimulate the participation of other faith communities in prison chaplaincy* (Beckford and Gilliat 1998:91-2, emphasis added).

In the case of institutions of higher education, some universities have come to regard a full complement of religious professionals as a necessary part of their image as providers of facilities and a wide range of support services for students. Likewise, some hospitals have encouraged the expansion of the chaplaincy 'team' to include religious leaders from other traditions. In this way, they can be seen as fulfilling the expectations set out in the Patients' Charter about religion. In a competitive market, more means better.

The example of the Imam above reflects how the process of approximation has taken place in one particular instance. But there is other evidence that suggests that the process is widespread and sometimes takes on an organisational character. For example, 'Angulimala', also known as the 'Buddhist Prison Chaplaincy Organisation' was founded in the mid-1980s to provide pastoral care to Buddhist inmates in British prisons. Volunteers associated with the organisation, few of whom are full time religious professionals, prefer the title 'Buddhist chaplain' rather than the Prison Service Chaplaincy's more neutral terminology for them, 'Visiting Minister'. Members of Angulimala are aware of the Christian history of the word 'chaplain', but feel it signifies status and some degree of equity with other religious professionals, and particularly Christian chaplains.

The emergence of 'chaplaincy' organisations, as well as 'chaplains' in the Jewish community is even more evident. The longer historical presence of Jews in

Britain naturally means that they have had longer to be influenced by the traditions of Christian chaplaincy in public institutions. The Jewish community has founded a number of distinctive chaplaincy organisations concerned with patients, prisoners, and students, and the emergence and remit of the latter are discussed in Appendix 7.

It is difficult to measure precisely the extent to which approximation is taking place, but data gathered about Visiting Ministers serving prisons does begin to chart a growing trend.

> Seven of the thirteen Muslims under the age of forty who serve as Visiting Ministers are also Imams; an eighth is currently a student. These relatively young men manage to combine their duties in mosques or Muslim organisations with visiting Muslim prisoners on a part-time (but extensive) basis. One of the Imams visits prisoners in six different establishments, while another visits four.

> ...Eight of the eighteen Sikh Visiting Ministers are also full-time Granthis or priests. One of them visits prisoners in four establishments, one visits five establishments, and one visits ten establishments. Being a Visiting Minister must constitute a major part of their professional life. Similarly, three of the seven Hindu Visiting Ministers were, until recently, priests in Temples. One of them visits five establishments (Beckford and Gilliat 1998:93-4).

There is also evidence besides the case study of the Imam, to suggest that those individuals serving as Visiting Ministers in prisons (or hospitals or universities) may also take on 'chaplaincy' work in other public institutions. In the 'Church of England and Other Faiths Project', there was some degree of overlap in the database of respondents from other faiths working in prisons and hospitals. The precise mechanics by which these individuals are promoted or recruited by their faith communities to take on work in public institutions or become known to Christian chaplains/institutions are not clear, but it seems that informal networking processes bring certain religious advisers/professionals/community leaders into chaplaincy work, rather than others.

It is difficult to predict with any degree of certainty what the ultimate course of this approximation will be, and even how to fully interpret it sociologically. At this point in time, it appears to be one dimension of a wider process of convergence. Gerd Baumann's study of young Southallians found that Hindu and Sikh families are increasingly celebrating Christmas and undertaking many of the rituals associated with this festival, and likewise there is an increasing emphasis upon worship at the temple or gurdwara on a Sunday. That these 'moments of convergence are orientated on Christian templates' (Baumann 1996:179) is obvious, but the different patterns and degrees of convergence between the faith groups will be interesting to monitor in the future.

As things stand, a concern for their public image leads some universities (and hospitals) to continue to promote religious diversity, as part of their marketing profile. Chaplaincy teams, presently ecumenical, are likely to become even more multi-faith in character, and the boundaries in terms of who is 'in' and who is 'out' of the team will become more flexible. Chaplaincies have over time expanded their parameters, to include Christians of other denominations, gradually Jews and increasingly other faith professionals and advisers.[16] They presently stand on a blurred outer boundary between inclusion and exclusion. The degree to which they become fully included within the institution is likely to rest to some degree upon their willingness to embrace the inclusive pastoral identity of many Christian chaplains.[17]

In this closing section, I wish to turn to America for some insights from chaplains who have written about their own vision for religiously diverse university communities.

Lessons from America

When it comes to religious diversity in higher education, there is much to learn from American experiences, though the discourse of debate in the States is inevitably framed by a different kind of language and discussion. However, the same question of how to reconcile different claims and build community remains the same. In her book *The Spirited Campus: the Chaplain and the College Community*, Barbara Brummett (1990) gives an account of a new chaplain arriving to serve in a small, liberal arts college in the United States. In the Introduction, Brummett reproduces a portion of a letter written by the new chaplain to the college's Dean of Student Affairs. It is clear that an awareness of religious diversity shapes the pastoral and professional identity of the new chaplain. Towards the end of her letter she writes:

> I would expect the Winfield chaplain be charged with overall responsibility for administration of and co-ordination with all religious groups on the campus. I do not see chaplaincy as a proselytising occupation, but instead one that would facilitate each group in its own direction.

> The purpose of such administration would be to co-ordinate an effective overall campus religious life in its traditional parts and in its pluralistic whole. The dilemma of groups as different as those struggling for identity on the college campus (even when it is as small as Winfield) is that each must deal with its own particularity. However, the hope inherent in pluralism lies in allowing each group to struggle openly side-by-side with others with the promise that, if effectively facilitated, we may discover our common humanity. An effective chaplain should be such a facilitator (Brummet 1990:xxi).

But the new chaplain soon realises that the particularly American ideal of religious life, with 'members of diverse religious groups maintaining autonomous participation in their particular faith communities within the broader cultural context common to all' (Brummet 1990:90), is sometimes hard to preserve. The Chaplain's test comes in relation to the display of religious symbols and decorations, such as a Christmas tree, in public parts of the institution, e.g. the library. In these kinds of situations, the Chaplain finds it difficult to reconcile the competing perspectives and particular religious sensitivities. Despite the difficulties, Brummett holds to the ideal that it is

> the chaplain's responsibility to hold an umbrella over the ongoing experiment in religious pluralism on the college campus. There is no way that he or she alone can insure the healthy and creative functioning of campus religious life. It takes community effort, and strongly invested and cohesive leadership. But more than likely it is the college chaplain whose task it is to find ways to balance the religious interests of the one and the many, to establish and maintain the organic and vital functioning of religious life, to somehow keep it whole (ibid).

This is a challenging vision for how chaplains might serve multi-faith universities.

An inter-faith perspective for higher education is exemplified in an article by another American chaplain working at The American University in Washington DC (Thornton 1990). She begins by describing what one might experience on a typical Friday afternoon at the Kay Spiritual Life Center in the university.

> Your interfaith experience might be more than you bargained for. Mouth-watering aromas emanate from the kitchen as the Jewish community prepares for their Shabbat dinner; all quiet upstairs while Buddhist meditation is in progress. Meanwhile, the Muslim community is getting ready for their service and Muslim women have taken over the ladies room for washing their feet. In the hallway, someone from the Gospel Choir might be practising a hymn…scheduling can get tight at times. Rooted in our own faith traditions, we have a joint mission to foster spiritual growth on the campus (Thornton 1990:27).

The author describes the positive experience of learning about different traditions within the Center, and the inter-faith events and ceremonies that have been held. In many ways, the issues and challenges that arise in devising such events, such as beginning-of-year services or memorial services are not exclusive to the higher education setting. Involving different traditions in ways that preserve the integrity of each, and finding words and rituals that are meaningful, will exercise any group of people trying to organise an inter-faith event. But the article is a positive reminder that inter-faith co-operation can and does work in the context of higher education, though it is no doubt supported by the willingness of chaplains and religious advisers to foster co-operation and trust, whilst preserving the distinctive traditions and norms of each faith.

The ethos of higher education institutions in Britain, despite the changing and often contested nature of student life, is still conducive to having new experiences, experimenting, learning about different aspects of life and meeting different people. This ethos is especially favourable for the meeting of people of different faiths, and from time to time new initiatives take place and interpersonal friendships grow which foster good relations and break down barriers of exclusion and misunderstanding.

In this chapter, chaplains and religious professionals/advisers from different faiths working within university chaplaincies have been the main focus. The following chapter moves away from issues connected with personnel and finance, to the more material question of religious facilities and the way that institutions meet student needs. We shall begin by looking at how and where universities physically accommodate religious activity, if at all, and why issues of space and accommodation are so significant.

Notes

1   Hammond (1965 and 1966) found, for example, that chaplains in higher education were significantly different from their parish colleagues in being politically more liberal, more interested in world affairs, more supportive of ecumenism, critical of their own denomination/church, more formally educated and more favourable to greater church involvement in social affairs (p.42). Their 'unorthodoxy', particularly within their own churches, is not so much a rejection or ignoring of their traditions, but a criticism of them from within. There is clearly scope for a contemporary study of higher education chaplains in the USA, in order to ascertain whether they still carry a reputation for 'radicalism', perhaps in comparison to UK chaplains.

2   This high turnover was also observed by Hammond in his study of United States higher education chaplaincy in the 1960s.

3   The ambiguity involved in chaplaincy and the lack of clear-cut responsibilities, were identified by Hammond (1966:19) as possibilities.

4   For a brief history of this word 'chaplain', see Beckford and Gilliat (1998:25-6).

5   See appendix 1 for a good example of an institutional statement emphasising an inclusive approach.

6   This research was carried out in the Department of Sociology at the University of Warwick by Professor James Beckford and Dr Sophie Gilliat between 1994-6, with the generous financial support of the Leverhulme Trust and the Church of England Central Board of Finance. The project aimed to discover how far the Church of England enabled people from 'other faiths' and philosophies of life such as Buddhists, Hindus, Jews, Muslims, and Sikhs to participate in the publicly funded aspects of religion in Britain, these being prison and hospital chaplaincy, and civic religion. The main findings of the project are described in a summary report (Beckford and Gilliat 1996b).

7   The extent to which religious, and more specifically Christian activities are funded in Church Colleges is well documented in Brighton (1989).

8   Members of the chaplaincy team in this institution did include religious advisers from a variety of faith traditions. This response indicates that they qualified for an honorarium to cover their expenses.

9   Modood and Acland (1998:169).

10   A Hindu priest may also be referred to as *'pandit'*, *'swami'*, or *'maharaj'*. There are other titles for Hindu religious professionals which refer more specifically to particular functions, such as one who undertakes life-cycle rituals within the home, known as a *'purohit'*. For further information see Weller (1997:305-6).

11 Clearly, the value of this information is in presenting an overall pattern of distribution. Data was not received from **all** universities, and there is no other independent source of data about the numbers of religious professionals of other faiths active in higher education.

12 Based on 68 useable responses.

13 See Davie (2000) for a further discussion of this question of scope.

14 Other terms for 'religious professionals' in Sikhism include *giani*, meaning someone who has a sufficient knowledge of the scriptures to interpret them to the congregation. Musical worship within the *gurdwara* is undertaken by *ragis*, or singers/musicians.

15 During December 1994, I spent three weeks in the Punjab area of Pakistan interviewing administrators and religious 'professionals' associated with prisons and hospitals. On 29th December, I carried out an interview (interpreted by the medical superintendent of the hospital) with the Imam of the Lahore General Hospital.

16 This gradual accommodation of other Christian and religious traditions is to some extent evident in the responses of Visiting Ministers in the 'Church of England and Other Faiths Project' to questions about the length of their service in prisons. 'Five out of the eight longest serving Visiting Ministers who supplied information about the date of their appointment are Jewish. Buddhists and Sikhs did not begin to be appointed frequently until the mid-1980s; the first Hindu in our sample was appointed in 1988' (Beckford and Gilliat 1998:99).

17 Support for this assessment is based upon observation of chaplaincy work in American prisons and hospitals. For example, chaplains are appointed without any reference to a specific religious tradition. Thus, chaplains who happen to be Muslims, for example, are increasingly becoming full-time members of institutional chaplaincy teams. They are expected to work with all religious traditions, including Christians (though obviously they do not undertake any Christian liturgical functions).

Chapter 5

Meeting Student Needs

Religious spaces

In most, if not all institutions of higher education today, accommodation is at a premium. Departments often compete for a limited number of seminar rooms, laboratories, staff offices, and lecture rooms. Decisions about who gets what facilities, and where, are often shaped by fierce competition and internal politics. Chaplains and student religious societies have engaged in the struggle as much as academic departments. According to the chaplains whom I interviewed and surveyed through questionnaires, the question of providing prayer rooms for Muslim students is at present one of the most pressing issues facing universities when it comes to the location and provision of religion on the campus.

As we have already seen in Chapter 2, in the life of the ancient universities the academic and religious ideas of 'congregation' were interwoven. Sacred space was located centrally in the life of the community in the form of a college chapel. Many Church colleges also reflect this tradition, with chapels at the heart of the campus. In many of today's universities, religious spaces (where they exist at all) are often a reflection of how successfully Churches have historically managed to get a foothold on the campus and liaise with institutions about the provision of facilities. With Churches as the main driving force behind the location of religion on many campuses, not surprisingly, they have generally reflected a Christian ethos.

Major faith traditions have different ways of naming, understanding, and approaching the arena of ritual activity, usually shaped by a particular theology or philosophy. Even in those religions that regard all life-contexts as sacred, some places eventually acquire greater sanctity over time, and perhaps become sites of pilgrimage. Spaces used for religious activity within public institutions, such as universities, are generally very different compared to other religious buildings and 'sacred' sites. Precisely what makes a place sacred differs between and within different religions, and is to some extent individual and experiential. However, a chaplaincy, a multi-faith centre, or a prayer room in a university will not constitute 'sacred space' in quite the same way as a major cathedral, a temple, or synagogue (the exception is of course campuses with purpose-built, consecrated or dedicated chapels, as in many Oxbridge and Church colleges). The locations for religious activity in public institutions will (in most cases) rarely have been designed – architecturally – for prayer or worship. As generally plain, undecorated rooms, unfurnished with artefacts from a particular tradition, they will often be devoid of the layers of history, meaning and significance that accrue following worship by different generations from one faith tradition over time. It is possible however, that they acquire some degree of 'sanctity' by virtue of the fact that they are subsequently designated as places of 'otherworldliness' and simply decorated with natural or 'neutral' objects such as flowers or candles. For example, their use may be subject to various norms and rules about conduct, such as an expectation of silence at certain times. To take a postmodern view, the users of 'multi-faith rooms' or 'quiet rooms' bring a diversity of perceptions with them, and necessarily impose their own individual, temporary, meanings upon the space.

How then are we to regard the various locations for religious activity in public institutions, such as universities? It appears that the way universities regard religion *per se* is often reflected in the quality, size and location of religious facilities on campus. Some universities provide no religious facilities for any faith group, and this is often an extension of a secular, or in some cases, a more anti-religious stance. For example, it was clear from one of the university chaplaincies that I visited that the premises, occupying a run-down, damp and smelly basement on the fringes of the campus, without any access for disabled students, was a clear reflection of the way the institution regarded religious life in general. Universities that make some investment in suitable premises for religious activity send out a very different message about their view of religion on campus. Furthermore, the kind of religious facilities provided for the various faith groups, and the perceptions of these spaces by the worshipping communities themselves vis-à-vis others, are also highly significant. In a context where space is often contested, inter-religious rivalries can take on new dimensions when it comes to perceptions of equity. A chaplain at a London college found that

> pressure from [the] Islamic Society to have rooms reserved for their prayers, led to a Jewish member of staff saying that he would then request kosher kitchen/meals on campus. The college is keen to preserve its secular, non-sectarian nature – hence the move to find a multi-faith solution.

Leaving aside the equation of 'secular' with 'multi-faith' for the moment, the claims of different religious groups clearly place institutions in the complicated situation of managing a range of collective claims.

Besides simply having suitable spaces for religious activity, there are a number of reasons why the location of religious activity is so symbolically (and politically) significant. The facilities provided for faith groups are also sites of communal identity. They are the spaces where, amid the facelessness and anonymity of the institution, religious identity can be expressed most fully. Identity and territory are closely interwoven, and a prayer room or chaplaincy centre is a protected arena vis-à-vis the institution, where religion can be affirmed and 'secular' forces resisted. Campaigns for suitable prayer rooms involve much more than simply the facility to pray. They also involve the marking out of a territory where religious identity can be protected 'from corruption by otherness' (al-Azmeh 1993:27) in a hostile environment. Hence the considerable dissatisfaction with temporary, 'secular' facilities such as teaching rooms for religious activity. The provision of religious spaces for faith groups also marks the institutional recognition, if with some resistance, of group identity and distinctiveness, as opposed to the toleration of difference in the private realm. Sacred sites and religious buildings have been associated with all the political and religious connotations of the word 'sanctuary' over the course of history, and the powerful connection between identity and space has been well established (see for example Eade 1993). Spaces – formal or informal – also provide a valuable forum for networking. For example, a group of tables in a canteen that was used by a group of Afro-Caribbean and Asian students had 'a variety of educational and political functions...it was the arena where black students had their own space to devise strategies and work through problems encountered within the institution' (Allen 1998:90).

Pressure for permanent prayer rooms in universities, or 'quiet rooms' in other major public institutions are a reflection of wider religious trends, and they recast normative assumptions about institutional religious spaces being the exclusive domain of Christianity. Struggles for campus prayer rooms are about forging a sense of 'place', imagined community, and belonging in the locality of the campus. 'Such places are vested with identity, an identity which involves both the supernatural sphere and the power of social self-identification and personal self-identity' (Ucko 1994:xviii). The vigorous campaigning and sense of institutional political agency that lies behind campus mosques or prayer rooms clearly suggests that they involve much more than simply the ability to observe *salat* (prayers). They are strategic 'sites' for empowerment, the defence of honour (*izzat*) in a society widely regarded as 'Islamophobic', and the activist process itself is part of a process of fashioning and affirming identity and solidarity. Place and space are crucial in the formation of collective identity and institutional recognition, and seen in this light, it is unsurprising that Islamic societies are often in a state of continual struggle with their institutions regarding either the provision or the improvement of prayer facilities. The struggle for an identifiable 'place' on campus is a clear reflection the centrality of religious identity for many young Muslims, and the desire to be 'visible' and recognised as a distinctive religious group (albeit with internal ethnic and demographic diversity). Just as chapels made an imprint on the academic landscape of the ancient universities, so prayer or other religious facilities on today's campuses are beginning to indicate the new identity and character of student populations.

Apart from collegiate university colleges and to some extent Church colleges where there is an explicit bias towards Christianity, the other types of higher education institution (such as 'old' or 'new' universities) do not show discernible patterns in their provision of, or attitudes towards, religious spaces. However, when it comes to prayer rooms, chaplaincies, and other spaces for religion, universities claiming to be 'secular' have very different conceptions of what this actually entails. This will be explored towards the end of this section through a discussion of four specific case studies.

As a foreword to a more detailed examination of the nature of religious space in universities, a brief note is warranted concerning religious facilities *beyond* the confines of the campus. Firstly, some faith traditions in Britain, principally the Jewish and Muslim communities, have followed the early pattern of the Churches' activity in higher education by providing hostels in some cities with significant numbers of student members. Where there is a 'Hillel House' (in effect a Jewish hall of residence) for example, it is likely to be the focus for a good deal of religious activity among some Jewish students. In such a context, they are less likely to look to their universities or chaplaincies for religious facilities. Secondly, students of different faiths who attend universities situated in large multi-faith cities are more able to have their worship and other religious needs met by local communities. This of course does not necessarily lessen their legitimate wish to meet with other students who share their faith, but in some cases, it may reduce their demands upon universities themselves. Some students from different traditions specifically take into account the ethnic or religious communities located near to the university when they make choices about institutions to apply to, mainly for the availability of specialist shops and religious centres (Acland and Azmi 1998).

Chaplaincy centres

The nature of, and the degree to which institutions allocate space for religion, serves as one indicator of how universities in Britain have responded to religious diversity. Whether spaces are shared by different faith groups, allocated for the permanent and dedicated use of one tradition, leased to a single faith community, or whether the institution maintains these premises, are all significant. As with the titles of chaplains, the names of religious sites are similarly meaningful for conveying implicit messages about religion in the institution. The activities contained within a Church-owned 'Anglican Chaplaincy' suggest something very different compared to those in an institutionally owned and maintained 'Multi-Faith Centre'.

In most universities, religious activity revolves around a chaplaincy centre, this being a dedicated/allocated building and/or room/group of rooms within a building that serve as a focus for religious meetings, worship, or social activities. The centre will usually be simply known as 'the chaplaincy', though in some institutions, chaplains committed to a multi-faith approach have sought to name and identify religious spaces in such a way as to clearly reflect the diversity of the student population. Most chaplains work in chaplaincy centres, apart from those in collegiate university colleges. Here, the chapel serves as the focus for religious activity, and the chaplain's own room(s) in college usually provide the facility for social or more informal gatherings. The statutes governing many

Oxbridge chapels preclude their use by other faith groups, though individual members of any tradition may use them for private reflection.

Chaplains who work in chaplaincy centres have access to very different physical environments. In general, most chaplaincies have a place of worship, a chapel, or a quiet room, and in some cases, a number of such spaces, often integral to the chaplaincy centre itself. The ownership of the building – by the institution or a Church/denomination – may determine the layout and accommodation. Sometimes the same physical space is adapted for a variety of different uses; a sitting room may be transformed into a place for meetings, worship, or even parties. Most chaplains have an office, or at least access to one, though it may not necessarily be within a chaplaincy centre. In some universities, the chaplain's office will be located with other staff offices in Student Services.

The extent to which chaplaincy facilities are used only by Christians, or shared with different religious groups reflect a number of variables, not least the views and theology of the chaplain, the attitudes and expectations of the institution, the demand on facilities by faith groups, and the physical adaptability of the existing premises for multi-faith use. Where chaplaincy space is shared by a variety of faith groups (in about one third of institutions), Buddhist and Muslim students tend to benefit from inclusion. Some of the ways chaplaincies are used include the following:

> 'used frequently by Muslims, less often by other faiths'
> 'Buddhists meet once a week for meditation class in chapel'
> 'it is open to all...and has been used by Sikhs regularly...'
> 'twice a year multi-faith event'.

Overall, few chaplaincies provide dedicated worship space for particular religious groups, but where separate space has been allocated within the chaplaincy, this is usually to accommodate the prayer requirements of Muslim students. Only one university provides separate space for more than two faiths within the chaplaincy centre.

There seem to be some specific conditions that point to whether the same facility can be successfully shared by different religious groups. Some of these relate to practicalities, while others are a matter of attitude. For example, an effective booking and timetabling system help to avoid clashes; likewise, clear guidance about religious artefacts and symbols. A chaplain from a new university in the north wrote, 'our experience proves that, provided artefacts and equipment are not given a permanent place, it is acceptable to use space interchangeably'. The success with which religious facilities are shared by different faiths can also be dependent upon the kind of expectations and relationships fostered within the chaplaincy centre itself, such as negotiation, tolerance, and co-operation.

Despite some excellent examples of multi-faith sharing of chaplaincy spaces, there is also considerable unease about their shared use. Reservations are sometimes a reflection of general uncertainties about shared space, while in other instances, the hesitancy relates to difficulties for specific religious groups. A good example of the former comes from a chaplain who said:

> the chapel is designed, fitted and used for Christian worship. It would be strange to conceal the traces of its being inhabited in this way. Places of worship are identity-shaping and importantly build up associations for people through the objects and actions that occur there.

Naturally, chaplains in Church colleges are often particularly concerned to promote and protect a clearly identifiable Christian identity in their institutions, thus precluding the sharing of space with other religions.

The emergence in some universities of 'multi-faith centres' where religious spaces are shared between different groups raises some interesting questions about their meaning and 'sanctity'. Indeed, the question is also pertinent to other public institutions where faith groups must necessarily share the same space. One university chaplain felt strongly that,

> to be meaningful, religious spaces must be shaped and decorated according to the traditions they serve – they are part of the experience and the message. Non-specific spaces seem empty of meaning.

However, in a multi-faith society, meaning and significance – and perhaps even sanctity – can also be acquired by and accrue to spaces that are shared by different faiths. The very fact that they are shared is part of the experience. Spaces that are shaped and decorated with imagination, such as with candles or plants can be meaningful even if 'non-specific'. Their use by different faith groups over time can confer a different quality of significance compared to a sacred space shaped and used by one tradition only.

Regardless of the extent to which good relations are fostered between different faith groups, sometimes the traditional physical spaces available make it difficult for more than one religious tradition to use them. For example, the particular spatial and ritual requirements for Islamic prayer mean that it can often be problematic for Muslims to share limited religious spaces with other faiths.[1] To what extent have institutions attempted to meet this issue?

Other facilities for religion

Questions surrounding religious facilities in higher education, particularly for Muslim students, have arisen during previous research on minority groups in higher education. In many ways this is not surprising. Muslim students often form one of the larger groups of students from a faith background outside the Christian Churches, and they also have particular requirements related to their regular patterns of obligatory prayer and associated ablution needs. The concerted efforts of Muslim students to have prayer rooms on campus in many ways mirrors the priority that Muslim communities in the post-war period gave to establishing mosques. The centrality of prayer in the life of observant Muslims meant that long before campaigns for such things as voluntary-aided Islamic schools, permission for mosque premises were a priority.[2] As the number of British Muslim students in higher education has grown, their concern for suitable prayer facilities on campus should come as no surprise; they are simply reflecting what their parents and grandparents also regarded as a priority for their communities in previous decades.

The findings of research carried out at an institution of higher education between 1993 and 1996 found that

> the strongest views on specialist facilities were expressed by Muslim males who were concerned with the provision of prayer rooms for males and females, with appropriate washing facilities. The institution's policy of permitting ordinary classrooms to be booked when available was considered to be inadequate. With increased numbers of Muslims in the institute, including overseas students, demands for such facilities increased during the period of the study (Acland and Azmi 1998:82).

Where universities have provided space for religion as an alternative to, or in addition to a chaplaincy centre, Muslim students tend to benefit the most. Approximately one third of the chaplains in the study reported that their institutions are providing prayer facilities for Muslims, separate from the chaplaincy. However, when the data from the 1995 Derby University research is compared with my findings, surprisingly few institutions which were *not* making provision for Muslims in 1995 have since gone on to provide prayer facilities. Only two institutions (out of 29 supplying usable data) have made additional provision for Muslims between 1995 and 1998. The findings from the research at Kingston University suggest a much higher number of universities are providing prayer space for Muslims. Thorne (1998) reports that nearly three quarters of universities are providing a dedicated room for the exclusive and permanent use of Muslims. However, this research only investigated sizeable universities in England; Scottish, Welsh, Northern Irish universities, Church colleges, the various collegiate university colleges, and the specialist institutions (drama, agriculture etc.), were all missing from the survey, hence the different findings in Thorne's research and my own.

However, the adequacy of Muslim prayer rooms is as much of an issue and the number of institutions actually providing space. The suitability of facilities appears to be extremely variable. In some universities the rooms are too small, especially at certain times of the religious calendar, such as Ramadan. In other institutions, there are no washing facilities or separate spaces for men and women. Inconvenient locations can also make access difficult, particularly on large multi-site campuses. In making provision, some universities have clearly not given enough thought to the nature of Islamic prayer.

Despite the evidence that there are difficulties when it comes to providing suitable religious spaces in universities, a number of institutions have plans to make significant improvements for the future. The acquisition of new buildings, refurbishment of existing premises and the building of 'multi-faith centres', are in progress at some institutions. Muslim students are likely to benefit considerably from much of this investment.

Some universities have been offered sizeable donations by outside Islamic organisations towards the cost of purpose-built washing, prayer and kitchen facilities for Muslim students. These offers have in many cases been met with reservations, especially when land owned by the institution is involved. However, religious life in many universities has a history of being funded and 'housed' by religious organisations themselves (sometimes within the estate of the institution) so the sponsorship of facilities for Muslims, by their own communities in Britain or overseas, would simply be a further development of an existing pattern of provision.

The extent to which religious spaces are provided in 'secular' universities raises some interesting issues which, if nothing else, indicate that the term secular can be interpreted in very different ways. Four different universities all claiming to be secular, have the following approaches to religious spaces, largely being an extension of their more general attitude to religion on campus:

Anti-religious. For example, one old, civic 'secular' university makes no provision for religious space for any faith group and, incidentally, its statutes explicitly forbid the teaching of theology. The university does not even tolerate a Church presence on the campus. The stance of this institution is openly anti-religious, and it is by no means alone in taking a hostile approach to religion.

Tolerant. Some 'secular' universities tolerate religious activity on the campus, and may even make some investment in the maintenance of religious spaces. However, the provision of these spaces is not promoted, and the institution does little more than the minimum by way of maintenance. The institution is keen not to be regarded as supporting *any* religious activity, so what provision there is, is often a grudging tolerance of Church involvement. Any provision for other faiths is likely to be temporary allocation of a room, booked in advance. Nonetheless, some provision is made for religion, despite the 'secular' character of the institution.

Anti-denominational. Some 'secular' universities willingly accommodate religious spaces within the institution, but with the clear proviso that they should not be regarded as the preserve of one faith group alone. Essentially, there *is no regard for the differences between faith groups*. All traditions must operate within the same context irrespective of particular needs. Any facilities which might appear to be for the benefit of one religion rather than another – such as ablution areas – are designated as 'religious washing facilities', rather than 'Muslim washing facilities'. Here 'secular' is more about ignoring differences between faiths, rather than making no provision at all.

Multi-faith pragmatist. One new university in the north of England, whilst being secular in foundation and in its day-to-day life, has provided the facility for a 'Multi-Faith Centre'. This is a facility used by all religious groups, but with a separate specially designated area for Muslim prayers. The university interprets secular to mean that special *privilege* should not be accorded to particular religious groups, *while also recognising distinctive needs*, notably of Muslims. It promotes its religious spaces as one aspect of student provision and equal opportunities, and goes beyond neutral tolerance of diversity towards a positive recognition of different religious identities. This interpretation of 'secular' is moderate, rather than radical, and the integration of faith groups into the campus community is a two-way process of adaptation.

From these examples, it is clear that questions of religious space on university campuses are far from straightforward, and reflect very different approaches to religion *per se*. There are no doubt many different factors determining where, if at all, religious facilities are located, and their size and use. Regardless of how institutions perceive religious space or provision (or lack of it), some appear to view the spiritual and religious needs of students as more akin to leisure activities for individual pursuit, rather than a legitimate welfare need for religious communities on the campus. Grace Davie has argued that religion is indeed a *leisure* activity for an increasing proportion of the nominally Christian population (Davie 1994:194). However, her observation does not square with the perception of religious observance in the minds of many young Muslims or Jews at university. For many of them (but certainly not all) religious practice is more in the realm of an obligation, and not a matter of choice, or a leisure pursuit among many others. For universities to view religious activity as simply a leisure pursuit, particularly for students from minority faith traditions, would be an inaccurate and short-sighted approach. This is especially the case since ethnic minority students, when choosing an institution in which to study, 'hope for information on facilities and services, such as attention to special dietary or religious provision, as well as evidence of suitable societies or clubs' (Acland and Azmi 1998:79).

> The provision of Muslim prayer rooms in a secular institution, may be easily lost in a resource-conscious university. However, there is one economic argument which might persuade institutions to make efforts to improve services and facilities for ethnic minorities. A number of universities compete to increase their overseas student admissions, with markets particularly buoyant in countries with Muslim populations. Provision of such facilities, accurately advertised, could result in increased overseas admissions (Acland and Azmi 1998:84).

It is unfortunate the needs of indigenous students from minority faith communities is only likely to be improved on the back of efforts to recruit more overseas students. Furthermore, it does little to change perceptions: 'we suspect that there is in the minds of many academics a continuing association between "ethnicity" or "blackness" with foreignness – a perpetuation of colonial images rather than an acceptance of multiracial Britain' (Williams *et al* 1989:14).

Further evidence of this can be found in a textual analysis of prospectuses from 53 universities, with specific reference to the mention of religious facilities (Jewson *et al* 1991). Their findings are worth recounting, but it is significant that they continually assume that those who belong to and practice faiths other than the Christian will be from ethnic minority communities or from overseas, thus ignoring British, white 'converts' to different world religions. This misplaced assumption aside, they found:

> Twenty nine (54.7 per cent) prospectuses referred to facilities available to students who practised non-Christian religions. Of these Judaism was mentioned in twenty three, Islam in twenty two, Buddhism in four, Hinduism in three and the Sikh religion in one. The most common type of information concerned the availability of prayer or meeting rooms. Forty-six (86.8 per cent) prospectuses referred to provision for members of Christian denominations (Jewson *et al* 1991:187).

They surmised that provision of religious facilities was likely to be aimed at the perceived needs of overseas students, rather than indigenous ethnic minorities. They also suggested that 'ethnic minority candidates who, attracted by the visual images of the prospectuses, look more closely for information about the range of facilities and services directed at their needs are likely to be disappointed' (Jewson *et al* 1991:198). Universities are working hard on their 'shop windows' where minority ethnic traditions are concerned (Jewson *et al* 1991), but as this chapter has indicated, certainly with regard to worship facilities, the reality of the promised goods doesn't always meet the expectations fostered.

Religious dietary provision

There has been growing sociological interest in food consumption in recent years, largely reflecting the increased social and cultural significance of food in affluent industrial societies (Marshall 1998:234). However, in many world religions, rituals and norms associated with food and drink have often been (and still are) pivotal in religious life for individuals and communities. For example, traditions of hospitality and the sharing of food with guests are particularly strong in Islam, and in Indian religions such as Hinduism and Sikhism. The prohibitions and prescriptions regarding food and drink are one element of difference between various religious groups.

For many of Britain's faith communities, food has retained its significance as part of the continuity of tradition, belief and practice, and as a marker of identity. In most communities, there is a full spectrum of observance and the way in which food laws are interpreted illustrates the variety within religious groups. Jacobson's research among young Pakistanis in Waltham Forest found that 'with respect to what they eat and drink, both the more *and less observant* respondents are engaged in a collective process of boundary construction and maintenance' (Jacobson 1998:131, emphasis added). The observance of dietary laws was, for them, one way of defining themselves and their community as *different* from others. 'What Hindus eat and their ideas about food are a significant strand in Hindu tradition' (Nesbitt and Jackson 1993:57). It is therefore not surprising that in wider society, and in many public institutions, religious diets and food (particularly meat) are charged with a good deal of political significance. Ronald Kaye regarded the question of 'the religious slaughter of animals...as a barometer of multi-culturalism in Britain' (Kaye 1993:235) and closely allied to the wider issue of the political effectiveness of faith communities. The politics and tension of religious food laws in public institutions often reflect wider community concerns. For example, the authenticity of *halal* meat has been subject to extensive scrutiny by different sections of the Muslim community, following isolated revelations of fraud. It is only in recent years that Muslims in Britain have begun to establish a system to certify meat that is verifiably *halal*. The background of uncertainty surrounding the legitimacy of *halal* sources in the wider Muslim community clearly has implications for the supply of ritually acceptable foodstuffs for Muslims in public institutions.

Within universities, the consequences of mistakes when it comes to religious dietary provision are often costly and inconvenient, as the Manchester Institute of Science and Technology (UMIST) found during November 1995. Despite the fact that the university was supplying *halal* meat for its Muslim students, upon enquiry they found that the meat was being cooked in steam boilers that had previously been used to cook non-*halal* food. The boilers had to be ritually cleaned under the supervision of the Islamic Student Society and a Muslim elder before they could be re-used for *halal* food (British Muslims Monthly Survey 1995). The provision of religious dietary requirements in prisons and hospitals has been similarly contentious. Over 80 Muslim prisoners at Strangeways Prison, again in Manchester, went on a hunger strike after they found that their '*halal*' food was being cooked in bacon fat (*Eastern Eye* 14th January 1996). These examples show that religious dietary requirements in public institutions are therefore not simply a matter of individual preference, but rather a matter of collective religious and ritual importance, the significance of which cannot be overlooked without considerable repercussions.

However, questions of religious dietary provision in universities have in some ways become less, rather than more, pressing. As institutions of higher education have expanded and diversified over time, the idea of residence being an integral and necessary part of university life has begun to diminish. Whilst there has been an increase in the number and diversity of students of other faiths in higher education, there is now also a greater range of choice for students about where to take their meals. Some students will have the choice to live in halls of residence, either on a self-catering basis, or with access to refectory catering. Others will prefer to eat at privately run catering outlets on the campus. Many students living in privately rented accommodation will be responsible for their own catering arrangements. The increasing availability of Hillel Houses, and Muslim hostels, provides further choice for Jewish and Muslim students in some cities. So the decisions students make about their lifestyle and diet are now shaped by a range of possible options. In a telephone interview with a catering officer from a Welsh university, he noted that students from different faith communities often chose to live in university self-catering accommodation, in order to meet their religious dietary requirements themselves. Another catering officer from a large new university in London also noted that the cost to the students and to the university of providing *halal* or *kosher* meals meant that it was not economically viable. He implied that Muslim students, for example, would choose a cheaper vegetarian dish rather than a more expensive *halal* meat dish. Although the catering provided by the university was 'in-house', it still had to be commercially viable.

Despite these considerations, the question of the extent to which universities meet the religious dietary needs of students, particularly in institutionally-owned and managed refectories, remains significant for a further assessment of their response to religious diversity. The table below indicates the range of provision.

Table 5.1 Provision of religious diets

'All types of religious diet are possible' (general statement)	19
'Only vegetarian diets are possible'	17
'Halal/kosher diets possible *by special request*'	10
'Halal/kosher diets only possible *for special occasions*'	7
'Vegetarian and kosher diets only'	1
'Vegetarian and halal diets only'	3
'No catering for religious dietary requirements'	4
'Don't know'	3
'No institutional catering'	4
Other	12
TOTAL	80

The figures in the table are largely self-explanatory. However, what these figures fail to reveal is the striking evidence that many universities are unable or unwilling to meet precise religious dietary needs on a day to day basis, largely because of expense both to the institution and to the 'consumers'. Even the apparently widespread availability of vegetarian food should not be regarded as straightforward. For some observant Hindus from particular *castes*, for example, their food should not only be vegetarian, but should also be cooked in a separate kitchen (or using separate utensils), and should not contain certain non-meat products.   None of the institutions indicated that they could meet such requirements.

However, the comments from chaplains (some based upon information supplied by catering officers) indicated a good deal of effort and innovation in some universities. Some of the responses represented in the 'Other' category are interesting for the evidence of pragmatic experimentation.   For example, one institution had placed a second 'kosher' fridge in a number of self-catering flats for the benefit of Jewish students, while another had set aside a dedicated kitchen for the preparation of *kosher* food.   Some chaplaincies have also co-operated in providing space for *kosher* refrigerators.   Chaplaincy noticeboards have also been used in some universities for advertising sources of locally available *halal* and *kosher* meat, and one university was considering supplying *halal* meat in its own campus supermarket.   A student union at one university was providing *halal* meat for Muslim students on Fridays, since Friday prayers were held in a large student union hall.   These examples of pragmatic experimentation appear to be more successful than attempts at regular provision of different religious diets alongside mainstream catering arrangements.   Even in a large university with a significant number of Muslim students, 'the catering department...gave up an earlier attempt to meet religious dietary requirements, especially *halal,* because the customer take-up was very poor'.   However, if the number of students from different religious traditions continues to grow, institutional provision for religious dietary needs may well need to be revisited and more systematic provision explored.   It is already clear that some universities are willing to listen to, and to explore the needs of students from different faiths when it comes to religious diets.

The examples above indicate that some institutions (and chaplaincies) have empowered students to make their own arrangements for observing religious dietary needs by providing information about local suppliers of appropriate food. Most universities do in fact make a point of providing students (especially those new to the institution) with more general information about religious facilities on campus, usually in conjunction with chaplaincies and/or student unions.   Some local student religious societies, especially Christian Unions, are also active in 'welcoming' new students with leaflets about local churches and places of worship. One of the best examples of good practice however was at one of the older Scottish universities where 'a welcome leaflet [is] sent by [the] chaplaincy on behalf of Christian societies and Jewish and Muslim groups'.

Accommodation and religious needs

Where accommodation is concerned, few universities have been able to keep pace with the growing number of students being admitted each year.   Demand rarely matches supply, and more and more students now tend to live in privately rented shared houses, especially those beyond the first year of undergraduate study.

However, many universities try to provide the choice of institutional accommodation to new and/or overseas students.

In some religious traditions and cultures, free mixing of the sexes is prohibited and unrelated men and women are required to live separately from each other. In faith communities where women in particular are regarded as the bearers of family honour and reputation, the availability of single-sex accommodation for women may be a critical factor in determining whether their families will permit daughters or wives to study away from home.

A small number of universities are acutely aware of the need to provide some single-sex accommodation on religious grounds. At one new university in the north, 'the accommodation service regularly meets the requests of numerous female Muslim students (and a number of women students from overseas) for single sex accommodation...It designates a number of university-owned houses for this purpose...'. Collegiate universities which retain the tradition of having some single-sex colleges are also able to meet the need for separate accommodation for men and women. Some universities also provide the facility for students who share a religious identity to live in the same flats or halls. For example, Manchester University provides kosher flats for Jewish students in its Oak House hall of residence (Wolfe 1998).

However, the majority of British universities will provide the option of living in single-sex institutional accommodation as a matter of choice for *all* students, even though they may be unaware of the need to do so on religious grounds.

Conclusion

Students from different faith communities who observe the norms of their tradition have a range of practical needs. Some universities have been reluctant to meet this new challenge, while others have embraced the possibilities, particularly in terms of recruitment. For example, a study by the European Access Network, sponsored by some of the main national higher education bodies, such as the CVCP, has been auditing institutions' access policies with religion as an important dimension of the study. Its research has revealed a particularly interesting initiative to recruit Muslim women into higher education at Lancaster University. At Lancaster, Access Officers have been building links with the Muslim community, encouraging young women to take up the opportunities open to them in higher education. At the same time, Access Officers have been reassuring their families (especially their mothers) about any worries relating to their daughters whilst in higher education. 'It is a fear of losing cultural and religious identity, a fear of picking up Western moral behaviour and a fear of racism' (Julia Preece, interviewed in the *Times Higher Educational Supplement*, 7th August 1998). One of the ways of reassuring Muslim families about their daughter's welfare has been showing them round the University, showing them the campus mosque, and inviting them to meet with members of the student Islamic Society. The 'Families into Higher Education Project' is a particularly interesting example of innovation on the back of institutional provision for Muslim students. Lancaster's initiative also indicates some degree of competition to recruit students from ethnic and religious communities, where religious facilities on campus can be used as a significant incentive.

Muslim women are also likely to benefit from another interesting initiative recently launched by the University of Birmingham following an award of £154,000 by the HEFCE.[3] The aim of the project is to provide local, community-based higher education programmes for women who, for a variety of reasons, are unable or unwilling to travel to a university or college. The project also involves other local institutions, such as the University of Central England, and some local further education colleges. 'Funds will be used to include more Moslem women in learning, to offer progression routes to those already studying, and to extend the use of Information Technology facilities' (*Black Country Evening Mail*, 19/11/99). In this instance, the initiative lies in appreciating the distinctive interests and needs of women in general, and Muslim women in particular.[4]

This chapter has concentrated upon some of the practicalities of religious needs and lifestyles, and the significance that these often have for religious identity and practice. It is clear that the provision of religious facilities is far from a straightforward matter, though provision of religious facilities is a significant indicator of how universities view religion, and diversity. The following chapter looks at what might be regarded as the 'public face' of universities, and the extent to which religious identities are recognised. There are clearly a number of possible approaches to this question. For example, extensive research has been carried out on undergraduate prospectuses, to assess their textual and visual appeal to ethnic minorities (Jewson and Mason *et al* 1991). My concern is rather with two distinctive public 'faces' of universities, namely institutional ceremonies, and equal opportunities policies.

Notes

1	Muslims are required to wash prior to prayer, and men and women should pray in different spaces. Given that the times of Muslim prayers vary throughout the year, Muslims need virtually continuous access to prayer space.
2	Other faith communities also prioritised the establishment of places of worship.
3	From an article in the *Black Country Evening Mail* (19.11.99) and cited in 'Muslim women to benefit from new project', British Muslims Monthly Survey, 7(11), November 1999, CSIC: Birmingham.
4	This initiative seems to be a particularly good example of the kind of development that higher education needs to make for the future. Flexibility and community-

based learning for women are identified by Milojevic (1998:693-703) as crucial to the future of the university as an institution.

Chapter 6

Religion and the Corporate Life of Universities: Equal Opportunities?

As British society has become more diverse, those who have historically been marginalised are making broader claims for equality, representation and power. With increasing access to higher education by minority groups, issues of race, gender, and religion have taken on a new urgency both as academic issues and in the day to day life of institutions. The previous chapter considered aspects of religious provision and recognition of religious needs that are usually daily concerns for members of different traditions. This chapter is more concerned with the relationship between religion and what might be called the 'public face' of universities, particularly activities and practices that have equal opportunities implications.[1]

My understanding of 'equal opportunities' is interpreted in the widest sense. For example, it encompasses occasions when different religious groups are formally and publicly 'recognised', and given the chance to contribute to institutional ceremonies as more than token participants. It includes the protection of different religious identities from harassment, ridicule, stereotypical prejudice, or unfair treatment, by the institution or any of its members. The focus of this chapter is upon institutional ceremonies and equal opportunities policies, both of which provide indicators of formal, public institutional recognition of religious diversity. An examination of institutional rituals and policies reveals not only some examples of good practice, but also much wider questions of structural and procedural exclusion, and hidden institutional cultures, values and assumptions.

Functions and ceremonies

Most organisations punctuate their calendars with regular as well as one-off functions and ceremonies. Christmas parties, celebrations of promotion, or the launch of new products, are all institutional rites of passage. However, some institutional ceremonies have

> a long history of obscure origins. Their deep-rootedness has given them a meaning, momentum and integrity; they "need" to happen simply because they have always happened. Ancient ceremonies associated with parliamentary procedure, royal occasions, military protocol or a school's traditions are of this ilk...they reveal, sometimes starkly, organisational values, politics and

relationships. The "dressing" or staging of different functions is itself as symbol of image (Fineman and Gabriel 1996:48).

Many of the ceremonies of academe indeed have a 'long history of obscure origins', and their continuity is embedded in the life of the university. 'Certain ritual occasions of university life (like degree ceremonies) might still conform to medieval protocols, marking off a kind of sacred space and time in contrast with the decidedly profane priorities which govern the institution for the rest of the time' (Cohen 1995:1). Examples include services to start the new academic year, as well as graduation ceremonies. They are celebrations of academic life, scholarly rites of passage, revealing not only widely shared values, but also indicators of less clearly identifiable structural exclusion. Not surprisingly, the attitudes and approaches to corporate celebrations among the different types of institution make for interesting points of contrast.

Due to the religious origins and foundations of the Church colleges, and many of the ancient and civic universities, these institutions often include a religious dimension to formal, ceremonial occasions. Chaplains have often had a long historical role in contributing to university celebrations, such as saying prayers at graduation ceremonies (Fern 1997) or leading 'beginning of year' services. Even in institutions that are explicitly secular and where there is no reference to religion in the business or ceremonial life of the university, from time to time, religious occasions take place.

When it comes to the ceremonial life of collegiate university colleges, students of other faiths would be unlikely to feel involved or comfortable with either university or college occasions which incorporate a religious dimension. The traditions and statues governing such ceremonies are exclusively Christian, and in most cases, specifically Anglican (though tempered perhaps by some degree of ecumenism). Despite lip-service to inclusivity, little attempt is actually made to reflect other religious identities.

Sometimes however, the nature of the ceremony can influence the degree to which other religious traditions can be included. In particular, memorial services introduce the possibility of much greater flexibility. A chaplain from an Oxford college commented 'what springs to mind as introducing diversity is the humanist, non-religious memorial service or event which is now fairly common and which may take place in chapel'. This clearly implies however, that while a *non-religious/'humanist'* ceremony is acceptable, a ceremony that clearly reflects a *distinctly different religion* would be unacceptable. But a non-religious ceremony would be quite inappropriate to mark the life of an individual from a committed faith background. Little prospect for change here. When it comes to other academic occasions, consider this reflection:

> although the university [Oxford] consists of a federation of colleges, at the same time it has an over-arching structure of its own. This too has its quota of ecclesiastical symbols and customs....Upon admission to the degree of MA, the ceremony in the Sheldonian has the distinct flavour of an ordination service.

Candidates kneel in front of the vice-chancellor who inducts each of them into the MA status by tapping their heads with a book and pronouncing the admission formula which starts and ends with ecclesiastical language (Gay 1981:143-4).

The corporate life of the collegiate university colleges maintains established traditions, based upon Christianity, which in many ways celebrate the prestige and longevity of the university. The structural exclusion of other faiths is explicit, and shows little sign of change.

In contrast, the 'secular' character embedded in the ethos of many of the new universities is interpreted in very different ways when it comes to academic and ceremonial occasions. There are varying degrees to which religion *per se* and religious diversity are recognised. At one end of the continuum, approximately half of the chaplains made comments of which the following is typical: 'official university occasions do not incorporate *any* religious dimension...it is purely secular and avoids any religious issues/recognition wherever possible' (emphasis original). Some new universities strictly limit their ceremonial/religious occasions to an annual carol service, which is of course, by definition, Christian. The middle ground is occupied by institutions that are *trying* to adapt their corporate ceremonies, where they occur, to be more inclusive of other religious traditions. This comment from a chaplain at a new Scottish university was typical: 'there is an attempt to respect the faiths of others to be as inclusive as possible without offending. But it is a difficult balance to strike. Leaders of other faiths are unwilling to take up initiatives and many Christians experience real difficulty with inclusivity'. One can begin to hazard a number of guesses as to who precisely might be offended, what makes involvement unattractive to members of other faiths, and why some Christians are unwilling for corporate occasions to reflect other traditions. There is clearly a degree of discomfort surrounding religion and ceremony in some new universities.

At the opposite end of the continuum, some new universities, despite being 'secular', nevertheless seem to regard certain occasions as exceptional in the corporate calendar, and this in itself appears to warrant a religious ingredient. Examples include the opening of a new campus or the installation of a new chancellor. For many new universities, their acquisition of university status was marked with a religious ceremony, despite their 'secular' foundations and character. A departure from institutional norms apparently calls for the involvement of those with ritual expertise *par excellence*. A chaplain from a new university in the north of England remarked of institutional ceremonies involving religion:

> such occasions are rare in a secular institution. Two such have related to the institution's acquisition of university status and the installing of a Chancellor. On each of these occasions I took part as chaplain and my Bishop was also present. But some care was taken to recognise the strength and diversity of religious standpoints.

Having clearly stated that 'no university occasions incorporate a religious dimension', this Scottish chaplain then went on to add, 'at the University's Inaugural Service, Christianity, Islam and Judaism were represented in a very exciting and moving act of worship conducted in [the] Cathedral'. Those new universities which marked their acquisition of university status with a religious ceremony, apparently took care to reflect the religious diversity of the university community.

The evidence from the new universities suggests some degree of ambivalence about *when,* if at all, to include religion in the corporate life of the institution, but there are at least no explicit structural (or historical) barriers preventing the recognition of the religious diversity of the university community. These new universities tend to reflect an 'all or nothing' approach, and questions about *how* to include different traditions appear to be easier to resolve than the larger issue of *when*, if at all, there should be a religious dimension to corporate occasions.

Like most of the new universities, the large majority of old institutions also ensure that their ceremonial occasions are devoid of any religious dimension, on the grounds that they are 'secular'. Where there are regular corporate religious ceremonies, these tend to be start-of-year or carol services in a nearby cathedral or civic church, and exclusively Christian. Unlike the new universities that acquired university status, there have been fewer occasions in older civic universities when it might have been appropriate to include a religious element to a corporate celebration. However, old universities also exemplify a general pattern apparent in the new universities. *One-off* occasions or celebrations are more likely to involve a religious dimension, and they often reflect the diversity of the student body. The following example from a technological university in the Midlands illustrates the point: 'we had a superb multi-faith/culture celebration of 100 years of the college/university'.[2]

Outside of the collegiate university colleges, there are three striking conclusions regarding academic ceremony and religion. Most universities conduct their corporate celebrations without any reference to religion, in keeping with their secular foundations. However, where institutions hold regular religious ceremonies, such as 'start-of-year' services, these tend to be exclusively Christian occasions. Regardless of secular foundations, one-off corporate ceremonies tend to be much more sensitive to religious diversity. This is however, unsurprising. Regular events are much more likely to be bound by tradition and established understandings about format, content and degrees of inclusion, while one-off events can be more responsive to the nature of the occasion and the make-up of the institutional community.

Equal opportunities policies

'Over recent years, formal equal opportunities policies have assumed an increasingly prominent role in the affairs of institutions of higher education in

Britain' (Sharp and Winch 1994:163). As part of this process of engagement with equal opportunities issues, universities are beginning to give more formal consideration to questions of religious discrimination, religious identity, and inter-religious relations. The publication of *Extremism and Intolerance on Campus* by the CVCP in 1998 is likely to be just one force for change in raising awareness of the issues concerning religion in higher education over the coming decade.

However, a case for including a religious dimension to institutional policies and codes of practice was voiced some years before the CVCP report:

> an increasing number of institutions throughout higher education have evolved and adopted policies designed to redress inequalities of opportunity which are related to race and gender. However, whilst race and gender are major determinants of individual and group identity, religion is also of significance. This is particularly the case among minority ethnic communities where, in some cases, religion is increasingly replacing ethnicity as the basis for self-understanding and self-organisation (Weller 1992b:53).

In this section, I will be exploring the extent to which different types of universities have begun to include religion as part of their equal opportunities policies, thereby recognising the distinctive nature of religious identity. However, it is essential to locate my findings on this issue within the context of equal opportunities in higher education more generally. In the next few pages, I will be considering some of the broader questions about equality in universities that will inform the later discussion about religion in particular.

Equal opportunities policies usually cover areas such as recruitment, harassment, discrimination, and discipline. However, some are what might be called 'employee relations practices which, while rarely included in formal equal opportunities policies, have the intention of promoting equality of opportunity…these include provision for extended leave, minority religious holidays/observance…' (Gibbon 1992:236). The development of policies and practices is a way of exerting control on new social realities, placing them within existing frameworks of employment practice, outlining the mutual rights and obligations of institutions and its constituent members, and marking the boundaries of acceptable and unacceptable conduct.

The expansion of higher education in the 1960s coincided with the emergence of a discourse about equal opportunities policies in many other public sector institutions. As marginalised and excluded sections of the workforce became more vocal in their protests, so the need for equal opportunities policies became more apparent. Additionally, different professional groups increasingly began to define organisational procedures, in order to present a more progressive public image, and, to pre-empt costly tribunals. However, organisations that proudly declared themselves to be 'equal opportunities employers' did not necessarily have corresponding policies on paper.

Higher education institutions did not themselves begin to engage with equal opportunities debates in any significant way until the mid to late 1980s. It was not until universities had relocated from the periphery to a more prominent place in national life, due to the growth in student numbers, that higher education began to participate in the discussion (Neal 1998). But there are also other reasons why equal opportunities in higher education has only come onto the agenda in a significant way in the past decade or so. William *et al* (1989) regard the failure to act earlier as a reflection of the 'complacency of liberal institutions'. But it is also, they argue 'symptomatic of a research paradigm which freely investigates the beliefs and values of society at large, but too infrequently considers its own context and practice as problematic, and hence open to critical review, evaluation and change' (Williams *et al* 1989:8). Universities have been resistant to turning the focus inwards towards their own structural inequalities.

Other researchers have observed and analysed the reasons for the apparent resistance of traditional, ancient universities to equal opportunities issues. Heward and Taylor (1993) observed that engagement with current equal opportunities questions strikes at the very heart of the elitist cultures in these universities.

> Higher education in the UK is hierarchical with Oxbridge at the apex, large provincial and other established universities ranked above the former polytechnics and colleges of higher education. Elite institutions maintain their position by exclusivity. Assumptions about academic merit underlie prestige...The prestige hierarchy with Oxbridge at its apex and the values underlying it are highly resistant to change (Heward and Taylor 1993:79-80).

> Institutional inertias inevitably compound active resistance to organisational change in universities which see their role as conserving an intellectual heritage (Cohen 1995:1).

With the rise in the number of universities adopting equal opportunities policies, the limitations of these documents have been exposed through a number of recent studies (such as Weiner 1998; Neal 1998). This book is not the place for a detailed account of the growing body of research into equal opportunities more generally, except where it illustrates practices and particularly corporate *attitudes* to equal opportunities which have a bearing on the way universities have recognised religion as a basis for possible discrimination. For example, Cockburn's (1991) study of women in employment found that organisations were apt to choose 'high profile, cost-free measures and neglect the more expensive changes that would improve things for a greater number of women' (Cockburn 1991:215). The survey of policies covering religion over the next few pages will therefore be alert to grand but perhaps unrealistic statements of intent, minus clear evidence of strategy or structures for implementation. It is worth noting at this point that none of the existing research on equal opportunities in higher education has so far considered *religion* as a basis for discrimination, despite the fact that more institutions are formulating policies and guidelines on this issue. The 'religion-blindness' that prevails in so many studies of race or ethnicity in academic research is clearly evident in studies of equality and policy in higher education.

Much more research would be needed, particularly among those living and working in university communities, to establish how equal opportunities policies are implemented, how effective they are, and the way in which they are perceived. Within the limits of my research, I was simply concerned to discover the existence, or not, of policies covering religious identity and practice, and the focus of attention was the *scope* of these policies, in terms of coverage and application. However, my survey of equal opportunities policies is carried out with an awareness of a range of factors that often limit the effectiveness of such policies.

For example, the principles that underpin equal opportunities polices are rooted in theories of classical liberalism which often favour the status quo. The policies that stem from this broad philosophical perspective fundamentally 'rest upon a belief in a pluralism of purposes such that none is entitled to special privilege, and...that law and state should preserve an institutional framework of equal justice' (Barry 1996:468). With a vision of the individual as prior to other collectivities, liberal policies

> assume that the removal of collective barriers to the expression of individual talent will enable the best person to win and, more generally, permit all individuals to make the best of themselves. This view ignores, or has great difficulty in accommodating, the *structural sources of social capacities and skills – and, hence, the structural sources of social inequality* (Jewson and Mason 1992:221, emphasis added).

Thus, through my analysis of religion in higher education equal opportunities policies, I am mindful that the structural arrangements concerned with religion in many institutions of higher education have been constructed in a setting that has historically privileged the liberal hegemony and, implicitly in some universities, the Christian tradition. These traditions and privileges have often been unchallenged.

Jewson and Mason contrast the aim of liberal equal opportunities policies with a more radical approach which is more concerned with 'the outcome of the contest rather than with the rules of the game' (Jewson and Mason 1992:222). A radical view of equal opportunities focuses more upon collective and group discrimination, rather than on individual instances of inequality or exclusion. Though 'liberal' and 'radical' are exemplified as ideal-types, Mason and Jewson emphasise the fundamental importance of understanding that regardless of labels and typologies

> groups formulating and implementing policies do so in social contexts characterised by struggles for power [and] these struggles for power are themselves historically contextual and are, thus, concerned as much with the general structure of the organisation as they are with the specific detail or objective of particular policies (Jewson and Mason 1992:230).

Again, this quotation points to the importance of being aware that equal opportunities policies covering religion are formulated (or not) in specific contexts, and often serve the interests of particular groups. They are not constructed in a vacuum, but against the background of different institutional politics, histories, cultures, and power struggles. And of course, it is the 'majority' who tend to define the parameters of equality, opportunity, discrimination and difference, and for whom.

Equal opportunities policies are broadly concerned with procedures and social mechanisms for ensuring that individuals are treated with fairness and justice. Regardless of what is set down in rules and regulations, the implementation of policies is another issue. They may or may not be effective in actually eliminating prejudice or inequality. For example, by neglect or manipulation, procedures may become ineffectual in reality. Therefore, my assessment of religion in equal opportunities policies will also be concerned with their potential for application, their gaps in coverage, and what their different emphases suggest about the institutions that have constructed them.

Higher education has a long-standing tradition of humanitarianism and liberal associations, and it would be easy to assume that they are receptive to equal opportunities issues (Neal 1998). But if we look at institutions of higher education 'as informal organisations with unwritten institutional cultures and practices' (Bowser *et al* 1993:1) then the perception of equity becomes less persuasive. 'There are the "rules" and then there is the way things get done: practice, the informal "rules" and institutional culture...relatively few of the rules and practices that define a tradition-laden institution such as a university or an academic department are spelled out (Bowser *et al* 1993:2).

Universities are characterised by an environmental culture of hierarchies, competition, and individualism. Equality for different student needs and interests represented in the institution is often far from the minds of many academics and senior managers, unless it is a matter of serving the interests of the university. Furthermore

> evidence of religious discrimination against individuals or small groups is much easier to detect than more fundamental but less obvious structural and process biases. Discrimination is usually blatant, whilst bias is deep-seated, subtle and complex (Gay 1981:158).

Once equal opportunities policies are constructed, their implementation is clearly another matter. 'Equal opportunities policies may be broad or narrow in their scope, and can espouse goals that range from marginal adjustment [of] procedures to far-reaching changes...Given that such goals represent a range from the immediately achievable to the intrinsically difficult, it is a matter of some importance that a given policy commitment can be understood very differently by different people within the same authority' (Young 1992:260).

The growing inclusion of religion as a basis for discrimination in equal opportunities policies reflects the fact that such policies are often incremental in nature. The initial consensus that a particular characteristic should not be the basis for unfair treatment or harassment, such as race or gender – provides the framework for the addition of other characteristics that could lead to exclusion or discrimination. The addition of newly defined areas, such as religion, are bound to be contentious in that they address new social realities in a dynamic institutional context, with a mindfulness of corporate image. The degree to which policies define corporate image, or are seen as the concern of specialists within the organisation, is likely to vary between institutions. The scope of policies and the way in which they are perceived is likely to be closely connected to the particular mores of an individual organisation.

Equal opportunities and religion

My research was concerned to discover whether institutions had formulated policies or codes of practice about a number of aspects of religious identity and practice. Firstly, I wanted to discover whether institutions had formulated policies or codes of practice on three *specific* issues: respectful interaction between faith groups on campus; authorised absence from lectures to attend religious festivals; and, scheduling of examinations to avoid major religious holidays. The scope of these policies, whether in terms of staff, students, or the entire institutional community was also of interest, where relevant. Secondly, I wished to know whether religion was mentioned as part of *general* institutional equal opportunities policies.

When it came to the three practical areas of university life and business listed above, I interpreted the concept of a 'code of practice' or policy statement as widely as possible, so as to cover not only formal policies, but also faculty handbooks, institutional 'guidelines', or what I cited earlier as 'employee relations' practices. Chaplains were specifically asked to enclose relevant documents or examples with their questionnaires.

The tables that follow represent the findings in relation to the three issues that I have referred to above. The more general issue of where religion figures in equal opportunities policies is explored further on, when I discuss my findings in relation to the different types of universities. Unfortunately, only two chaplains from 'other' types of institutions, such as music, or drama colleges, or institutes of higher education, submitted any useable information on the subject of equal opportunities, hence their exclusion from the tables. Fortunately, one of the institutions that did submit information had formulated a comprehensive policy regarding religion (see appendix 2). There are a number of conclusions that can be drawn from the 'silence' from these 'other' institutions, but their relatively limited diversity in terms of faiths and cultures is likely to be a significant factor.

Leave of absence for religious festivals

Two of the main holiday periods during the academic year in British universities correspond with two major Christian festivals, Christmas and Easter. However, a significant number of celebrations and holy days in the other major world religions do not coincide with these vacation periods. For example, the Jewish festivals of Yom Kippur and Sukkot regularly fall in late September/early October, just as the academic year is beginning. The Jewish community has long pressed for the needs of Jewish students to be recognised at this time of year, and the Union of Jewish Students was instrumental in the adoption of a policy by the NUS opposing 'principal union events on religious festivals or holy days' (letter, *Jewish Chronicle* 23rd October 1998). If students from different traditions are to observe their faith traditions, they have an inalienable right to request a period of authorised absence from the institution. In recognition of the religious diversity of the student body, some universities have developed policies governing leave for religious purposes. Others are in the process of formalising existing informal procedures, such as at this small specialist college in London:

> for the first time last year a (Jewish) student asked for time off for attendance at religious festivals and this was granted. I am currently working to have this *de facto* acceptance made *de jure*. College closes at Christmas and for Good Friday and Easter Monday – I do not think the significance of this should be ignored.

The table below indicates how chaplains from different types of institution responded to a question on this matter.

Table 6.1 Policies authorising absence for religious festivals

	Yes	No	Don't know	Total responses
Collegiate university colleges	9 (4)	6	8	23
New universities	8 (3)	10	4	22
Church colleges	2 (0)	3	0	5
Old universities	8 (0)	9	8	25
University of London colleges	2 (1)	0	2	4

N.B. The numbers given in brackets in the 'yes' column show the number of positive responses *supported* by examples of established procedures, or quotation from/or documentary evidence of, a policy or code of practice.

Examination timetabling and religious festivals

For much the same reason that students may request absence from lectures, some universities have become much more aware of the difficulties that are caused due to the scheduling of examinations on major religious festivals and holy days. Again, some institutions have devised policies or codes of practice, either for the re-scheduling of the exam, or to enable students to sit their paper(s) at a different time. There is also evidence of institutions formalising existing informal arrangements. The Academic Registrar at one old university wrote at length to a chaplain (in response to the questionnaire):

> We have agreed to operate a formal policy on examinations and religious festivals from 1998/9 onwards. Up to now we have dealt with requests *ad hoc*. The revised Code of Practice for Students will say, "the University will seek to avoid scheduling an examination to coincide with a major religious festival, in accordance with the published procedure for such arrangements". The published procedure (final version yet to be drafted) will tell students that they must contact the Examinations Office by a set date each year if they know that there will be a major religious festival during the examination period. These arrangements will be publicised to students in the Student Handbook and by notices. We also ensure that appropriate arrangements are made for other major events e.g. when Registration coincides with a Jewish festival in October we allow Jewish students to attend late registration without penalty.

Table 6.2 Policies for scheduling examinations to avoid conflict with major religious festivals

	Yes	No	Don't know	Total responses
Collegiate university colleges	14 (0)	6	4	24
New universities	6 (2)	13	3	22
Church colleges	0	5	0	5
Old universities	11 (4)	8	5	24
University of London colleges	2 (0)	0	2	4

N.B. The numbers given in brackets in the 'yes' column show the number of positive responses *supported* by examples of established procedures, or quotation from/or documentary evidence of, a policy or code of practice.

Respectful interaction between faiths

In the Introduction to this book, I referred to some of the inter-religious tensions that have been evident in some British universities, particularly in the past decade. An awareness of these difficulties has led some institutions to formulate clear codes of conduct that include references to respectful interaction between members of different religions. Table 6.3 below summarises the findings.

Table 6.3 Policies for respectful interaction between faiths

	Yes	No	Don't know	Total responses
Collegiate university colleges	7 (2)	10	7	24
New universities	7 (1)	10	5	22
Church colleges	2 (0)	1	2	5
Old universities	9 (3)	8	9	26
University of London colleges	2 (0)	0	2	4

N.B. The numbers given in brackets in the 'yes' column show the number of positive responses *supported* by examples of established procedures, or quotation from/or documentary evidence of, a policy or code of practice.

In assessing the figures from these three tables, there are a number of general comments that can be made, as well as more direct observations relating to the particular types of institutions. Firstly, from a general perspective, the number of 'don't know' responses was surprising. Some chaplains were apparently ignorant about institutional practices or policies on religious matters and were also, it seems, unprepared to find out more in order to answer the question more precisely. This approach was typified by the comments of a chaplain from an Oxford college:

> I really don't know the answer to this! My ignorance speaks volumes about the non-issue status of religious identity in the college. No-one is remotely bothered.

Secondly, the relatively high proportion of chaplains who replied positively that their institutions had relevant policies, procedures or codes, but who then failed to supply the documentation or examples of established procedure (which had been explicitly requested) to support their claims, was disappointing (and surprising).

Thirdly, some chaplains indicated that there were no policies or codes of practice in place because the issues were 'not applicable' to their institution, usually on the grounds of there being relatively few 'other faith' students. Chaplains did not seem to be aware that it is precisely their status as religious minority groups that warrants their protection by formal codes or policies. Other researchers have discovered a similar 'not applicable' attitude in their investigations of equal opportunities in higher education, and one team concluded that 'it is in such ways that the moral superiority, ignorance and complacency of higher education manifests itself' (Williams *et al* 1989:12).

Religion and equal opportunities in collegiate university colleges

In the ancient universities, matters such as examination timetabling and other policy issues usually constitute *university* business, rather than being a matter for individual colleges. However, some colleges also have their own particular statutes, especially in relation to religious matters. For example, an Oxford chaplain noted that:

> the college is described in the statutes as "a place of religion, education and learning", and Fellows take an oath to uphold this. In 1971 the governing body decided that this requirement was to be interpreted as allowing *everyone* to practise their religion freely. We stress the religious pluralism of the college during Freshers' Week and underline equality of respect for all faiths.

The evidence from the collegiate university colleges suggests much goodwill towards religion and an expectation that religion *per se* will be respected, regardless of tradition: 'The religious ethos of this college could lead to all people of faith being respected and treated fairly by the institution'. However, we have already seen that there is considerable structural inequality when it comes to matters of religious provision in collegiate universities. Respect and good intent towards all religions has not translated into equity in matters such as prayer facilities. Only one chaplain from a collegiate institution could supply evidence that religious identity was covered in college (or university) equal opportunities policies.

When it comes to practical issues, such as examination timetabling and religious festivals, collegiate university colleges rely heavily on established, taken-for-granted procedures, rather than codified policies. Particularly in relation to examinations on Jewish holy days, or the Sabbath, these universities have a long-standing tradition of 'chaperoning' Jewish students in order that they can take exams at another time. Chaplains from these institutions regularly used words such as 'discretion', 'flexibility', 'sympathy, and '*ad hoc*' to describe how cases where religious needs clashed with university business would be regarded. These universities tend to approach such needs on a case-by-case basis, rather than as a matter affecting a collective minority group. None of the responses from chaplains in collegiate institutions referred to policies that are relevant or applicable to staff.

Religion and equal opportunities in new universities

In direct contrast to the collegiate institutions, a number of new universities have formulated policies about religion that *only* have employees in mind (see appendix 3). However, where a policy does exist, the scope is generally the entire institutional community of staff and students (see appendix 4). A policy that does more than simply add religion to other unacceptable criteria for discrimination is the exception rather than the rule, and the 'incremental' nature of equal opportunities polices is evident from the first three examples given in appendix 4. Nearly two thirds of chaplains from new universities indicated that religious identity is covered by equal opportunities policies, and 41 per cent of these chaplains were able to substantiate their claims with written evidence. It was also clear that questions of religion and equal opportunities were in the process of discussion at the time of my research.   A chaplain from a new university in Bedfordshire reported:

> The equal opportunities group is 1) looking at timetables avoiding clashing with Friday Muslim prayers 2) inviting speakers from various faiths to equal opportunities meetings with a view to understanding and sensitivity growth and 3) display of all festivals of world faiths in [the] foyer of [the] university.

This was not the only evidence of on-going efforts in new universities to formally address religious needs and issues.

Compared to other types of university, it is clear that on balance the newer institutions are giving more thought to the question of religion as an equal opportunities issue. This assessment squares with other research findings (such as Powney and Weiner 1992). 'The association of the former polytechnic sector with equality issues can be understood in the combined context of a history of local authority control, the types of courses offered, more flexible entry requirements, and the geographical locations of polytechnics, which were often in urban, industrialised areas' (Neal 1998:30).   Though only a small number of new universities have written comprehensive policy statements regarding religion, these must be seen as important for their 'catalytic' potential in raising awareness of good practice across the higher education sector.

Church colleges

Even from the limited number of responses from Church institutions, it is clear that equal opportunities and religious identity issues do not figure strongly on their agendas. Without further research, it is difficult to assess whether this is a reflection of these institutions in particular, or a reflection of the limited diversity within them. None of the chaplains from these universities/colleges cited evidence for policies covering religious identity or practice.

Old universities

The incremental nature of equal opportunities policies was even more strikingly apparent in old, civic universities, compared to other types of institution. Among chaplains who reported that religion was covered by policies, in most instances religion was simply listed along with other criteria upon which discrimination or prejudice was forbidden, such as race or gender. However, this raises a serious question in terms of implementation, and this is discussed in more depth in the following section.

One old university had considered the Inter Faith Network document *Building Good Relations with People of Different Faiths and Beliefs* (see appendix 5 that reproduces this in full) as a code that could be adopted as a statement of

University policy. However the Senate and Council decided to maintain an existing and very general statement in the institution's regulations which simply listed religion as one dimension. 'Students should note that the University deplores all forms of intolerance and discrimination, especially those which demonstrate prejudice with regard to race, nationality, gender, sexual orientation, religion, disability, age or class, and will take appropriate disciplinary action against students who fail to acknowledge the cultural diversity embodied in a university environment'. There were various reasons behind the decision to retain this general statement, rather than adopt the Network document. In particular, it was felt that the existing statement on conduct in the regulations of the university was sufficiently powerful, and there was a concern that religious intolerance should not be singled out as distinctive from other forms of intolerance.

To some extent, this stance, and the decision made in other universities to omit even the mention of religion in equal opportunities policies, indicates a profound failure to understand the nature of intolerance itself, let alone religious discrimination or prejudice in particular. Unless distinct forms of oppression are clearly identified, there is little scope for marking the boundaries of acceptable or unacceptable conduct. A 'religion-blind' approach systematically fails to recognise an entire section of the population who feel themselves to be vulnerable to prejudicial behaviour or intolerance on specifically religious grounds, or an account of their religious identity. '...[A]ny oppressed group feels its oppression most according to those dimensions of its being which *it* (not the oppressor) values the most' (Modood 1990:92). Universities that ignore religion in their policies are failing to recognise the fact that religion is a core dimension of identity, not least for the growing ethnic minority population of students.

The chaplaincy at one old university in the North West had written a 'charter' outlining the mutual responsibilities of the chaplaincy/institution, and its members (see appendix 6). This constituted the most comprehensive statement on religion from an old university. 'Given that the "old" university sector has operated within a different ideological context of higher education provision, it is not surprising that its incorporation of an equal opportunities agenda has been a slower and more reticent process' (Neal 1998:30).

Religion and equal opportunities: implementation

Where equal opportunities policies address religious issues and needs, there is evidence across all types of higher education institution of reliance upon good intent, minus clear indications of how policies are to be implemented. Phrases such as 'appropriate consideration', 'seek to ensure,' 'accommodate', 'take account of', and 'discretion' were common. These efforts are not to be dismissed, particularly as they begin to stake out the importance of recognising different religious identities and needs. Furthermore, all institutions have clearly begun the process of formulating equal opportunities policies from different starting points, in different contexts. However, as they stand, policies that rely on these words and phrases are simply statements of good intent. Clearer evidence of strategies for implementing policies are limited but can be found, for example, in the policy at a university in London, which specifically requires staff involved in selection and recruitment to undergo training on how to recognise stereotypical views and assumptions on matters such as 'race, colour...religion or political belief'.

For all the good intent surrounding religion and equal opportunities in universities, there is still a significant problem in terms of implementation. At present, a student or staff member who felt that they had been discriminated against in terms of their religion, and who felt the matter had not been dealt with satisfactorily within the institution, would find little support from the law. At present, the Race Relations Act (1976) only protects individuals who are members of distinctive racial-ethnic groups, such as Jews and Sikhs. There is presently no direct protection for most other religious groups, such as Hindus, Muslims, or Buddhists. The complexities of the current scope of the law in relation to matters such as housing, education or employment and religion is outlined in a government document published by the Inner Cities Religious Council (1996), and discussed in more detail in Modood (1994a) and Weller (1997).

A study by Powney and Weiner (1992) of women and ethnic minority managers in educational institutions found a continuum of attitudes and approaches to equal opportunities among different institutions. Their study was concerned to establish the degree to which equal opportunities permeated the ethos of the institutions, and the spectrum ranged from no interest whatever, to full awareness of obstacles barring progress and equality. In between these extremes, there was 'commitment', 'predisposition', and 'lip-service'; terms which indicate a gradual decline in awareness or interest in equal opportunities questions (Powney and Weiner 1992). This spectrum of approaches is also evident in my findings. At one end of the continuum, some universities have drafted documents and guidelines that attempt to make a commitment to equal opportunities and religion an institution-wide concern, permeating all aspects of university life (see for example the document from the University of Derby – appendix 4). This policy at Derby is implemented through a Religious Resource and Research Centre which acts as a central service unit, providing advice and resources across the institution on a wide range of religious matters. At the other end of the continuum, some universities regard equal opportunities questions in relation to religion as 'not applicable'. 'Some institutions deem it sufficient to assert their commitment to equal opportunities through mission and policy statements whereas others have developed rigorous programmes and structures focused on achieving equal opportunities' (Weiner 1998:323). The University of Derby can be clearly regarded as taking the latter approach. What is fundamental to Derby's initiative, as with a small number of others like it, is the recognition that 'if an institution sees equal opportunities as a holistic philosophy which should permeate both the staff and student body, it would seem imperative to design new groupings, units or structures to promote this' (Williams *et al* 1989:18). Derby has achieved this through the 'Religious Resource and Research Centre', but a possible future role of chaplaincies could be a more proactive approach to equal opportunities questions in relation to religion.

The framework for this to occur already exists in some universities. Just over half of chaplains reported that their institution has a committee meeting regularly to discuss religious matters. At present, chaplaincy team members and student religious society representatives form the core participation of most of these committees, but in some universities, senior members of the institution also take part. Multi-faith issues already have a prominent place on most agendas.

It is clear that many of the policies and codes cited in the appendices have the scope to deal with individual cases of victimisation. However, what is also apparent is their inability to tackle more systematic discrimination directed towards religious groups. For example, there was frequent reference in the policies cited of the potential for discrimination in matters between an individual and the institution, such as selection, admission, recruitment, assessment, or promotion. One of the valuable contributions of the report *Extremism and Intolerance on Campus* is its recognition that some forms of unacceptable behaviour or discrimination may be directed from one group to another within the student community.

Some universities emphasise their commitment to equal opportunities as a direct marketing strategy. At this point, the framing of policies can become a more contentious matter. During her research on equal opportunities policies in higher education, Neal (1998) recorded a conflict of interests between those wishing to include sexual orientation in the categories the university would not discriminate upon, and those concerned with the effect this might have on recruitment of potential overseas students. One of her interviewees recounted the difficulty with this inclusion in the institution's policy, mainly for its potential to deter students specifically from Muslim countries and from the Indian sub-continent: 'they are worried to come and study where there are things about sexual orientation going on...this is a *nightmare* for some of them' (Neal 1998:71 – emphasis added by Neal). Neal's analysis of the general 'social drama' surrounding the issue, and the comments of her interviewee were highly perceptive: 'the entire rationale of this respondent's position rests on new racist discourses using "illiberal" and "pre-modern" Muslim/other and liberal modern "western" stereotypes' (Neal 1998:71).

This incident also illustrates a number of the more general points raised at the beginning of this section on equal opportunities. These policies and codes of practice emerge in specific contexts, against the background of institutional politics and power group struggles. Their construction is not a 'neutral' matter, even if these policies are not as politicised as other issues in higher education. To some extent, this may be deliberate, in an effort to maximise consent, and minimise disagreement.

Regulation of religious activity on campus

A litmus test of the ability of universities to ensure religious harmony and respectful relations between different faiths on campus, are the measures taken when things break down or when there is any kind of religious disruption. As the student population has expanded and become more diverse in the past decades, so too it has become harder for institutions to keep a watchful eye on student activity (or indeed the activities of outside religious groups operating on campuses). In small communities, informal mechanisms for discipline and regulation of conduct are perhaps effective enough means for ensuring that behaviour is kept within the bounds of respect. However, as the size of universities continues to grow and diversify, effective disciplinary measures and procedures are more likely to rest upon formal policies and codes of practice for ensuring the safety of members of the community. The following table broadly indicates how chaplains responded to a question about how religious activity is regulated on campus.

Table 6.4 Regulation of religious activity

No regulation	17
Ad hoc regulation as necessary	10
Ban of religious groups when necessary	3
Institutional harassment policies	10
Responsibility of chaplaincy	11
Regulation of room bookings and outside speakers	3
General assumptions of decorum/respect	9
Don't know	2
Issues have not arisen	2
Total	67

What is striking about these findings is the range of different mechanisms for regulating conduct with respect to religion, and the fact that a quarter of chaplains stated that there was 'no regulation' *at all*. Institutions appear to largely rely upon informal, *ad hoc* devices for managing religious conflicts. It will be interesting to see how many universities take up the advice in *Extremism and Intolerance on Campus* and how effective this is in the regulation of religious conduct on campuses in the future.

Conclusion

The extent to which universities regard religion as an equal opportunities matter is extremely mixed, especially when actual codes of practice on specific religious issues are brought into consideration. Universities appear to be ambivalent about equal opportunities in general, and Neal observed the clear 'de-politicised character of equal opportunities in the 1990s' (Neal 1998:32). Equal opportunities policies and codes of practice serve a variety of purposes, and attention should be paid to what lies below the surface of good intent. 'An institution's willingness to demonstrate a commitment to equal opportunities can become divorced from issues of social justice and become tangled up with public relations, marketing concerns and the projection of a desired image' (Neal 1998:72). While in some cases there remains a mismatch between what is promised and what is actually delivered, universities might consider the potential implications of raising expectations that cannot be met, particularly in view of the 'consumer' attitude fee-paying students now demonstrate.

Notes

1   I have deliberately chosen not to examine another significant 'public face' of universities, namely prospectuses, largely due to the fact that extensive research has been carried out to examine the way in which universities have tried to appeal to ethnic minorities via brochures and publicity. See for example Jewson *et al* (1991).

2   Despite this example of successful multi-faith worship, nevertheless, corporate worship involving different religious traditions can raise complex issues for all involved. Considerable care is necessary in the planning and hosting of such events. Some of these issues are raised in the General Synod Board of Mission (1992) document *Multi-faith Worship?*

Chapter 7

Student Voices

An important human reality is the experience of defining oneself as "a member of a group" in this strong sense of sharing goals and a discursive practice. Another important experience is being treated by others as a group member (Kennedy 1995:159).

This chapter turns the focus away from universities towards students themselves, and particularly the national student religious organisations that have emerged to support students over the past century.[1] Some of these were founded in the 19th century, and others have been created as recently as the early 1990s. Acland and Azmi found that:

> for many students, Students' Union societies...helped them enormously to find friends, develop support groups and share experiences. They found these self-support groups to be much more successful in addressing ethnic minority needs than the formal mechanisms of support provided by the institution (Acland and Azmi 1998:81).

The formation of some of the newer student religious organisations is, in part, a consequence of the dissolution of pan-Asian youth movements, especially in large, multi-ethnic cities, in the late 1970s and 1980s. Chetan Bhatt ascribes this decline to 'local authority racial equality [and] multiculturalist policies' (Bhatt 1997:127), and notes their replacement, especially in London and northern towns, by

> explicitly Muslim-identified youth groups, student *dawa* associations and Islamic students' associations, and in London and Birmingham by Sikh and, later, Hindu counterparts. Youth organisations that were primarily formed in response to racial violence and policing were replaced by organisations primarily identified by ethnic-religious, sect or national affiliations (Bhatt 1997:127).

For Bhatt, this amounts to an explicit 'desecularisation of Asian youth politics' (Bhatt 1997:127); a process which has become evident in many British universities in the formation and growing popularity of a number of student religious organisations.

In the formation of student religious organisations, locally and nationally, we can identify a process of what Steven Vertovec calls 'ethnic mobilisation'. He defines this as a strategy 'through which ethnic groups self-consciously define themselves by specific criteria of "belonging", compile and co-ordinate financial and symbolic resources, formalise social networks, institutionalise selected social practices (often by way of invoking – or, indeed, "inventing" – "tradition"), and engage the wider public sphere in order to advance group-specific causes' (Vertovec and Peach 1997:10). In other words, defining group difference on the basis of religion can be used to advance material and social benefits for the group. Implicated in the defining process is the fact that

> social identities exist and are acquired, claimed and allocated within power relations. Identity is something *over* which struggles take place and *with* which stratagems are advanced: it is means and end in politics (Jenkins 1996:25).

Jenkins' observation highlights if nothing else why student politics involving religion are so contentious. Furthermore, essentialist assertions of identity can be highly strategic in power struggles vis-à-vis other religious groups and within institutions, and thus inherently political. However, behind the united front generated by the outward appearance of unity there will be differences of worldviews and other fundamentals among and between members, in much the same way that faith communities in wider society are characterised by considerable internal diversity. Student religious groups, like faith communities, are not monolithic entities.

Social identity theorists regard social categories and groups as the primary means by which people define themselves. Theories of social identity and social categorisation 'therefore place great importance on the group as a source of identity for the individual' (Tsui, Egan and Xin 1995:210). New students may therefore gravitate towards religious groups for anchorage and community in the unfamiliar social world of a university. Furthermore, research carried out on the link between religion and well-being among university students has identified a positive relationship between faith group involvement and various aspects of health status. Frankel and Hewitt (1994) found that students who belonged to campus faith groups were healthier, happier and better able to handle stress than a group of students with no such affiliations. The research suggested that faith groups in universities often provide a crucial support mechanism for their members.

The next sections of this chapter will provide a comparative discussion and analysis of the national student religious organisations, and will focus in particular upon their historical emergence and development over time, their activities and aims, their co-operative links with other organisations, and their views about religion in higher education. This comparative survey is followed by a more analytical discussion of what the strength and growth of student religious organisations might tell us about the increasingly politicised character of religion in many public institutions, including universities.

The formation of student religious organisations[2]

The first student religious organisation founded in Britain was the 'Student Christian Movement' (SCM) in 1894. Throughout its history, it has been identified with a broadly liberal approach to the Christian faith,[3] and indeed, this self-definition as 'liberal' was one of the reasons for a division in SCM within 34 years of its foundation. Those with more evangelical views and practices claimed that the SCM had moved 'too far from its evangelistic and missionary orientation' (Worrall 1988:271), and they decided to form their own association. In 1928, the Inter-Varsity Fellowship of Evangelical Christian Unions (IVF) was established, later to be renamed the Universities and Colleges Christian Fellowship (UCCF) in 1974. The UCCF is the body behind today's 'Christian Unions'.[4]

The SCM was the largest student organisation in Britain prior to the formation of the NUS in 1922, and was most active and vibrant between the First World War and the late 1950s. It was a significant influence in student life during this period, and most university campuses had a well-supported SCM group. However, its apparent change of focus in the 1960s – to radical politics rather than Christian mission – appears to be one reason for its downfall and virtual disappearance (Worrall 1988). But there were other compounding factors behind the dwindling fortunes of the SCM. The formation of denominational chaplaincy posts in universities, from the 1960s onwards, had the effect of diluting the ecumenical emphasis of SCM, and led to the fragmentation of Christian activity into denominational groups, such as Methodist Societies (often known as 'MethSoc'), or Anglican Societies. Denominational chaplains naturally galvanised the specifically denominational identities of students. Since the 1980s, interest in Christianity in universities appears to have been directed into the more conservative CUs, and a particularly non-denominational and charismatic form of Christianity.

> Towards the end of the century [1900s] problems of church unity do not seem to be a major issue with Christian students; indeed many of the most committed seem impatient of any denominational labels. They are concerned about Jesus, about individual discipleship... (Worrall 1988:221-2).

However, the SCM has seen some growth over the past decade, and my interviewee in July 1998 reported the re-formation of a number of SCM groups on campuses, and the recruitment of new staff to co-ordinate national activity.[5] However, this 'revival' within the SCM appears to be overshadowed by the continuing strength of CUs, which according to an article by Charlotte Raven for *The Guardian* ('God: the remix', 28th September 1999), are now the fastest growing societies in universities and colleges.

The activity of Jewish student organisations in Britain has a similarly long history, but again with periods of varying fortune. The Inter University Jewish Federation (IUJF) was established in 1919, but even prior to this date, there were active Jewish societies in a number of universities,[6] with the first being at

Cambridge in 1902. The first Hillel House[7] for the educational and religious welfare of Jewish students was opened and consecrated in London by the then Chief Rabbi, Dr Israel Brodie, in October 1954 (Webber 1993), amid considerable press coverage. During the 1960s, there was an active programme to establish other such houses around the country, in Oxford, Cambridge, Leeds, Manchester, Birmingham, Sheffield, and Glasgow. There are now some 23 Hillel Houses in the UK, as well as a number of other Jewish organisations concerned for student welfare (these are mostly concerned with chaplaincy,[8] and are not run by students themselves). As a response to the considerable anti-Semitism and anti-Zionism in British universities in the mid-1970s (Webber 1993) a new organisation was formed out of the IUJF, namely the Union of Jewish Students (UJS), and this became the Jewish organisation – organised by and for students – with which we are familiar today.[9]

The first national organisation for Muslim students in Britain came into being with the formation of the Federation of Students Islamic Societies in the UK and Eire (FOSIS) in 1962.[10] Representatives from different student Islamic Societies decided to form a national federal body to protect the interests of Muslim students and to enable nationwide collaboration. 'The subsequent years have seen the emergence of FOSIS as a well-knit and committed body of students with a growing role among students and the Muslim community in general' (Ally 1979:9). Apart from anecdotal observation, the early years of FOSIS do not appear to have been extensively documented,[11] and it is difficult to find other sources of information about the work and activity of FOSIS during the 1960s and 1970s. It is likely that much valuable data lies largely forgotten in unpublished newsletters and conversations.

The National Hindu Students Forum (NHSF) came into being in 1991, with just two 'chapters' (local societies) in Sheffield and LSE. But over time, the organisation has become the representative body for Hindu students in British universities, and there are now links with over 75 institutions of higher education around the country, affiliated to the main body.[12] The NHSF is the largest Hindu student movement in Europe, and it aims to provide a platform for debate and education about Hindu *Dharma*.

The late 1980s saw Sikh students in British universities begin to organise for the formation of a national body, the British Organisation of Sikh Students, but it was not until 1992 that a distinctive association and identity emerged.[13] The interviewee for my research reported only a 'handful' of Sikh societies in institutions of higher education in 1992, but by 1998 this number had risen to over 50. As with the NHSF, the picture that emerges from BOSS is rapid (but unsurprising) expansion over a relatively short period of time, and little documentary recording of the early history.

As yet, there is no national body for Buddhist students. This is in many ways surprising given the extent of activity related to Buddhism (mainly meditation groups) reported by chaplains in a number of universities. The possible future developments in this regard will be interesting to observe.

Nearly all of the student religious organisations emphasised their self-governing independence and their freedom to formulate their own policies and devise their own programmes. They appeared keen to emphasise their freedom from the influence and interference of the wider faith communities from which they are drawn. This said, how have their defined their role, and translated their aims into practical initiatives?

Aims and activities

The aims and activities of student religious organisations are largely self-evident, but some generic comments were made by many of my interviewees.[14] These might be summed up in a general statement as the local and national support, co-ordination and representation of students in higher education through a leadership infrastructure, and the provision of learning materials, advice and information. Examples include the production and provision of literature for distribution at Freshers' Fairs, support in establishing new campus faith groups, and the organisation of annual conferences and regional events. Over and above these general aims, two organisations explicitly refer to a *missionary* dimension to their role, namely UCCF and FOSIS, though there is no published evidence to assess their claim of success when it comes to proselytism. However, in both the academic years 1994/5 and 1997/8, the UCCF collaborated with the Bible Society[15] in the production and distribution of about 38,000 copies of St Luke's and St John's Gospels for UK students living in university accommodation, as part of its missionary endeavours. Interestingly, the UCCF was the only organisation that reported direct opposition to the work of CUs on campus, mainly coming from (it claims) those hostile to evangelical Christian beliefs.

All the student religious organisations host some kind of annual national conference, with levels of participation varying from about 100 in the case of SCM,[16] to approximately 500 in the case of the UJS, and the duration lasting from one day (NHSF) to one week (BOSS). Only one student religious society conference has specifically addressed the theme of religious diversity, namely the SCM during its 'Celebration of Faiths' conference held in Leicester in 1996.[17]

One of the student religious organisations has a significant involvement in the publishing of books. The UCCF has its own publishing house, known as IVP (Inter-Varsity Press), which in turn has imprints for academic and popular Christian publications. A particular anxiety of the organisation appears to be the spiritual welfare of Christian students who are studying academic Theology and Religious Studies. Out of a concern that such teaching will be excessively 'liberal', UCCF publishes a journal called 'Themelios' which presents alternative and more evangelical (though scholarly) arguments on religious subjects.

Regionally and nationally, the different student religious societies organise a wide range of social, sporting, and academic events. Members are informed about these through local newsletters, termly magazines, and increasingly, the Internet. The quality and volume of printed information varies widely, as does the extent of technology on each of the web sites (some sites had not been updated between early 1998 and the beginning of 2000).

Most of the organisations rely upon considerable volunteer and sabbatical staff support, and again, the qualifications and number of people involved is diverse and often reflects regional patterns of organisation. Unlike most of the other student religious societies, the UCCF has full-time, salaried professional staff. This is a reflection, in part, of the considerable financial support for UCCF. Donations from past members, local evangelical churches, and students themselves help to support the salaried staff in the organisation. Given the emphasis upon tithing (the donation of a percentage of one's resources) in the evangelical, charismatic church traditions, this financial support (even by students) is not surprising. None of the other student religious organisations were prepared to reveal, even generally, the sources of their income.

However, the interviewee from SCM admitted that the assets of their organisation had dwindled considerably from the era when SCM owned a number of student hostels, only to be sold during the 'difficult' years for the organisation in the 1970s. The Movement has also been affected by the gradual passing away of supportive ex-members who remember the organisation's vital years in the early part of the 20th century. In the light of a constant concern with fundraising, SCM is beginning to take on some of the characteristics of other voluntary sector organisations in seeking strategic advise from local government voluntary sector advisers.

Through the Hillel Foundation, some university towns and cities are able to provide a Hillel House for Jewish students, while FOSIS funds a number of hostels for its members. Hillel describes its hostels as a resource against the '3 A's of anti-Semitism, apathy and assimilation' (http://www.ort.org/hillel). In the past, SCM also owned a number of houses for its members. Some universities have also taken the step of setting aside particular properties, or halls of residence (or 'corridors' in halls), for students from the same faith background. However, the provision of such halls/corridors or faith-community hostels echoes a much earlier but parallel development and debate within the Roman Catholic community.

When Catholics were first admitted to Oxbridge colleges in the 19th century, there was considerable discussion as to whether Catholics 'should reside one by one within the walls of the existing Colleges and halls, or that a Catholic college and hall be founded to receive them' (H.E. Manning, July 1863, *The Dublin Review* cited in McClelland 1973:184). The pros and cons of this matter were extensively debated, the arguments *for* chiefly resting upon the need for Catholics to engage as fully as possible with the intellectual and social culture of the university. Others were less supportive of this position, and argued that 'the anti-Catholic atmosphere of Oxford and Cambridge cannot fail to be secretly and deeply injurious to the faith and morals of the Catholic students' (McClelland 1973:186). In today's multicultural, multi-faith society, I would suggest that religious hostels and 'halls' are founded less upon a negative fear of 'contamination' by, or prejudice from, the rest of the student population, and more positively upon enabling students to observe the practical norms of their tradition, and sustaining their religious identity in shared surroundings.

Co-operative links

All of the student religious organisations currently active in Britain appear to be well-connected to a wide range of other religious, voluntary, student, and charitable associations, both within and outside their own tradition. For example, SCM is affiliated to the main national ecumenical body 'Churches Together' and with the Society of Friends (Quakers), while FOSIS sends some of its executive members to the newly formed 'Muslim Council of Britain' (http://www.mcb.org.uk). The UJS has formed closer ties with the NUS in recent years, and was consulted by the CVCP as part of its report *Extremism and Intolerance on Campus*. It has also formed connections with a number of organisations working to eradicate racism on campus, such as the '1990 Trust', and, in particular the National Black Students Alliance.

These links are becoming increasingly international. For example, SCM is affiliated to the World Student Christian Federation, while the NHSF has ties with a sister organisation in India, the Akhil Bharathya Vidyarthi Parishad (ABVP). More interestingly however, Britain's student religious organisations are becoming increasingly well connected with each other. Over the past few years, stronger cross-cutting collaborative links have been formed, and the Inter Faith Network for the UK has helped in a number of instances with the development of these. It is only the two Christian organisations, SCM and UCCF that have not been part of this networking process between student religious organisations, and neither gave any particular reason for this. Currently, the closest ties appear to be between the UJS, the NHSF, and BOSS, though links between the UJS and FOSIS have also increased over the past few years. This collaboration, as well as being a worthwhile exercise in its own right, has also enabled the different national student bodies to recognise common areas of concern, such as examination timetabling and religious festivals, thus increasing the potential for the successful lobbying of institutions and academic bodies. Sikh students interested in founding their own campus group are advised by BOSS not to alienate themselves from other religious bodies; the Sikh society should 'promote unity between all students irrespective of race, religion or colour' (www.waheguru.demon.co.uk). A similarly inclusive statement can also be found on the SCM web site. Thus, nearly all the student religious organisations are highly aware of the diverse environment in which they must operate, and the potential collective strength that might be derived from this diversity.

A number of interviewees expressed concern that more could and should be done to strengthen the link between individual campus faith groups, and local religious communities. BOSS is critical of the way that the British Sikh community has 'failed to recognise the needs of their youth', while the NHSF interviewee also noted the need to bridge the gap between the needs of Hindu students and the support that could be offered by local temples (*Mandirs*). SCM wanted to see an increasing 'partnership' between students and local Christian communities. However, FOSIS, and some of the Jewish chaplaincy organisations have perhaps done the greatest amount of work so far in matching the potential resources of local communities and congregations, and students in nearby institutions of higher education. The Reform Synagogues of Great Britain, for example, has sent information packs to local congregations with details about how to work with students, and has encouraged them to nominate a 'link' officer to liaise with Jewish students in the area. FOSIS has strong connections with the regional networking done by the Islamic Foundation in Leicester, and some campus Muslim groups have used local Imams for Friday sermons. It will be interesting to see whether other organisations follow these examples in the future.

Views and issues

I was keen to establish from interviewees what they considered as the most pressing or immediate issues facing their organisations, as well as their more general views about religion in higher education.[18] Questions on these issues elicited a range of reflections, suggestions, criticisms, and aspirations.

All the organisations felt that institutions of higher education had some responsibility for meeting the religious needs of students, including the protection of more vulnerable students from some religious groups (especially those from outside the university). The ways in which universities might act on behalf of, or for the benefit of students, included the following:

- effective mechanisms to monitor religious activity on campus
- chaplaincies affiliating to the national student religious organisations (some chaplaincies are already affiliated to SCM)
- publicity about the national organisations in chaplaincy/institutional information about religion.
- better chaplaincy/institutional links with local faith communities
- new chaplaincy posts which have a more explicitly 'co-ordinating' dimension, working to implement the above suggestions
- wider recognition and implementation of the good practice and inclusive multi-faith approach to chaplaincy currently evident in some universities
- a national forum for institutions to share and discuss good practice with student faith groups.

Some of the interviewees had mixed feelings about the general adequacy of current arrangements for religion on campus. They felt strongly that where institutions fail to meet the needs of students from particular traditions, this has the effect of alienating students from that faith group. Furthermore, where students have met with hostility or indifference about their religious needs, or where institutions have been obstructive in making provision, feelings of resentment and disappointment may be carried into adult life.

The balance of positive suggestions against 'complaints' is an indication of the willingness of the national student religious organisations to co-operate with chaplaincies, and with institutions, to meet the religious needs of students and to help develop good inter-faith relations on campus. This is a valuable resource for universities, especially since student religious organisations have proved their worth in recruiting new students from local faith communities.[19]

Besides these generic comments, two of the student religious organisations voiced concerns that were internal matters, distinctive to each organisation.[20] Firstly, the UCCF was concerned that a general indifference and contempt for committed Christians on campus and hostility to some CUs was ultimately 'limiting religious freedom in higher education'. Universities, it claimed, should maintain an environment of 'liberty for all religious groups to engage in proselytism', and there should be 'fair play' for all, and 'no preferential treatment for some faiths rather than others'. Within these comments was a perception that sometimes, 'minority' faiths were treated in some institutions with greater respect than Christianity.

FOSIS expressed frustration that 'Islamophobia'[21] was still a problem in a number of universities, manifesting itself as, for example, 'offensive/racist graffiti on prayer room walls'. The organisation felt that universities had a responsibility to take a 'pro-active approach to anti-Muslim prejudice'. FOSIS was also concerned that a small, but often vocal minority of Muslim extremists was leading to wider perceptions of all Muslim students as 'fundamentalist'. This small minority hampered the efforts of other moderate Muslims who wanted to make 'positive contributions to the life of the wider institution'. The FOSIS interviewee felt that as the Muslim community in Britain develops and matures these difficulties should recede.[22] However, at the time of interview, the organisation was sensitive to its recent exclusion from the consultation process that preceded the CVCP report, *Extremism and Intolerance on Campus*. The NUS and UJS were both consulted, and FOSIS regards its exclusion as a "blatant omission". Despite its 'reminder' to the CVCP of its existence and willingness to co-operate with the report, FOSIS felt the lack of consultation as "insulting". It meant that 'Muslim students with constructive ideas about tackling common concerns were not heard'.

Overall, a clear sense of energy, pride, and organisation emerges from the national student religious organisations. They share some common aims and objectives and wish to serve students in broadly similar ways such as holding regular events, publishing newsletters and magazines, and acting as a resource for information and advice. Each of the organisations aims to meet religious, social, and educational needs, whilst also facing the restrictions of limited funding. The longer history of the Christian, Jewish, and Muslim organisations is reflected in their more formal structures and more developed committee and sub-committee work. However, out of the distinctive history of each organisation, the national student religious groups share some common characteristics.

Shared perspectives

Some of the challenges facing the organisations and their members are a reflection, in microcosm, of issues facing faith communities in wider society more generally, such as extremism or racism. This link between the experiences of student faith groups and their home communities appears to be stronger given that students from different faiths are now increasingly from the UK, rather than from overseas. It is almost inevitable that challenges and difficulties faced by faith communities in Britain are reflected in student religious organisations in universities. So the apparent divisions within student religious groups, especially those that represent different philosophical schools of thought, simply reflect similar divisions within wider faith communities. It is often difficult for university administrators, or chaplains to keep up with the turnover in religious society Presidents and/or committees, and indeed the philosophical differences that may exist between the work of a committee one year and the next. The fluidity and fluctuation of different groups can sometimes make it difficult for the good inter-society, inter-personal relations accumulated during the life of a committee to be sustained once key student leaders leave the institution. Similarly however, this turnover also means that new student religious society committees can bring new energy and commitment to co-operative work with others, build upon past success, or if necessary, transform past difficulties.

Most of my interviewees reported increasing membership and participation, locally and nationally and it would appear that student religious societies represent an area of vibrant religious activity in Britain. To some extent, this is a reflection of the growing numbers of students entering higher education more generally, particularly from ethnic minority backgrounds. Nevertheless, the formation and strength of new organisations has reversed a trend of declining religious activity among students. Many students of Muslim, Hindu, Sikh or other religious backgrounds are twice or three times removed from the migration experience of their parents or grandparents. It is not adequate to suggest, as proponents of the secularisation thesis might claim, that increasing religious activity among migrant families is simply a way of handling cultural transition or easing the process of integration, and not about the more fundamental relationship between the individual and the supernatural (Hamilton 1998:30). For every young Muslim or Jew who discovers simply an 'associational' identity through their faith, there is likely to be another who is actively concerned with matters of religious practice, lifestyle, and 'meaning'. This appears to be especially the case among young Muslims in contemporary Britain. Jacobson's research found that Muslim youth are 'resisting the secularising trends that are manifest in wider society (Jacobson 1998:154). They are taking an individual, personal, thoughtful and disciplined approach to their faith, and combining this with 'unquestioning belief in the absolute "truths" of Islam; truths which inform Muslims of the predetermined, unambiguous and constant constraints within which they all should live' (ibid). Islam is, for them, a vital source of meaning. The vibrancy of student religious activity also challenges the widespread assumption in sociology of religion circles that older people tend to be more religious than the young (Davie 1994). Hanif Kureishi's 1998 film *My Son the Fanatic*, is more than a stereotypical cliché in its depiction of the tension between the religious apathy and taken-for-granted attitudes of some older, first-generation Muslim migrants to Britain, and their deeply committed young offspring.

The national organisations, and their constituent societies, are increasingly focusing upon the needs of 'home' students, though not to the exclusion of members from overseas. This is an inevitable consequence of the increasing numbers of ethnic minority students from the UK entering British universities, and with it, their sense of Britain as 'home' (Jacobson 1998). For example, most of my interviewees emphasised the importance of increasing their links with and participation in national student politics. This change in focus is paralleled in Britain's faith communities, as more resources and energy are channelled into ventures that will benefit future UK-born members, and an increasing engagement with national political life.

Student religious organisations: contesting religion on campus

On occasion, some student religious societies, especially at the local level, have profoundly challenged the normative assumptions of their institutions. Academics and administrators – assuming the 'secularisation' of society and higher education – have apparently been caught unawares by the refusal of some religious groups to accept a marginal place in campus life or to observe their traditions in the purely private realm. The CVCP report, *Extremism and Intolerance on Campus* might in some senses be seen as a first response to some of the problems arising on campus relating to religious identity. Its focus, at the title suggests, was the negative dimension of student religious expression. The report did not, unfortunately, analyse whether inadequate provision for responding to religious identity on the part of institutions of higher education might have contributed to difficulties on campus, but the CVCP went on to circulate the short report on the 'Higher Education and Student Religious Identity' research project and has shown an increasing awareness of the significance of faith in campus life.

Many of the student religious organisations in various universities at different times have had a prominent public profile in the civic culture of the campus, and as such, exemplify the 'deprivatisation' (Casanova 1994) of religion within the sphere of higher education. By lobbying the NUS, or protesting to institutions about religious issues or needs, student religious groups have occasionally brought religion squarely into the centre of public campus life. For example, some CU groups have in the past assumed the 'moral majority' position on matters such as abortion, and publicly campaigned against the NUS position on the issue. Islamic societies have lobbied universities on issues such as prayer room provision. Furthermore, as I found in my research, the perception of 'preferential treatment' to some faith groups, rather than others (especially at the local level) has, on occasion, led to protest by members of *other* traditions. However, as Casanova suggests, instead of seeing some of these periodically prominent groups as 'antimodern fundamentalist reactions to inevitable processes of differentiation' (Casanova 1994:43), they might be better understood instead as 'counterfactual normative critiques of dominant historical trends, in many respects similar to the classical, and feminist critiques' (ibid).

> By crossing boundaries, by raising questions publicly about the autonomous pretentions of the differentiated spheres to function without regard to moral norms or human considerations, public religions may help to mobilize people against such pretensions, they may contribute to the redrawing of the boundaries, or, at the very least, they may force or contribute to a public debate about the issues (Casanova 1994:43).

The periodic deprivatisation of religion in universities can be justified when it enters the 'public sphere' of the campus to question and contest established practices and the claims of the so-called 'secular' sphere. In this way, responding to religious claims and counterclaims on campus are part of the collective self-reflection of universities in a modern, global, multicultural world. To suggest that religion and any discussion of its claims should be confined to the private sphere alone, thereby assigning discussion in the public realm as 'neutral', excludes from public debate a wide range of so-called 'private' issues. The feminist critique that 'the private is political' is a parallel example. Seyla Benhabib suggests that

> the model of a public dialogue based on conversational restraint is not neutral, in that it presupposes a moral and political epistemology; this in turn justifies an implicit separation between the public and the private of such a kind as leads to the silencing of the concerns of certain excluded groups (Benhabib 1991:82).

Despite the secularisation of higher education and the many other social changes which have increasingly pushed religion into the private sphere, nevertheless, religion in public life generally, and in higher education particularly, continues to have a critical and forceful public dimension. The foundation of new student religious organisations, and the enduring strength of older ones, is only likely to ensure that the religious views and needs of students remain on the agenda of local universities and higher education more generally. Some of the ways in which universities might view and respond to this scenario are discussed in the following, final chapter.

However, questions are sometimes raised as to why there is *differential prominence* between the various faith groups in the public sphere of the campus.

Some faith groups can appear to be more 'public' than others at different times. To the observer of campus life, there may not be a clear explanation for these variations, and, lacking obvious empirical justification, in such a situation it becomes much harder to resist the labelling of particular faith groups, or elements within them, as simply 'fundamentalist'. However, there are a number of possible explanations for the differentially 'public' character of faith groups on campus.

Firstly some faiths, by tradition and doctrine, have a stronger public, community identity than other religions. It is natural that they should wish to maintain the assumption of this public character, and thereby resist marginalisation or pressures to become 'privatised' (Casanova 1994). Those faiths which prescribe a 'way of life' covering politics, economics, family life etc., as well as individual conduct and devotions, will be much more likely to inject their concerns and interests into the various aspects of 'public' life. A second explanation for the differentially public character of faith traditions – related to the first – lies in the extent to which they are tied to particular national identities, and, connected to this, the extent of their claim to be a 'universal' and absolute soteriology transcending national, ethnic, historical boundaries. Those faiths that make ultimate truth claims about matters of salvation are likely to take a more public role in defending the rights of followers to observe the practices that stem from these truths. Thirdly – and again connected to the two previous points – the ability of different traditions to assume public roles is greatly furthered by processes of globalisation. The communications revolution heightens awareness of the already strong transnational, global character of particular faith traditions. In these circumstances, the dynamics of international events connect believers in majority and minority contexts into an overarching global sphere of action and media-driven public prominence. The dynamics within and between religions on campus are likely to reflect the on-going pattern of international affairs, and these dynamics will necessarily give more public prominence to some faiths rather than others, at different times.

Conclusion

From the survey of the activities of student religious organisations currently active in Britain, it is possible to identify the dynamics of 'mobilisation' identified by Steve Vertovec and Ceri Peach (Vertovec and Peach 1997:10) at the start of this chapter. Each of the student bodies has defined themselves by various criteria of 'belonging', and they have successfully co-ordinated both financial and symbolic resources in order to further their aims. Furthermore, those national student religious organisations that provide training for their local and national executive members see themselves as preparing a future generation of leaders who will be suitably equipped and skilled to participate in British life, whether as 'community leaders' or as religious professionals. The organisations meet many immediate short-term needs of students, but they can also be considered as furthering the longer-term need for the recognition of different religious identities in higher education and, ultimately, in wider society.

Notes

1   Much of the material for this chapter is derived from the original telephone interviews that I conducted during the summer of 1998 for the research project upon which this book is, in part, based. All the student religious organisations gave permission for an account of these interviews to form part of the project research report, and any publications arising from the study. The accounts included not only factual information, but also evaluative, and to some extent 'promotional' statements about their work. Rather than simply reproduce the accounts of these interviews again here, instead, this chapter critically surveys the organisations in terms of their formation, aims, funding, activities and so on, and in places, refers to other texts and sources. Statements of fact are derived from the interviews unless otherwise indicated. Analytical comment or observation from these facts are *entirely* my own. More detailed information about the organisational structure and profile of the different student bodies can be found on their respective web sites. These are sequentially noted in this chapter. Further information about the chaplaincy bodies for Jewish students is given in Appendix 7.

2   This survey covers the historical emergence of the various organisations, and thus departs from the usual alphabetical reference to each student organisation.

3   One of the four objectives of the SCM recounted to me during interview was 'sharing and learning about Christianity in a liberal, non-proscriptive way'. The other stated objectives of the organisation were: support and empowerment of Christians in the exploration of their faith; creation of a positive environment and opportunities for meeting; concern for issues of peace, justice and social provision. See also the web site of SCM (http://www.charis.co.uk/scm). The web site also outlines the organisational structure and activities of SCM.

4   More information about UCCF can be obtained from its web site (http://www.uccf.org.uk).

5   The interviewee from SCM reported to me that there were now approximately 70 SCM groups in UK universities (July 1998), of which 20 were actual SCM groups; the rest affiliated chaplaincies, or Chaplain-led groups.

6   I am grateful to Dr Alan Webber for sending me his (unpublished) paper outlining the history of the Jewish Societies in UK universities, written for the 75th anniversary of the Inter-University Jewish Federation. See his 1993 book for a more detailed history of activity by and for Jewish students.

7   A Hillel House is what might be called a 'Jewish hall of residence'. It enables students to live in a kosher environment and observe the norms and traditions of their faith. The name 'Hillel' derives from a sage in the Talmud, noted for his open-minded outlook. A number of chaplains in my research made reference to the availability of Hillel Houses for Jewish students studying at their institutions (mainly in large cities). These houses often act as the focus for Jewish activity and worship, rather than rooms in universities or colleges. This goes some way

towards explaining the comments of some chaplains who noted that they had limited contact with the Jewish chaplain serving in their area. The web site for the B'nai B'rith Hillel Foundation is (http://www.ort.org/hillel).

8   See Appendix 7 for more details about a) the National Jewish Chaplaincy Board and b) the Youth and Student section of the Reform Synagogues of Great Britain.

9   The UJS web site is (http://www.brijnet.org/ujs).

10   The FOSIS web pages give much information about structure and activities (http://www.fosis.demon.co.uk).

11   There appears to be little reference to FOSIS itself in books or articles that document the recent history of Islam in Britain. For example, Philip Lewis (1994) makes only one reference to FOSIS in his well regarded study of Islam in Britain, namely its collaboration with the UK Islamic Mission to found a hostel for Muslim students in 1967 with funds from King Fahd of Saudi Arabia (p.103). Likewise, Nielsen (second edition, 1995) makes only a brief passing reference to FOSIS (p.47). There are no references to FOSIS or specifically Muslim student activity in higher education in either Joly (1995) or Raza (1991), but Jacobson (1998), does mention the activity of *Hizb-ut-Tahrir* in some institutions (p.36), and the high degree of activity of Islamic societies in universities (p.54).

12   For more information, see the web page:
     (http://www.cg-shah.dircon.co.uk/nhsf/about_nhsf.html).

13   For more details see the web page (http://www.waheguru.demon.co.uk).

14   Three of the six different organisations I surveyed had bulleted 'objectives' either on their web sites or on publicity information. For example, **UCCF** states its aim as: MISSION – proclaiming the gospel of Jesus Christ where God has placed us and to the ends of the earth; MATURITY – growing in our relationship with God as we submit every area of life and thought to the authority of the Bible (UCCF Annual Report 1998). **FOSIS** describes its objectives to: unite all existing student Islamic societies in the UK and Eire on Islamic principles; to encourage the formation of new Islamic societies on campuses and to support the activities of existing ones; to protect and promote the interests of Muslim students; to develop the Muslim student's understanding, character and skills; to invite students from other faiths to Islam, as a complete, balanced and comprehensive way of life; to initiate mechanisms for regular communication and co-ordination among Islamic societies (http://www.fosis.demon.co.uk). **BOSS** describes its aims as follows: to organise and assist individual members in setting up local groups/societies by providing information, materials and resources, and literature for distribution; to develop packages, resources and literature which are targeted at members, of suitable content and proficient quality (it is anticipated BOSS will provide training for members in administration and positive enhancement of groups' activities); co-ordinate and network national Sikh society/local group activity through conferences and tournaments (http://www.waheguru.demon.co.uk).

15   The Bible Society is an interdenominational organisation that began in 1804 and which aims to make the Bible as widely available as possible (www.biblesociety.org.uk).

16   SCM also holds a joint annual conference with Catholic Student Council and the body which co-ordinates Methodist students on campuses (often known as 'MethSocs').

17   One of the mission statements of the SCM is its 'openness to people of all faiths and none'. The conference involved visits to places of worship and visiting speakers with expertise on inter-faith relations.

18   Each national student religious organisation was contacted during July 1998, and asked to nominate an interviewee (usually the President or Chair) to take part in a recorded telephone interview at an arranged time. Interviewees were sent a copy of the interview schedule in advance, with brief instructions about the format and procedure for the interview. In particular, they were reminded that some consultation about the interview questions with other executive members might be required in order that an *organisational* response, rather than personal comments were given. It is difficult to assess the degree to which this distinction was fully understood, so as much as possible I have tried used any evaluative statements (with care) to contribute to my own more general discussion and assessment (for which, of course, I am solely responsible). I have also tried to make it very clear when the views of the student religious organisations/interviewees are being directly recounted. After each interview, a written account/summary was sent to each interviewee so that they could ensure that the information in the account had been accurately recorded, and understood/interpreted. Subsequently, some interviewees asked for minor errors/misunderstandings to be corrected. The 'final' accounts of the interviews were documented in full in the original project report.

19   See the conclusion to Chapter 5 for more evidence of this.

20   The following paragraphs recount as closely as possible the comments as they were told to me by interviewees and the single quotation marks indicate the *paraphrasing* of recorded statements. Double quotation marks indicate *direct statements or phrases.*

21   'Islamophobia' is a relatively new word that has now become part of the vocabulary of discussion about Islam in Britain. It first came into parlance in the late 1980s and appeared in print in 1991 for the first time in the USA. Its standard place as a tool to describe anti-Muslim prejudice became widely recognised in Britain when used as the title of a report published by the Runnymede Trust 'Commission on British Muslims and Islamophobia' in October 1997, *Islamophobia: a challenge for us all.* The report gave many examples of prejudice and violence against Muslims in Britain, and one of the incidents presented to the Commission was the planting of a hoax bomb in the foyer of flats mainly occupied by Sudanese students (p.38).

22   This seems to be rather an optimistic assessment, since nearly all religions/worldviews throughout the course of history have had their 'extremist' elements.

Chapter 8

Religion in Higher Education and Public Life: Some Conclusions

> With the ethnic population set to almost double in just a few years from 5 per cent to over 10 per cent of the UK population, the needs of ethnic minority students will remain on the agenda for change (Adia *et al* 1996:71).

Many of the questions and issues that I have explored in this book are unlikely to disappear. My research is not the first, nor is it likely to be the last, to discover that 'the higher education scene in both the United States and in England [and Scotland, Wales and Northern Ireland] consists of a diversity of types of institution varying along the spectrum from explicitly religious to implicitly anti-religious' (Gay 1981:157). The implications of religious diversity on campus will continue to affect universities, and the dynamics and debates surrounding religious activity in higher education will continue to provide sociologists of religion with data that amplifies both general religious trends, and perhaps some unexpected patterns.

Diversity and de-secularisation

In this final chapter, I shall demonstrate how different universities both individually and as members of a generic group (such as 'new' or collegiate) are often far from secular. Even those that have adopted a radically secular approach still tend to privilege some faiths rather than others, or allow religion into university life in ways that conform to a definition of religion held by a dominant power-holding minority. Universities operate with very different understandings of where religion 'fits' into their civic campus culture, and have responded in different ways to the increasing religious diversity that has come about in the past two decades. Regardless of the way universities have viewed diversity and difference among students, the presence of different faiths on campus has been a powerful force for change in de-secularising the university environment, both in visible ways, and in more subtle invisible ways. Some perspectives on this situation are explored later in this chapter.

A current preoccupation of sociologists of religion is the relationship between individual belief and affiliation (see Davie 1994), and the so-called 'privatised' dimensions of religious practice (Beckford and Gilliat 1998:204). A study of religion in higher education marks a shift in focus by placing the corporate dimensions of religion at the centre of the discussion. Additionally, a study such as this exposes the way in which the historical and organisational dynamics of public institutions – in this case universities – shape the opportunities and constraints for relative newcomers on the religious scene.

The presence of different religious groups on campus, with their different requests for recognition and accommodation highlights both the implicit and explicit historical dominance of Christianity in higher education.   There is no escaping the imprint of the medieval Church upon university education, and this is still evident today in the collegiate university colleges.   The extent of this dominance is well illustrated by the following observations:

> A visitor looking down from the top of the university church in Oxford gains the distinct impression of an ecclesiastical landscape – quadrangles, towers, spires, stained glass windows, pointed arches and chapel buildings…somewhere in every college will be the chapel; not the centre of life for most students but nevertheless a close and accessible symbol of Christianity. Daily services and Sunday sermons preached by the distinguished are likely to impinge upon a high proportion of resident students in a way that would be impossible in a polytechnic. [V]irtually every college has a designated chaplain.

> The role of Visitor of a college has symbolic importance which is easy to minimise. Most other universities choose a prominent secular member from the "great and the good" but in Oxford, sixteen of the colleges have a bishop. The Bishop of Winchester is Visitor to five colleges, the Archbishop of Canterbury to four, and the Bishop of London to two.

> The titles of twelve of the colleges are religious, comprising six saints; Jesus, Trinity, All Souls, Corpus Christi, Magdalen, and Christ Church. The merging of the religious and the academic is highlighted by Christ Church…[with] the college chapel also the cathedral for the Diocese of Oxford and the head of the college also dean of the cathedral.   At the student level several places, academic clerkships, are awarded to those who sing in the cathedral choir (Gay 1981:143-4).

Some institutions have been decidedly reluctant to confront the historical legacy of Christianity in higher education, and to consider how a multi-faith student body can (and should) affect and alter established practices and norms. I would argue that some degree of equity between religious groups on campus is important if universities are to regard themselves as institutions espousing the ideals of equal opportunities. As I have shown, universities are not the 'neutral' arena of fair play that we might suppose, particularly when it comes to religion. It will be difficult to begin a debate of the issues until this fact is acknowledged. Most institutions, even 'secular' ones, have in-built structural biases that empower and privilege some faiths and worldviews rather than others.   This presents a challenge, since the expectations and practices that become encoded in institutional processes work against change.

Research conducted on campus codes in American evangelical colleges found that 'both secularizing and *resacralisation* forces' were evident (Wheeler and Schmalzbauer 1996:241). Secularisation was evident in the declining membership of some student religious societies, while resacralisation could be identified from the growing membership of others and the return of religion into the public sphere of the campus. These same trends are evident in British universities, with the process of de-secularisation largely coming about through the presence of students from other faith communities. They have, from time to time, brought matters of religion squarely into the forefront of debate. Furthermore, the identification with, and/or observance of their faith by members of minority faith groups now appears to be outstripping Christian activity, certainly in some universities (Fern 1997). The forces of de-secularisation appear to be overtaking those of secularisation in a number of universities, particularly in regard to student religious belief and activity.

De-secularisation has taken place at two levels: at the public and political level and at the internal and practical level. To take the former, Chapter 6 illustrated that more institutions of higher education, even those with an explicitly secular ethos have begun to incorporate religion as part of their equal opportunities policies. Clearly the implementation of these policies is another question, but I wish to point to the *significance* of the incorporation of religion into institutional policies at this time. Someone, or a group of individuals has at some stage, persuaded a committee that religion and a commitment towards challenging religious discrimination, should now be considered as a dimension of corporate identity and policy. Furthermore, at the public level, many universities, even the 'secular' ones, either regularly or occasionally hold religious ceremonies that are taking religious diversity into greater account.

In a much less public or obvious way, universities have necessarily had to respond to the needs and claims of different religious groups, if only for the purposes of student recruitment (and particularly the lucrative overseas market). Over time, more and more universities, even the secular institutions, have begun to appoint (and pay for) chaplains and to include religious professionals and advisers from other faiths within their structures. Some universities in Britain are currently following the example of other public institutions in developing new, sometimes purpose-built, 'multi-faith' centres or spaces. The time of committees, and individuals in some universities is now being given to decisions about allocation of institutional resources for worship space, dietary provision, examination timetabling, and personnel. Discussions about religion and provision for different faith groups are of course only likely to take up a small proportion of management or committee time, but the fact that religion is on the agenda in a new and prominent way is a significant reversal of trends. Religious diversity has disturbed an earlier, gradually secularising, status quo.

Far from religion losing its significance or influence on the activities of universities, the reverse appears to be occurring as religious issues become more evident and contested. At the student level, it is evident that religion is not only the basis for identity for many students from minority faith communities, but that it is being used as a significant cultural resource in order to secure certain rights and meet needs. Religion in universities has proved itself to be 'a potent cultural resource or form which may act as the vehicle of change [and] challenge [and its] capacity to mobilise people and material resources remains strong'. Beckford is right in his prediction that it 'is likely to be mobilised in unexpected places and in ways which may be in tension with "establishment" practices and public policy' (Beckford 1989:170). As we have seen in Chapter 7, the vigorous campaigns for prayer rooms by Muslim students, for example, contest widespread sociological and institutional assumptions that religion is purely a matter for the private domain. Furthermore, the growth in the activity and number of some student religious organisations (but not all), challenges the taken-for-grant 'secular' norms governing many universities and the specifically Christian traditions of collegiate university colleges and Church institutions.[1]

Clearly, higher education does not 'need' religion for its purpose, direction, or for the integration of the campus community, and there has been a clear secularisation of higher education from the era when Christianity had a foundational place in the life of the early universities. The methods and assumptions of learning, and the lifestyle of the first collegiate universities, had religion, and more specifically Christianity, at their core. However, at the turn of the millennium, religion in universities cannot be relegated as insignificant or unimportant. Universities are being forced to consider the needs and implications of the life-world of a new generation of students from a variety of different religious traditions. Much the same can be said about other large public institutions, such as hospitals that, for a variety of reasons, are becoming more responsive to a variety of religious needs and values. The presence of diverse religious communities in universities is challenging the boundaries and assumptions about the 'sacred'/private and the 'secular'/public. As the previous chapter has shown, student religious groups are challenging and contesting this boundary, forcing debate and, 'like feminist critiques of modern developments, they will have functioned as counterfactual normative critiques' (Casanova 1994:43).

Some universities and large corporations are beginning to respond to the religious and spiritual aspirations of their members, and thus to allow the supposedly 'private' sphere of religion into the 'public' arena of work. In particular, the 'workplace' and those institutions, such as universities, where people spend considerable amounts of their time (periodically, or over a length of time), are increasingly responding to a variety of religious and spiritual claims. 'It is finally being recognised that companies need to appeal to people's souls as well as to their minds and pay-packets' (Hilpern 1999). More and more employers provide their employees with opportunities to benefit from the increasing popularity of holistic/spiritual/well-being techniques and practices, from yoga to T'ai Chi. My own institution, Cardiff University, an avowedly secular institution, now provides its staff and students with the opportunity to benefit from the 'Well-being Clinic' which offers a range of complementary services, which, it is claimed in a glossy brochure 'illustrate our holistic approach to health and fitness'. After a hard day in the lecture theatre, one can take refuge in the Well-being Clinic and benefit from Reflexology or Aromatherapy. Both of these alternative therapies have emerged as part of a growing interest in non-conventional spirituality and New Age philosophies during the 1980s and 1990s. The revival of interest in the spiritual consciousness embodied in the New Age movement has provided evidence for those sociologists of religion who have difficulties with the secularisation thesis, as espoused by Bryan Wilson, and others (Wilson 1966). What is interesting is the willingness of different corporate organisations to embrace privatised, holistic, 'safe', non-corporate, self-orientated, non-judgemental/moralistic therapies, based on their own definition of what counts as religion/spirituality. This contrasts, unsurprisingly, with their reluctance to embrace a less radically secular or less hostile approach towards the more corporate dimensions of religion. The reason for this contrast might lie, at least partially, in the fact that privatised religious phenomena *per se* do not pose any challenge to either the dominant structures or the dominant paradigms of the institution.

Religion is not the 'sacred canopy' it once was over society, or over the functioning of social institutions such as universities. Nonetheless, many large organisations are for various reasons taking increasing account of the individual religious and spiritual needs and aspirations of their members. I would argue that the strength of religious identities and practices within some of the more recently established religious groups in Britain has been a considerable force for change in the religious landscape of contemporary Britain. This is clearly out of all proportion to the numerical size of these communities. Whether this amounts to some degree of erosion of the gulf between the private and the public sphere when it comes to religion is debatable, but the evidence points to the fact that religion, though perhaps at marginal points of overall social activity, is a force to be reckoned with. Through their ability to influence institutional life, faith communities on campus are recovering a political territory previously lost through 'secularisation'. There is a parallel in public life more generally, in that those religious worldviews that do not distinguish between private and public are injecting religious concerns into the public sphere in a new way. The assertion of different and often marginalised identities is placing the dominant culture in the spotlight. Thus, the presence of Muslims, Hindus, Sikhs and other faith groups on campus highlights the historical legacy of Christian traditions and heritage, as well as the generally secular approach of today that is so taken-for-granted in many universities. The multi-faith campus confronts established practices, assumptions and even apathy.

Paradoxically, it seems that the legacy of Christianity in British higher education institutions is somehow 'invisible' to many decision-makers and authorities because it is so taken-for-granted. The established status quo is institutionalised as somehow 'neutral'; 'the avowedly secular point of view in

[many] universities has itself become generally unquestioned and uncriticized' (Turner 1996a: editorial introduction to interpretive essays, p.260). Over time, many universities have simply moved from one kind of 'establishment' (Protestant), to another (secularism). In his recent book *Varieties of Unbelief,* John Habgood (2000) asks us to reflect whether the comments of an American philosophy lecturer might also resonate in UK universities:

> "what was especially intolerable" he wrote, "was the absolutely unexamined assumption that, because I was a member of the academic community, I would, of course, regard sneering at God and the church as meet, right and even my bounden duty". He went on to describe himself as "simply revolted by the malevolent, self-satisfied stupidity of the attacks on Christianity that proceeded from..."the great secular consensus", by which he meant "just about everyone connected with the universities" (Habgood 2000:3).

Those who represented difference in the early 19th century challenged the exclusive, established status quo, in much the same way that religious diversity on campus is now beginning to challenge the dominance of unquestioned, uncriticised secular perspectives.

University administrators sometimes become indignant in relation to the claims of minority groups because they are perceived as more 'visibly' religious. In the political struggle for the 'recognition' of different religious identities and rights, it is becoming harder for some institutions to continue to assert their secular fundamentalism as 'neutral' or normal, and the identities of religious minority groups as deviant. 'Blindness to difference perpetuates cultural imperialism by allowing norms expressing the point of view and experience of privileged groups to appear neutral and universal' (I.M.Young 1995:203). The structural patterns of group privilege, and the elitism of a secular approach dominated by a majority become evident; remember, 'secularism' is itself a philosophy of religion. Powerful majorities, or a decision-making minority, have the power to define people, cultures, languages, or religions as 'different', which implies that their own ascribed or achieved characteristics or values are 'normal'. Belonging to the 'normal' group or to the group described as 'different' 'brings about something more than an unequal distribution of resources or opportunity among social groups: rather it defines the capability of being a full or second-rate citizen' (Galeotti 1998:268).

The 'secular' exclusion of religious concerns from the agenda and corporate thinking of some universities has not proved itself to be more effective in keeping the peace between religions, nor in maintaining real equity between traditions. My research as well as other work (see for example Marsden 1994) has proved this point. The radical secularism of some universities seems to be just as extreme as the religious exclusiveness of Oxford and Cambridge in the 18th and early 19th century. But perhaps there is a middle way?

Radical and pragmatic/moderate secularism

Some universities, and especially some of those with shorter histories as universities, have begun to espouse a 'secular' stance which, rather than being hostile to religion, or relegating religious matters to the private realm, have tried to constructively engage with diversity on campus. Theirs is a more pragmatically secular approach, and it again finds a parallel more generally. Tariq Modood has observed that:

> secularism has increasingly grown in power and scope, but it is clear that a historically evolved and evolving compromise with religion is the defining feature of Western European secularism, rather than the absolute separation of religion and politics. Secularism does today enjoy a hegemony in Western Europe, but it is a moderate rather than a radical, a pragmatic rather than an ideological secularism (Modood 1998:392).

Some universities are adopting an 'Indian' style of secularism, rather than an 'American' one, by which I mean that some institutions aim to respond to all religions fairly, rather than being suspicious of any association with religion.[2] I am indebted to Modood for this distinction.

> While American secularism is suspicious of any state endorsement of religion, Indian secularism was designed to ensure state support for religions other than just those of the majority. It was not meant to deny the public character of religion, but to deny the identification of the state with any one religion (Modood 1998b:92).

There are some values in the Indian-style 'secular' approach that, if interpreted in an inclusive way, can be profoundly helpful for the management of religious diversity in higher education. For example, 'a regulated competition between secularism and religious forces helps to preserve the freedom of religion and non-religion alike' (Beckford 1989:76-7). As we have seen, terms such as 'secularism' and 'secular' can contain a range of nuances and different points of emphasis. However, a hostile, anti-religious secular perspective (which is not liberal, as some might suppose) is different from a multi-faith 'secularism' that seeks to ensure equitable involvement between traditions in the public sphere, and ensures that voices of difference are audible.

The evidence from my research suggests that secular universities which recognise religious diversity and difference have been the most successful not only in attracting and recruiting students from different faith communities, but can often boast better overall inter-religious relations on campus. Charles Davis' definition of a secular society, (if the word 'university' is substituted for 'society') corresponds with the kind of university I have in mind.

> A secular society is a society or people that has not committed itself as a collectivity to a single set of ultimate beliefs and values. It is pluralist in the sense

that it embraces people who differ in regard to their adherence to ultimate beliefs and values. A secular, pluralist society is not secularist in the sense of embodying an ideology hostile to religion (Davis 1994:2).

This view of secularism is a long way from the combative, illiberal, and exclusionist attitude towards religion evident in some universities. The 'success' and potential of a Multi-faith Centre at a secular university, this time at Griffin University, Queensland, Australia is well illustrated by Patricia Blondell when she writes

> ...we need a public space where people from different religions can encounter each other. Where can we cultivate such public spaces? Universities provide ideal sites that are both neutral in the religious sense and safe in that the space does not belong to a particular religious tradition. Universities are already places where cultural exchanges take place and perhaps a secular university in particular offers the ideal venue for dialogue which take account of differences in religions' (Blondell 1999:153).

The challenge for universities is to build a collective corporate unity of belonging while valuing a diversity of beliefs and values. This is easy to advocate, but much harder to put into practice. But there is a danger of ethnic separatism and/or cultural isolationism when faith groups do not have the opportunity to contribute in a recognised way – perhaps through a chaplaincy/committee – to the shaping of the campus community. 'Isolationism becomes injurious to a sense of campus community when people decide that only their groups matter, when they lose (or fail to develop) concern and consideration for other individuals, other groups, the campus at large, and society as a whole' (Cortés 1991:12). Universities with a combative or hostile, 'hands-off' approach to religious matters are unable to shape through their structural arrangements, the kind of campus community that might help to foster unity while celebrating diversity. Such structural arrangements might include, for example, the promotion of student religious societies on campus to institutionally recognised committees so their voices heard through established channels of negotiation and discussion. These avenues could perhaps include the chaplaincy or other committee, so that these societies can become transformed into active participants engaged in the formation of the civic culture of the institution, rather than excluded, isolated, or 'problematised' groups on the periphery. The 'complex patterns of affinity and enmity' (Cohen 1995:5) between students of different faith backgrounds can be managed more openly and constructively in this kind of environment, and prevent injustice or conflict in one part of the community affecting the quality of life or sense of community for the whole. Separatist tendencies are much more likely to flourish when there are no opportunities to contribute to the public life of the campus, and inclusive structures do not make a heavy demand on resources.

> The key indicator of a campus that is building a multi-cultural community is the degree to which conflict is used to inform or improve campus decisions, the

degree to which processes are in place to "work through" the conflict, and the degree to which persons from marginalized groups feel that they have a voice in resolving the conflicts (Smith 1994:33).

Earlier in this book, I argued that religious trends in universities mirror religion in wider society in microcosm, largely due to the fact that in some ways, universities are societies and polities in miniature. This is the case not only in terms of patterns of religious activity, but also in terms of different perspectives about where, if at all, religion should figure in public life. Tariq Modood's comments about multiculturalism and establishment in the public sphere support my general findings about religion in universities.

> We have in Britain at the moment a three-cornered contest between a secular hegemony, a Christianity which, albeit in a dilute way, still gives to most people their understanding of divinity and moral conduct, yet is fading as an organised religion; and, thirdly, an emergent multi-faith society as the new religions establish communal and institutional foundations and seek accommodation from Christians and secularists alike (Modood 1994b:72).

In the wider society, the 'winners' in this contest often reflect regional or local trends; the 'multi-faith society' is, for example, much more evident in towns and cities such as Bradford or Birmingham, than in Truro or Norwich. The 'winners' in higher education are a reflection of ideological and historical factors. Very broadly, the collegiate university colleges tend to explicitly represent establishment Christianity and its privileges. Civic universities as a generic group tend to represent the secular hegemony, though with some concessions to religion on their own terms.

In marked contrast, the new, 'secular' universities have often (but not in all cases) been more willing to engage with the multi-faith society and student body in their midst, through an inclusive but secular approach where religious and non-religious voices can be heard. It seems likely that their ability to operate in this way is a reflection of the fact that the salaries of many chaplains in new universities (either before or after 1992) often (but not exclusively) reflect collaborative funding arrangements whereby chaplains are funded either entirely or partially by their institutions. *Institutional investment in, and ownership of chaplaincy* has broken the otherwise complete reliance upon Church resources, and with it, a gap has been bridged between Church priorities and consciousness, and the realities of diverse communities and campus environments. Moreover, many of the new universities appear to have adopted a moderate rather than a radical secularism, enabling a more creative approach to the religious diversity contained within them. This has often led to better relations between institutions and the student faith groups within them, and it paves the way toward some degree of mutual accountability. Many of the new universities, and indeed some of those institutions founded in the 1960s and 1970s were free to innovate. Speaking about Lancaster University, Eric Sharpe writes the university was brand new, and could make up the story as it went along, in a manner of speaking, without the need to defer to precedent, especially not to that of, say, a religious establishment (Sharpe 1999:228).

As organisations, newer institutions have often had more scope to establish organisational structures built upon the vision and norms of the times.

The paradox of these overall findings is clear. The collegiate university colleges and to some extent the Church Colleges, founded upon the traditions of Christianity and with religion at their core, are often the least accommodating to religious diversity. There appears to be little outright hostility to other religions, but it is difficult for students belonging to faiths other than the Christian, to benefit from the religious privileges in such institutions. The present structures, traditions, statutes, myths, rituals, and many procedures of the collegiate university colleges reflect the historical connection between higher education and the Church, and the strength of these connective ties does not appear to be weakening, even in the face of diversity. The religious 'umbrella' over many of the collegiate university colleges is giving little shelter to other traditions, and students from different traditions must rely upon more general university level provision and support. By contrast, the 'new' universities, largely founded without any reference to religion, are often the most willing to accommodate diversity. Their 'secularism' appears to entail an understanding that no one faith group will be accorded special rights or privilege. In between, we find the older, civic universities, where secularism is interpreted both radically and moderately. Students with religious commitments and needs will benefit, or more likely suffer together from the interpretation of 'secular' prevalent in their institution, regardless of their tradition.

Organisational change and identity

This exploration of the current situation points to a number of considerations about the way in which organisations might change – for the better – in relation to diversity: 'diversity theorists concur that effective management of diversity requires organisational change' (Ragins 1995:92). The questions and issues are more than just academic: feelings of exclusion are likely to find a vent somewhere, someday. The student or staff member who feels that their religious sensitivities or needs have been disrespected is likely to carry ill-feeling into the future. Furthermore, the defining of some religious groups or activities on campus as 'problematical' defines groups or individuals only according to these perceived 'problems'. It serves to distract attention from a more general need to consider organisational issues, change, and management. There is thus a need for further research which focuses upon the way universities themselves are designed and structured, formally and informally, to manage diversity.

Change may occur, and can be managed at a number of different levels. Culturally, attitudes towards diversity are bound up with the identity of the institution. The degree to which different universities respond to religious diversity among their members will be a reflection of their founding principles, the degree to which their structures accommodate change, openness to new ideas, and so on. The power-holders can critically affect the ideology, values and assumptions within an organisation. For example, one of my interviewees was anticipating a better future for her role, for the status of the chaplaincy, and for the opportunities of other faiths, with the appointment of a new Vice-Chancellor whom she knew to be sympathetic towards her work. Change in the cultural identity involves adjustment of an organisation's basic assumptions and ideologies, and those characteristics that define the identity of the organisation, in ways that are more supportive of diversity. This might involve, for example, the formulation of clear policy or mission statements. 'Simply respecting difference is an oversimplification that avoids concerns about genuine differences in values and approaches, and the ways in which institutional values must also change' (Smith 1989:iv). This necessarily implies structural changes in the organisation.

Structural differences in access to power can be seen to contribute to the emergence and sustenance of unequal power relationships (Ragins 1995). We have already seen in Chapter 4 that among those institutions that allocate or provide resources for religious activity (explicitly or implicitly), Christian students are the principal beneficiaries of this funding, seemingly out of all proportion to their numerical strength on many campuses. Christian chaplains remain the key personnel in matters of religion in many universities, and Christian students often have more opportunities to benefit from chaplaincy activities. The physical, financial, and ceremonial structures and norms of many institutions tend to privilege Christianity, and where religion has any power of influence in institution matters, it is likely to reflect Christian interests. Religion in higher education cannot deny its historical Christian identity. However, I would argue that on the multi-faith campus, students of other faiths are entitled to the same opportunities and access to structural and institutional financial resources that Christians have often enjoyed. The many 'hidden' and taken-for-granted ways in which some universities have supported and sustained religious activity on campus need to become more transparent and accessible to students of differing religious identities. A direct way to take this forward could involve the expansion of committees concerned with religious matters, so that inclusion from representatives of different faith traditions itself becomes taken-for-granted.

Behavioural analysis of institutions involves an examination of practices and policies concerned with issues such as stereotyping of minority groups, and the subtle, often unintentional behaviour which may marginalise or exclude certain faith traditions (what Rowe (1990) has termed 'micro-inequities'). As I showed in Chapter 6, the efficacy of equal opportunities policies can be highly variable in relation to implementation, and may even reinforce prejudice through being rooted in liberal Western stereotypical assumptions. Policies need to address attitudes, practices, and behaviour that might affect the inclusion of minority groups. Educating for diversity is a concern of a number of American writers on diversity in universities. One of the leading commentators and analysts on this subject,

Daryl Smith, regards programmes where staff and students are obliged to undertake courses about plurality and difference as necessary, not only for institutional change, but also for shaping the society into which students will ultimately enter. A number of British universities offer optional staff development courses about 'Religious and Cultural Diversity' for their staff, for example. However, the lesson from America is that more widespread programmes of education for diversity are also needed.

Naturally, the cultural, structural and behavioural attitudes to diversity within an institution are interdependently related to each other, but their separate analysis enables a clearer picture of how strategies for change might be constructed. Action at one level synergistically affects other levels, but change at one level only is ineffective in producing effective organisational change (Ragins 1995:94-5).

Change within organisations is critically linked to change in society as a whole, and it is apparent that

> organisational culture is shaped by the larger societal context in which the organisation is embedded. Societal values, assumptions, and beliefs regarding power relationships among groups are internalised and reinforced by the organisation (Ragins 1995:96).

This is evident in universities by the fact that many of the civic universities were often founded in a climate of secularism and reaction to the establishment Christianity dominating the collegiate university colleges. Their character today and certainly their perceptions of where religion 'fits' into higher education, are often a legacy of the cultural context in which they were founded. Newer institutions were established during a period when issues of diversity and equality in wider society were emerging, coupled with increasing awareness of ethnic, racial and religious diversity. This has resulted in less radically secular founding ideologies in some newer institutions.

Progress towards the recognition and inclusion of different religious identities on campus is likely to be closely related to these same issues in wider society. Present evidence suggests more rather than less recognition of difference in the public and institutional sphere, largely due to the increasing political awareness and activity of minority faith groups. For example, the new Welsh Assembly in Cardiff is seeking to establish links with different faith communities in Wales. The religious representation of the House of Lords has diversified over the past two years with the presence of two Muslims peers, namely Baroness Uddin and Lord Ahmed (Malik 1998:10). Other Muslims have entered the Lords more recently. Guidelines for religious celebrations of the millennium have been constructed with Britain's religious diversity in mind (Department for Culture, Media and Sport 1998). After a hard-won and bitterly contested battle, there is now a 'Muslim Adviser' at the level of 'assistant chaplain general' to oversee issues relating to the Muslim prison population (Bodi 1999). The increasing recognition and representation of other faiths in public life has something to say to those universities resistant to recognition of religious diversity, or to religion *per se*. Increasingly, religion cannot be ignored or relegated as unimportant to the functioning of some of Britain's major public institutions.

Universities and collective religious identities

The increasing religious diversity of many campuses has elicited a number of responses from different types of university. As I illustrated in Chapter 5, in relation to religious spaces, the spectrum of response ranges from distinctly anti-religious, to a more inclusive, multi-faith pragmatism. Some collegiate university colleges have accommodated sources of religious and pastoral support for members of other traditions in an environment that is architecturally and historically 'soaked' in religion. But provision for different faiths in these circumstances can be regarded as largely peripheral to the entire structures that explicitly privilege Christian students and Church establishment practices.

I suggest that there are a number of philosophical, economic, and sociological arguments that underpin the case that universities, regardless of their religious or non-religious foundations, should become more responsive (in terms of provision and structural 'recognition') to different religious identities. It is to the philosophical case that I turn in the first instance to argue the case for campus communities that are more inclusive and responsive to religious difference.

Facing all the different types of university is the question of how to reconcile the claims for recognition made by different faith groups, and the 'liberal' ideals of the academy. How can an educational system that represents individual competition, prestige, liberalism, free debate and argument, also respond to collective religious identities and to religious needs that may not conform to the exact parameters of this liberal vision? This is fundamentally a political (and frequently asked) age-old question: 'how to achieve a reconciliation between our collective needs as human beings and our specific needs as individuals and members of diverse communities, how to balance the universal and the particular' (Weeks 1990:89). Weeks proposes a 'radical pluralism' and a vision of politics as an ongoing process of discussion, negotiation and education through which difference and diversity can be accepted (Weeks 1990).

As part of a project of 'radical pluralism' for higher education there is scope for those universities hostile to religion to re-evaluate their 'radical secularism'. The older civic universities were largely formed by a vision of liberation from establishment religious dogmas and a freedom to pursue value-free inquiry. Recent scholarly and cultural discussions have suggested, however, that inquiry is rarely value-free and there is little reason to continue to insist upon the ideologies and scholarly models of the past; 'liberal universities were never as free from political, commercial, class, and gender interests as their rhetoric implied' (Marsden 1992:7; Marsden 1996). This suggests that there is room to re-evaluate a place for religious outlooks in higher education, not through the return to a dominant Christianity, but through the recognition that 'religious perspectives, if responsibly held and civilly presented, are as academically respectable as any other perspectives' (Marsden 1992:7). This implies a greater recognition of different religious voices; a collective process of establishing what constitutes 'civil' religious conduct; and, a greater sensitivity towards different religious lifestyles within the academy.

Collective religious claims upon institutions, such as the provision of prayer space, or the right to leave of absence on religious holidays, need not conflict with the ideologies of liberalism implicit in the world of higher education. Following the kind of arguments made by Will Kymlicka (despite the debate surrounding the qualifications for his perspective), for example, it is possible to claim that 'secure cultural membership is a primary good as essential to individual well-being as are the more traditional liberal goods, such as freedom of conscience, movement, assembly, etc.' (Weinstock 1998:283).[3] For example, the right of student religious organisations as legitimate members of the campus community to feel 'secure' within the university – perhaps through material provision and support – can be regarded as on a par with the rights of individual students (or staff) who may find support from other 'secular' agencies on campus. Institutional support for students or staff of different faiths – as individuals and as faith groups members – need not interfere with the rights of other individuals or groups within the university community, as long as resources are distributed justly. In turn, membership of student religious groups is validated by placing such groups on an equal footing with different support mechanisms within the university that other students or staff – without religious commitments – happen to find valuable. Institutional support, recognition, and provision for different religious identities and religious groups from which members find well-being – where it is sought – also brings with it the possibility of mutual accountability and responsibility, inclusion, learning, discussion and debate, with the latter as central defining features of higher education itself. This would necessitate a re-evaluation or reinterpretation of the radical secularism in some universities, and the privileged religious structures in others, thus ending the dominance of powerful (majoritarian?) interests, and providing protection to voices of difference, in this case religious.

Earlier in this book I pointed to the fact that students from ethnic minority backgrounds are now disproportionately represented in higher education. For a variety of reasons, students from different ethnic and religious backgrounds – not to mention overseas students – represent a significant proportion of the growing university population. Questions of access to higher education for minority groups, while still important, are being replaced by other discussions about the quality of the student experience. From an economic perspective it is now important for universities to consider the connection between the retention of students from different religious and ethnic backgrounds, and appropriate support on campus. Caplan *et al* examined student retention on a predominantly 'White' campus in the United States, and they found that:

students of color in this sample, as in other studies in predominantly White multiracial campuses, remain on the periphery of campus life because they differ culturally from the mainstream. Consistent with this interpretation, although perception of disrespect attributable to race, ethnicity, or religion was related to commitment for both minority and nonminority students, a larger proportion of the minority students reported having had experiences in which they were treated with disrespect by fellow students. Such experiences with racism have been shown to decrease social integration...When students perceived the environment as unwelcoming because of race, ethnicity, or religion, their desire to continue attending college diminished (Caplan *et al* 1997:149 and 157).

Despite some problems with unqualified and undefined use of a number of research terms, nevertheless, Caplan *et al* have proved a direct link between what can be called the 'quality of student experience' and the retention of students from different ethnic and religious backgrounds. A critical factor determining students' intention to remain in higher education appears to be to their sense of integration into the academic and social community of the institution. Students who feel involved and integrated into campus life show greater commitment to the institution and to academic achievement (Tinto 1993). Related to this is the perception that the *university is making an investment in them*. This evidence suggests that student religious organisations and religious facilities for different traditions *on campus*, are a key resource for universities in as much as they provide a further avenue of support and involvement in the university for some students (particularly perhaps, for those who might otherwise feel marginal or excluded). If students from ethnic and religious minority communities continue to look for information about religious facilities on campus when applying to university (Acland and Azmi 1998), and if universities are to attract *and retain* students from different religious backgrounds (particularly those from overseas, who pay high fees), appropriate responses to religious and spiritual needs become directly related to an important source of income for universities (Blundell 1999:149).

Both philosophically and economically therefore, it is possible to justify universities giving more thought to the question of religious provision on campus. However, there are also a number of important sociological arguments to be considered. Firstly, universities have an important social and cultural responsibility to engage in and with changing trends, including the claims of different religious identities. Universities are 'deeply implicated in the processes of social and cultural change...[and] most ideas of the modern university require that it should reflect upon the conditions and consequences of these processes as well as participate in their initiation, implementation and consolidation...It is only through engagement with them that they can sustain their relevance for modern society' (Filmer 1997:57). If a former polytechnic chaplain is right that universities 'represent the spirit of the age [and] they embody all that is best – and worst – in contemporary society' (Earwaker 1994), then healthy debate, reflection and perhaps re-evaluation about the place of religion on campus is warranted.

Secondly, though writing from an American perspective, Rosaldo (1994) argues that concern about diversity issues and change in higher education mirrors the same kinds of questions about diversity and plurality in wider society. Universities thus provide an opportunity, in microcosm, to engage with major questions about difference, diversity, and religion. Such a debate is unlikely to occur in institutions characterised either by radical secularism or hostility to religion, or in universities that regard religion as simply a leisure pursuit for an (unimportant) minority. Thirdly, from an organisational perspective, the changing composition of the population in an institution necessitates change. If a major public institution, such as the army, or the police, immediately recruited enough women for them to constitute 50 per cent of the total force, a whole raft of organisational changes would be needed. Likewise, with universities recruiting enough ethnic and religious minorities such that they are now disproportionately represented, structures, norms and procedures need to be reviewed to take account of this change and the needs of the new students. Crucially however,

> diversity and inclusion should eventually encompass most rooms, especially decision-making rooms. Always ask, "Who was not in the room when the consensus was reached?". Introducing diversity into decision-making rooms makes them less comfortable and a consensus becomes harder to reach. In the long run, however, the decisions usually prove more durable because they have been tested against a broader range of opinion (Rosaldo 1994:409-190).

From organisational and sociological perspectives, religious diversity in higher education deserves to be an area for on-going and future debate and re-negotiation, and an issue that is itself 'recognised' as a changing and dynamic dimension of campus life.

However, what answers do we find to the difficult question of 'what might equitable institutional support for different faiths groups look like in higher education'? I support Weinstock's assertion that collective rights and recognition can be 'tailor-made for specific groups in function of their needs...and capacities' (Weinstock 1998:301). By this, he implies that, for example, some faith groups may claim the right to prayer space, while others may be more concerned for recognition through the provision of facilities to observe religious dietary needs. Some rights are likely to be generic, affecting most religious groups equally – such as leave of absence to celebrate religious festivals – while others will be specific to different traditions, such as regular access to appropriate prayer space.

> Given the great variety of kinds of groups present in a reasonably multicultural and pluralistic society, it is illusory to argue that they will all fit into the same mould as far as rights are concerned. The language of rights in fact covers a wide range of liberties, claims, immunities and powers, and there is no reason not to help ourselves to the full range of rights-contexts which these terms denote in order to produce a more fine-grained and contextually sensitive theory of minority rights...(Weinstock 1998:301).

Such a 'tailoring' approach to religious needs on campus assures us that universities will not be overwhelmed by a multiplicity of different faith groups requiring exactly the same kind of facilities or provision, and enables an equity that ensures the specific needs of different groups are met fairly, on the basis of well-being for their members. This does not imply, of course, that thereafter confrontational and difficult questions will not arise. However, institutions that have made some investment in terms of commitment, thought and inclusion of those with a vested interest in the outcomes of change are likely to have more human resources at their disposal to reach satisfactory and more harmonious outcomes.

The future?

At the turn of the millennium, it is appropriate to raise the question as to how universities might change in the future. A special edition of the prestigious journal *Futures* was devoted to exploring this question,[4] and, not surprisingly, the issue of multiculturalism and diversity featured as a subject for discussion in several contributions (Inayatullah 1998; Kelly 1998; Wildman 1998).

Some of the driving forces for change in higher education include globalisation, multiculturalism, the Internet, and the increasing politicisation of higher learning (Inayatullah 1998:591). One of the consequences of these forces is that students themselves have begun to have a far greater impact on the shape of universities, and this is likely to continue in the future. The control of higher education is no longer solely in the hands of the providers; the introduction of tuition fees, among other things, has furthered the re-definition of students as 'consumers'. Universities need to re-think their mission and processes – currently set up for the convenience of the institution – and become more responsive to the needs and interests of the 'consumer'. The balance of power is changing as learning becomes more transactional and commodified, and consequently, as students become entitled to demand certain 'products' from the university, whether these are courses in particular subjects, religious facilities, or a right to expect evaluations of an essay by a certain date. Universities are losing their 'rights' to determine the use to which students put these goods.

> [M]any university administrators and many educators could not care less how women, Islam, Confucianism, Tantra, the Vedas and indigenous peoples and perspectives are treated in dominant texts. Students, however, do. Raised more and more in multicultural backgrounds – or at least having access to the Other, with postmodernity giving the ideological legitimacy to embrace the Other – texts that write that the only relevance of Islam is as a conquering force, or of India as the transcendental are ridiculed and rightfully labelled orientalist.
>
> …[T]he multicultural challenge to the future of the university has become more pervasive (moving beyond the catchphrase of "equal opportunity employer") and

> will not go away [and] the future is more and more about an ethics of inclusion instead of a politics of exclusion (Inayatullah 1998:593).

To this end, universities need to embrace the fact that multiculturalism and religious diversity means not only the expansion of the curriculum, a re-thinking of textbooks, or better representation of difference in the faculty. It also implies greater awareness of the different religious needs and lifestyles of students, more sensitivity to, and inclusion of, the unique perspectives that they can contribute to the civic culture of the campus. This change should occur organically according to the locality of the university or college and in keeping with the traditions of the past.

The issues that I have raised in this book might at present seem peripheral to some institutions. However, as universities become more global and more diverse their response to difference among the staff and student body, especially religious difference, will mark their creative ability as institutions for the 21st century.

> Somehow Universities need to harmonise diversity rather than centralise conformity. Difference must not merely be tolerated, but seen as a fund of necessary polarities, e.g. information and imagination, perception and apperception. These polarities can help our creative spark and generate new meanings through the operations of this dialectic equivalence (Wildman 1998:630).

If universities are to equip students to face the challenges of a rapidly changing global world – part of which means enabling students to recognise and learn from the racial, ethnic and religious diversity of the campus or learning environment – then universities themselves need to set the first example. This means creating inclusive institutional structures, and recognising and providing for the distinctiveness of various religious identities across the university community. However, it also involves some consideration of what the patterns of de-secularisation of the campus that I have identified in this book might imply.

> The re-sacralisation of the world in order to sustain it is a personal journey but it could also form a part of university life. It could transform the way a campus looks, both real and virtual; its institutional voice; the sights and sounds to which staff and students would be exposed; the rhythm of the day itself. Instead of cramming ever more activities into a day, one could create a meditation time and dedicated spaces to such activities (Kelly 1998:743).

In some senses, this suggests a return to the kind of holistic, community-based ethos that characterised some of the very first universities (but where community now means global, virtual, local and real), and bringing higher education back to some of its earliest roots and foundations. Though over 150 years old, Newman's 'idea of the university' and the place of religion in the higher education setting still present germane and prophetic challenges for the future.

Notes

1	However, the increased activity by some student religious organisations does have to be set against an overall decline in student religious activity, especially among 'mainstream' Christians. No doubt, the SCM looks back with some degree of nostalgia to the days when every university campus had a thriving Christian presence, and when a large proportion of students identified themselves as SCM members (Worrall 1988). The strength of CUs in some ways mirrors the growth of charismatic Christianity in Britain, and relations between CUs and chaplains can often parallel a tension between conservative and 'liberal' traditions within the Churches. In this respect, CUs function much more like an 'other faith' group in being prominent and often 'visibly' religious on campus.
2	This is a reference to the constitutions of India and the United States.
3	For a more detailed discussion and criticism of some of the limitations of Kymlicka's arguments, and for further references to his work, see Weinstock (1998).
4	Published by Pergamon Press (Cambridge, UK), *Futures* is a multidisciplinary journal covering the methods and practice of long-term forecasting for decision and policy-making on the future of humankind, culture and society, economics, technology, politics and environment. The special issue on universities was published in 1998, vol. 30, no.7.

Appendix 1

Chaplaincy Statement of Purpose – Bolton Institute

The Chaplaincy seeks to provide support for the spiritual and religious needs of all staff and students, irrespective of race, culture and religious belief and, wherever possible, to contribute to the fulfilment of the Student Services' mission with which it is associated.

The aims of the Chaplaincy include the following:

1. To encourage and nurture individuals in their understanding of their own spirituality, recognising this as an important part of their personal growth and development.
2. To offer spiritual support and pastoral care to all who seek it.
3. To encourage individuals and groups to reflect on their experience in the light of their religious, ethical or moral beliefs.
4. To engage with people in their work, supporting and affirming all that is good and creative, thereby encouraging within them a sense of self-worth and pride in what they are doing.
5. To show a care and concern for the quality of experience which is being offered by the institutions in its many forms and to contribute to the improvement of that as and when appropriate.
6. To be a 'link person' between groups, sectors and sites, thereby helping to develop a sense of community within the institutions.
7. To facilitate an understanding of the institutions' work and aims within the local community and particularly within the Christian Churches.
8. To liaise with churches and other faith communities so as to be able to help students and staff who wish it to find a spiritual home within a worshipping community.
9. To provide opportunities for prayer, worship and the exploration of faith as and when appropriate.

Volunteer Chaplaincy Assistants

[THE] Institute employs a Chaplain to meet the spiritual and religious needs of its students and staff.

To complement and further enhance the work of the Chaplain the Institute welcomes the support of volunteer chaplaincy assistants from within:

1.   member churches of Churches Together in Great Britain and N. Ireland

2.   other major world religions i.e. Islam, Judaism, Hinduism and Sikhism

Volunteers must have a genuine respect for other faith traditions and seek to promote dialogue and understanding between members of different faith groups in the Institute. (Volunteers from within the Christian tradition must be committed to ecumenism and not seek to promote any particular denomination.)

Job Descriptions

Two possible areas of responsibility are outlined below.

1.   To support students and members of staff of a particular faith by:

   •   building up a network of contacts through which a sense of community might be created
   •   fostering among them a sense of mutual support
   •   providing means and opportunities for nurturing people in that faith without in any way proselytising.

2.   To focus on a particular area of work within the Institute which reflects and draws on the interests and expertise of the volunteer (e.g. Engineering, Humanities etc.) where s/he would

   •   seek to support the staff in their work
   •   work with the staff in creating an environment where individuals are valued and their gifts affirmed
   •   form relationships of trust through which spiritual and moral values can be explored

Volunteers are accountable to the Chaplain with whom they will meet regularly to share and discuss their work. They are expected to provide a short annual report outlining their work and indicating how they hope to develop it in the future. Any appointment will be reviewed annually by the Chaplain and Head of Student Guidance and Support Services.

Appendix 2

Administrative Notice from Southampton Institute

Policy on Religion

1. The Institute recognises that many of its staff and students have a religious commitment which it will seek to respect. However, the Institute is a secular institution and will therefore conduct its affairs largely without reference to religion, systems of faith or worship.

2. The Institute recognises the diversity of religious traditions represented by staff and students from this country and overseas. In accordance with the Institute's policies for equal opportunities in employment and in education, the Institute will not discriminate in favour of or against staff or students who hold particular religious or sectarian beliefs unless those beliefs are:

   i) Incompatible with the purposes and operation of the Institute.
   ii) Seeking to deny free speech among staff or students.

3. The Institute's secular status and its recognition that its staff and students may be from widely differing religious backgrounds, requires that religious preferences, prayers and practices etc. should not form part of the Institute's business processes. For example grace should not be said at Institute sponsored meals, nor should there be prayers associated with meetings of Institute boards or committees. Religious allusions or terminology should be avoided in Institute documents.

4. The Institute will not impede its staff or students from following their personal religious beliefs. Limited modifications to Institute processes and procedures (with the exception of financial procedures) may be made at the discretion of the individual Dean of Faculty or Head of Centre/Service, to enable individual staff and students to fulfil obligations associated with their religious beliefs unless those beliefs result in a breach of criminal law.

5.   In accordance with the Institute's recognition of the place of religious commitment in the lives of its staff and students, it supports the provision of an ecumenical Chaplaincy within its network of Community Services. The Institute will also make available limited facilities for those religions and sects that are not proscribed by the Institute. The Board of Governors shall determine which religions and sects are to be proscribed on the basis of paragraph 2 above. The facilities to be made available (see paragraph 3 above) will be determined by the Institute Director within the following framework:

i)   No special accommodation is to be made available for religious assembly, though the recognised religions and sects may be permitted to use rooms in the Institute when they are not required for Institute business.

ii)   Office facilities may be provided for religious leaders or coordinators (e.g.: chaplains).

iii)   The Institute will not contribute to the salaries or expenses of such staff or their associated support staff.

iv)   The Institute may make available information through normal processes on facilities or events relevant to the recognised religions and sects.

Code of Practice for Staff from the University of Lincolnshire and Humberside

Code of Practice: Religious and Cultural Beliefs

Equal Opportunities Statement

The University aims to create an environment free from unfair discrimination and harassment. The University respects and values individuals and the diversity they bring to its community.

Through the implementation of the Equal Opportunities Policy and practices the University seeks to ensure that:

- staff are selected on the basis of their relevant merits and abilities;
- everyone is treated with dignity and fairness regardless of position and status within the University;
- under-represented groups are encouraged to join its community.

The University is committed to developing, maintaining, monitoring and reviewing detailed practices covering equal opportunities and to dealing with any complaints in a fair, just and open manner.

All staff should ensure their personal conduct conforms to the University's Equal Opportunities Policy and Codes of Practice. The University expects a similar standard of behaviour from all students as documented in the University Regulations.

Introduction

The University aims to create an environment where all members of staff have their religious and cultural beliefs treated in a respectful manner.

Managers of the University have a responsibility to respond reasonably and sensitively to any request from an employee in meeting their cultural and religious needs.

The University has made a statement of intent with regard to equal opportunities which is detailed above. Compliance with this Code is therefore important to ensure that both this statement and the Policy document are fully implemented.

Approved Absence for Religious Festivals

Managers should give appropriate and sympathetic consideration to requests for leave from employees specifically wishing to participate in their religious festivals.

At the commencement of the leave year, or on joining the department, staff should advise their line manager of religious leave requests for the coming year.

Managers should use the discretion available within the rules for granting annual leave, time off in lieu and, in exceptional circumstances unpaid leave to facilitate these requests. Whilst such requests will not be unreasonably refused, it must be appreciated that managers must always ensure the effective delivery of service.

Cultural Dress

The wearing of religious and cultural dress (including turbans, clerical collars, veils) is accepted and must not be discouraged. Although staff are responsible for their own actions, managers must strive to ensure that such matters do not become the basis of insensitive ridicule or humour from other staff.

The following points must be borne in mind:

- some religions determine a certain mode of dress;
- if necessary, a manager should explain any individual's requirements to other employees;
- no agreed rules exist regarding female or male attire at work unless it is a requirement of the post (e.g. wearing overalls, safety equipment), however, staff should bear in mind that there is a need for decency at all times;
- priority must be given to health and safety requirements.

Religious Observance

The requirement and need to pray is a matter of personal choice based on the nature and depth of personal belief. Individual members of staff should advise their line manager if they have any special prayer requirements.

Managers should make every reasonable effort to provide appropriate facilities for prayer when these are sought by an employee or group of employees (e.g. the provision of a quiet room or other suitable accommodation). Managers are responsible for ensuring that if other employees are affected by an individual's need to pray, a reasonable degree of respect and understanding exists among them.

However, no person using the University's facilities and/or premises may use these to enforce their own religious views or beliefs.

Complaints

If an employee feels that their religious and cultural needs have not received sympathetic support and understanding from managers and colleagues, they should firstly discuss this with their line manager or, if their line manager is not offering support, with their Dean/Director. If the issue is not resolved, they should, in the first instance, contact the Equal Opportunities Officer in the department of Human Resources. An acknowledgement will be made within 14 days of receipt of the complaint. This will detail a timescale for an investigation and formal response to the issues raised.

A member of staff may pursue a complaint through their trade union. In such circumstances the trade union should, in the first instance, contact the Equal Opportunities Officer.

Appendix 4

Examples of Institutional Statements and Policies on Religion from New Universities

1.   University of North London

A respondent wrote: 'religious belief is (the last of) listed areas of which the University's Equal Opportunities Policy says: "the University will function in such a way that it does not discriminate directly or indirectly in the admission, progress, and assessment of students; in the appointment, development and promotion of staff; or the treatment of any individual".'

2.   Oxford Brookes University

'The following are examples which contribute to diversity among the student population and which will not be used as discriminatory factors in selection or assessment decisions (except where the nature of study makes this essential and legislation permits)...religious and political beliefs....'

3.   London Guildhall University

'The University respects the wide diversity of the student body and will endeavour to ensure that systems and practices do not conflict with cultural and religious beliefs. Where there is potential for such conflict staff are encouraged to take a sympathetic approach and to seek advice where appropriate.'

4.   Derby University

'The University Equal Opportunities Policy includes a commitment to implementing measures to ensure that no staff or students are disadvantaged on the basis of "religious beliefs" as well as a commitment to "support for mainstream worship requirements" for staff and students within the University.'

In its *Second Review of the Race Relations Act 1978: A Consultative Paper* (Commission for Racial Equality, London, 1991, pp.17-18, 58-61*)*, the Commission for Racial Equality called for consideration to be given to making religious discrimination and incitement to religious hatred offences under English law. These recommendations may or may not eventually pass into law. At present, however, outside of Northern Ireland there are currently very few legal requirements laid upon institutions with regard to the beliefs or practices of their staff and students.

However, under the terms of the Race Relations Act "a common religion" is seen as being one of the elements of ethnicity which establishes a group of people to be a "racial group" in the meaning of the Act and therefore to be covered by its provisions against discrimination. Because of this, Sikhs and Jews are covered by the terms of the Race Relations Act in terms of the religious dimensions of their ethnicity, although Buddhists, Christians, Muslims, Hindus and others are not, unless they also happen to be members of a "racial group" in the meaning of the Act. The University's Equal Opportunities Policy therefore addresses the position of religious believers in the institution in terms of good practice rather than in terms of legal obligation.

The University's commitment not to disadvantage students or staff on the basis of "religious beliefs" includes those who do not have religious beliefs since the University is a plural community in which the integrity and contributions to University life of humanists, agnostics and atheists are also respected. In addition, the University's mission as an educational institution means that it is concerned to provide a supportive context in which all students and staff of all backgrounds and beliefs, religious, philosophical and cultural, can explore new ideas and experiences and engage critically with received and inherited beliefs and understandings. In its curricula, and by virtue of the social and religious mix in the wider life of the institution, the personal identities, beliefs and commitments of students and staff are subject to critique and questioning. This questioning can result in changes in such beliefs, understandings and identities in ways which are entirely proper in terms of the University's educational mission.

At the same time, a plural community can only function as an educative community when all its members feel affirmed and respected as well as challenged and questioned. The University's policy therefore advocates going beyond the meeting of minimal legal obligations with regard to the religious beliefs and practices of members of its community. The policy's section on Equal Opportunities and the University Environment therefore commits the University to providing "an environment and ethos in which all students, staff and visitors feel welcome and supported by...[among other things] evidence that people's cultural, social and religious practices are respected...[and in which there is] support for mainstream religious worship requirements".

In general terms this means trying to take practical account of the religious needs and obligations of students and staff where the organisation and experience of University life has a bearing upon these needs and obligations.

University staff should also attempt to ensure that such factors are taken fully into consideration during the negotiation of student placements with outside institutions.

In Summary:

- The variety of religious beliefs and practices among students and staff should be welcomed as a positive enrichment of University life rather then being seen primarily as a source of problems for the institution, or as a matter of indifference.

- The images which the University projects, the policies which it evolves and its work and study practices and patterns need to be regularly reviewed for the extent to which they take sensitive account of the religious identities, needs and obligations of students and staff of various religious traditions.

- The dates and significance of religious festivals and other observances should be taken into sympathetic account in the planning of courses, assignments, examination dates and institutional events, where these are under the control of the University.

- On those occasions when days which are religiously significant days for some staff and students are regarded by the institution as ordinary working days, requests for time off from employment and study to undertake religious obligations should be met with a sympathetic and consistent response.

- Where examination dates unavoidably clash with days of obligatory religious observance and may thus create problems of conscience for some students affecting their attendance or performance, then requests for individual alternative arrangements should be sympathetically considered where such decisions are under the direct control of the University.

- The planning, preparation and presentation of the food which is sold or provided by the University should evidence sensitivity to dietary requirements arising from the religious beliefs and practices of students and staff.

- Staff need to be sensitive to the religious dimensions and significance of items of dress in some religious traditions.

- Staff need to develop a working understanding of cultural and religious naming systems which differ from European and Christian ones.

- Staff need to develop a sensitivity to the community mores, social structures and gender traditions of students and staff from minority religious/cultural groups.

- The Equal Opportunities Policy commitment to "support for mainstream worship requirements" means that student and staff requests to book University rooms for the purposes of religious worship, prayer and meditation should be sympathetically and consistently considered and, where possible, facilitated'.

5.   Liverpool John Moores University (Equal Opportunities Unit) – Equal Opportunities Policy on Cultural and Religious Diversity

1. *Statement of Intent*

1.1   The University celebrates and values the diversity that is brought to its community through individuals and aims to create an environment where the religious and cultural beliefs of all staff, students and visitors are respected.

1.2   The University is committed to developing, maintaining, monitoring and reviewing detailed practices covering Equal Opportunities and in dealing with complaints in a fair, just, timely and open manner.

1.3   Through the implementation of its Equal Opportunities Policies and practices, the University seeks to ensure that:

    a)   staff and students are selected on the basis of their relevant merits and abilities;

    b)   each individual is treated with dignity and fairness;

    c)   under-represented groups in society are encouraged to join the University community;

    d)   where possible, appropriate services are provided to meet the cultural, including linguistic and spiritual, needs of all staff, students, and visitors;

1.4   All staff, students, and visitors should ensure his/her personal conduct and practice conform to the University's Equal Opportunities Policies and other relevant University regulations.

2. *Dress Code*

2.1 The wearing of religious and cultural dress (including clerical collars, head scarves, skull caps and turbans) is allowable and must not be discouraged. The exception to this protocol is where the health, safety and welfare of the wearer is compromised by the wearing of such dress and/or where this is likely to enhance the risk to other persons. The following points should be borne in mind:

a) some religions and cultures determine a certain mode of dress; for example, the wearing of compulsory items, such as bangles (kara) as worn by Sikh men and women.

b) where necessary, the Equal Opportunities Unit may be contacted to assist with disseminating appropriate information explaining cultural dress and customs.

c) no specific formalities exist regarding female or male dress code at the University, other than in circumstances such as the requirement to wear overalls, protective clothing, and in specific cases the wearing of JMU uniforms. The University does not prescribe the kind of clothes one wears, however, staff and students should bear in mind that there is a need for decency at all times.

d) wearing of T-shirts displaying obscene material, in any language, which may be considered offensive and are likely to breach national law, for example, racist slogans, will be considered a breach of this policy and other University rules and regulations. Appropriate disciplinary action can be taken by the University upon receipt of a complaint.

e) priority will be given to health and safety requirements, as laid down by national legislation. Where appropriate, you may seek advice from the Health, Safety and Environment Unit.

f) further guidance on un-resolved matters may be obtained from the Equal Opportunities Unit or Equal Opportunities Committee representatives.

3. *Cultural and Religious Observance*

3.1 The requirement and need to pray in a particular form is a matter of personal choice based on the nature and depth of personal belief. Practising individuals (staff and students) should advise their line manager or tutor, if they have any special prayer requirements. Line managers and tutors are responsible for ensuring that if other staff or students are affected by an individual's spiritual needs, a reasonable degree of respect and understanding exists amongst them.

3.2   Where facilities are sought by staff and students, such as provision of a quiet room, the University should make every reasonable effort to provide clearly signed appropriate accommodation, on site, with washing facilities nearby. Users of such accommodation will be responsible for the general upkeep of the accommodation. It will be the responsibility of the University to ensure that the accommodation meets with Health and Safety requirements.

3.3   Individuals will not be required to work for specified period of time such as mid-day on Friday, Saturday or Sundays where it conflicts with their religious beliefs and practice.

3.4   A calendar of Religious Festivals and brief information on practices will be made available by the Equal Opportunities Unit.

4. *Approved Absence for Cultural/ Religious Festivals*

4A Staff   A1 Appropriate and sympathetic consideration will be expected from line-managers to requests for leave from employees specifically wishing to participate in their cultural/ religious festivals.

A2 It would be helpful if at the commencement of the leave year, or on joining the University, staff could advise their line manager of their leave requests for the coming year. Line managers should use the current University regulations for granting annual leave or their discretion for time off in lieu, and in exceptional circumstances, unpaid leave to facilitate these requests.

A3 Whilst such requests will not be refused unreasonably without adequate explanation, it must be appreciated that managers must always ensure the effective delivery of service.

A4 Where difficulties arise and/ or inconsistency of practice is identified, line managers and concerned staff may seek advice and guidance from the University's Equal Opportunities Unit, and/ or the International Office.

4B Students   B1 When devising assessment and examination timetables, arranging open days etc., should take in to account the impact of significant cultural religious events.

B2 Students wishing to participate in cultural/religious festivals should give advance notice to the course leader or appropriate member of staff for abstention from classroom attendance. However, it remains the student's responsibility to make good any missed learning opportunities.

B3   Where difficulties arise and/or inconsistency of practice is identified, tutors and concerned students may seek advice and guidance from the University's Equal Opportunities Unit and/or the International Office.

5. *Implementation and Responsibilities*

5A *University Responsibility* The University, through its Equal Opportunities Unit and the International Office, in implementing this Policy, will aim to provide:

A1   Training to raise awareness for staff and students, the latter in liaison with the Liverpool Students Union;
A2   An annual calendar of religious festivals and brief information in both hard copy and electronically via the Campus Wide Information Service (CWIS);
A3   Where possible, appropriate accommodation and resources to meet the spiritual needs of its community;
A4   Service provision such as accommodation and catering that would be cultural specific, such as diets;
A5   That complaints are handled in a just, fair, open and timely manner;
A6   This Policy is reviewed every two years in consultation with appropriate services such as Employment Relations, Health, Safety and Environment Unit, Personnel and Welfare Services, Student Relations and the Students Union. At the time of review, Schools and Service Teams should be asked to evaluate their experience of implementing the policy and offer any observations to amend/improve the policy provisions. Ultimately, any policy changes will need to be approved by the Employment Committee of the Board of Governors.

5B *Individual Responsibility* Any student, staff or visitor to the University in supporting this policy will:

B1   Be responsible for familiarising themselves with the Policy in accordance with other University rules and regulations;
B2   Undertake responsibility for informing appropriate staff of their particular requirements;
B3   Be responsible for making alternative arrangements for opportunities missed as a result of absences for cultural/religious observance. For example, absence from lectures/tutorials;
B4   Voluntarily participate in any training courses provided by the University which support the consistent implementation of the Policy;
B5   Bring to the attention of the University's Equal Opportunities Unit and/or the International Office, any matters of unfair treatment.

Please note that any attempt at coercion/enforcement of others to comply with a particular religious viewpoint/approach, for example through distribution of hate literature, offensive remarks and/or misuse of the University's services or facilities, or actions that may bring the University in to disrepute, may result in disciplinary action.

Appendix 5

'Building Good Relations With People of Different Faiths and Beliefs' – Inter Faith Network for the UK

In Britain today, people of many different faiths and beliefs live side by side. The opportunity lies before us to work together to build a society rooted in the values we treasure. But this society can only be built on a sure foundation of mutual respect, openness and trust. This means finding ways to live our lives of faith with integrity, and allowing others to do so too. Our different religious traditions offer us many resources for this and teach us the importance of good relationships characterised by honesty, compassion and generosity of spirit. The Inter Faith Network offers the following code of conduct for encouraging and strengthening these relationships.

As members of the human family, we should show each other respect and courtesy. In our dealings with people of other faiths and beliefs this means exercising good will and:

- Respecting other people's freedom within the law to express their beliefs and convictions
- Learning to understand what others actually believe and value, and letting them express this in their own terms
- Respecting the convictions of others about food, dress and social etiquette and not behaving in ways which cause needless offence
- Recognising that all of us at times fall short of the ideals of our own traditions and never comparing our own *ideals* with other people's *practices*
- Working to prevent disagreement from leading to conflict
- Always seeking to avoid violence in our relationships

When we talk about matters of faith with one another, we need to do so with sensitivity, honesty and straightforwardness. This means:

- Recognising that listening as well as speaking is necessary for a genuine conversation
- Being honest about our beliefs and religious allegiances

- Not misrepresenting or disparaging other people's beliefs and practices
- Correcting misunderstanding or misrepresentations not only of our own but also of other faiths whenever we come across them
- Being straightforward about our intentions
- Accepting that in formal inter faith meetings there is a particular responsibility to ensure that the religious commitment of all those who are present will be respected

All of us want others to understand and respect our views. Some people will also want to persuade others to join their faith. In a multi faith society where this is permitted, the attempt should always be characterised by self-restraint and a concern for the other's freedom and dignity. This means:

- Respecting another person's expressed wish to be left alone
- Avoiding imposing ourselves and our views on individuals or communities who are in vulnerable situations in ways which exploit these
- Being sensitive and courteous
- Avoiding violent action or language, threats, manipulation, improper inducements, or the misuse of any kind of power
- Respecting the right of others to disagree with us

Living and working together is not always easy. Religion harnesses deep emotions which can sometimes take destructive forms. Where this happens, we must draw on our faith to bring about reconciliation and understanding. The truest fruits of religion are healing and positive. We have a great deal to learn from one another which can enrich us without undermining our own identities. Together, listening and responding with openness and respect, we can move forward to work in ways that acknowledge genuine differences but build on shared hopes and values.

Appendix 6

Charter on Religion from an Old University

Religion

In recognition of the importance of religious belief and practice for personal and social life, and as an enhancement to educational development, the University attempts to make reasonable efforts to provide facilities for the practice of religion.

In 1969 the Chaplaincy Centre was opened as a result of a partnership between a number of religious organisations, including the major Christian denominations and the Jewish community.

Our Commitments

- The University believes that students should have freedom of expression of their religious beliefs and allows students flexibility to express those beliefs, provided this does not interfere with the beliefs of others.
- All members of the University are invited both to use the Centre's facilities and to consult the team of Chaplains, irrespective of their own adherence to a particular religious tradition. In consultation, no attempt is made to persuade or convince students of a particular approach.
- In addition to the Chaplaincy Centre the University also provides a prayer room for Muslims.

Your Responsibilities

- You should respect the rights of others to hold, or not hold, and express their own religious beliefs.

Jewish Chaplaincy Organisations

The Jewish community is the only faith community (other than the Christian) in Britain with a network of national organisations linked to regional representatives (usually full-time religious professionals) solely concerned for the pastoral needs of its students. There are a number of separate (though sometimes inter-connected) organisations, most of which act co-operatively for the religious and pastoral welfare of Jewish students. The key organisations are the Union of Jewish Students, the National Jewish Chaplaincy Board, the B'nai B'rith Hillel Foundation, and the Youth and Student section of the Reform Synagogues of Great Britain. I conducted telephone interviews with spokespersons from the National Jewish Chaplaincy Board and the Youth and Student Section of the Reform Synagogues of Great Britain. The following pages give a brief outline of their work, organisation, and aims.

i) National Jewish Chaplaincy Board

Some 25 years ago, the present Chief Rabbi, Dr Jonathan Sacks approached the then Chief Rabbi, Lord Jacobovitz about the particular concern he had for the religious needs of Jewish students. Out of this concern came the foundation of the National Jewish Chaplaincy Board, an independent non-denominational organisation which both then and now is 'serving *all* Jewish students'.[1] Dr Sacks is its current President, and the organisation has close links to the United Synagogue. But despite this association, the NJC maintains its independence from any particular synagogue or other national body. The aims and objectives of the NJC as formulated in its Constitution can be found in the close of this section.

The NJC began in the north east of England, but its coverage gradually extended to other parts of the country with significant numbers of Jews, such as London, Manchester, Leeds, Birmingham, Bristol, and more recently Cambridge. The NJC now funds seven full-time Rabbis to work regionally with Jewish students in higher education. The cities and regions now covered by the NJC include:

- London
- Manchester – for Lancashire and Merseyside
- Leeds – for Yorkshire

- Birmingham – for the Midlands
- Bristol – for Wales and the West Country
- Cambridge – for East Anglia
- Glasgow – for Scotland

These regions broadly mirror the regional structure of the UJS, enabling a close relationship between the two organisations. Clearly, the present coverage of the NJC is not comprehensive and the existing gaps, such as the south coast region, are a priority for future development. NJC therefore operates through a national framework and a regional infrastructure, in co-operation with other organisations.

In some ways, the range of pastoral issues facing NJC chaplains has changed during the lifetime of the organisation. Whilst the essential task of providing pastoral care has stayed the same, certain challenges and issues have become more pressing concerns. Welfare issues such as substance abuse, are now on the agendas of Rabbis working with students, and at a recent conference for regional chaplains, there were presentations from experts in the fields of drug abuse, and other pastoral issues such as suicide awareness, bereavement and terminal illness.

One of the organisations that the NJC works with is the Hillel Foundation. This national body serves as the umbrella framework for local Hillel boards. These local boards provide a management body for what are known as Hillel Houses, or what one might call 'Jewish halls of residence'.

For the future, the NJC has identified five key areas for its work.

- Provision of Jewish experience e.g. Sabbath hospitality
- Liaison and fund raising with Jewish community organisations
- Educational programmes, in conjunction with the UJS
- Liaison with institutions of higher education
- Pastoral counselling

Aims and Objectives of the National Jewish Chaplaincy Board

The Revised Constitution of the National Jewish Chaplaincy Board identifies the following aims and objectives for the organisation.

- To promote and assist local chaplaincy boards in the appointment of full time or part time chaplains to serve Jewish students at universities, polytechnics and other institutions of higher education within the United Kingdom
- To concern itself with the spiritual, educational and social welfare needs of Jewish students at universities, polytechnics and institutions of higher education within the United Kingdom.

The stated 'functions' of the National Board include the following:

- The Board shall be available to provide advice, guidance and assistance on chaplaincy matters in particular and student problems in general
- The Board shall seek to work closely with all relevant communal organisations in promoting the well being of the Jewish student community
- The Board shall encourage the provision of training courses for chaplains

ii) Reform Synagogues of Great Britain (Youth and Student Section)

In many ways, the NJC has similar aims and objectives when it comes to Jewish student welfare as the Reform Synagogues of Great Britain which itself has a department concerned for the interests of students and young people. Its Director has written a short paper that gives an overview of its work. This document is reproduced at the close of this section.

The history of support for Jewish students from a Reform tradition is more recent. Four years ago, in 1994, the Reform Synagogues of Great Britain hired a Northern Student Chaplain to work in a one-third time post based in Manchester. He was the first Reform Jewish chaplain appointed to work with students. Two years ago, a further new post was created for a half-time Southern Student Chaplain. This post covered all institutions of higher education south of Birmingham. In January 1998, this half-time post was increased to full-time, with effect from September 1998, and re-named as 'National Student Chaplain'. The former Northern post has now terminated, but nevertheless, these changes mean that there are more hours going to Reform chaplaincy than previously. Given the obvious limitations of only having one Reform chaplain for the entire country, the National Student Chaplain hopes to work co-operatively with provincial Reform communities. This will entail a connection with Reform Rabbis and their congregations, encouraging them to make links with Reform Jewish students in their area. They in turn can refer pastoral matters in their areas back to the National Student Chaplain. Whilst only limited funding is available, the Reform Synagogues are keen to make the most of local networks and resources. To assist them in this effort, the Reform Synagogues are sending information packs to local congregations with details about how to work with students. In addition, they want to encourage congregations to nominate a student 'link' officer to be a regional contact in a particular locality.

The objectives of the new full-time position are clearly defined and focused. The new full-time post will concentrate upon meeting pastoral and educational needs at eight different campuses. The criteria for selecting particular institutions were that there needed to be substantial numbers of Jewish Society members (say, between 75-100) and gaps in existing provision for Jewish students, i.e. no full-time Orthodox chaplain. The eight institutions are:

- Edinburgh
- Liverpool
- Sheffield
- Nottingham
- Warwick
- Cardiff
- Brighton
- Canterbury

It is likely that out of the initial work with these eight different institutions, future efforts will concentrate upon four or five.

The National Student Chaplain works closely with the Union of Jewish Students, and both organisations are trying to encourage, involve and integrate Reform students into the UJS. In the past, the UJS has been incorrectly viewed as an Orthodox organisation, hence the active recent support being given to Reform students wishing to become involved in UJS, both nationally or locally. The National Student Chaplain from the Reform Synagogues also works with the Hillel Foundation, and there are prospects for closer links between the two organisations in the future. The National Student Chaplain has recently been appointed to one of the Hillel boards,[2] and both organisations would like to encourage more Reform Jewish students to live in Hillel Houses. The Reform Synagogues Youth and Students division also has good relations with the Union of Liberal and Progressive Synagogues, and the Masorti movement.

During interview, the National Student Chaplain affirmed that institutions of higher education have a responsibility to ensure that religious provision is available for students who want it. She was also concerned that any provision goes through university channels so that it is known to be safe and 'sensible'. In this regard, institutions have a particular responsibility to protect vulnerable students from the aggressive recruitment activities of some religious groups.

"Defining Reform Chaplaincy"

Introduction 'The purpose of Reform student chaplaincy is to ensure that Reform Jewish students on campuses throughout the United Kingdom are supported, cared for, and encouraged to become actively involved in the Jewish student community as Reform Jews.

At present, given the limited number of Reform chaplains, specific communities and campuses are targeted, in order to make the work as effective as possible. Targets are selected on the basis of various criteria, including numbers of Reform students, need and interest, and ease of access.

Undergraduates are the priority grouping with which to work, as they are the majority and often the most vulnerable. However, graduates are welcome to utilise any services provided by Reform chaplains.

Reform chaplaincy work is achieved through six fundamental techniques:

a) student education;
b) pastoral care;
c) leadership development;
d) outreach work;
e) developing external relationships;
f) developing rabbinic support.

Student Education   Providing Reform students with intellectual, spiritual and experiential learning opportunities is essential to Reform student work. Wherever possible, such students should be encouraged to events which offer possibilities for religious and spiritual development. Reform Jewish chaplains are also available to write articles, run shiurim, and attend central student events, notably UJS Conference and Spring Seminar.

Pastoral Care   Whilst most universities provide extensive welfare support for students, Reform Jewish chaplains offer additional care. This may include support on issues of Jewish belief, identification and faith, as well as more general assistance on any concerns students may have. In cases where students are referred on for expert support, Reform chaplains are required to monitor their progress.

Leadership Development   In order to ensure the future of Reform Judaism, it is essential that a future leadership is developed. Part of the function of Reform student chaplains is to serve as role models for Reform Jewish students, encouraging them to develop their Jewish literacy and skills and to take on leadership roles.

Outreach Work   It is not the role of Reform student chaplains to actively seek out non-Reform students and encourage them to become involved in Reform Jewish life. However, if invited to, Reform chaplains will work with Jews from across the communal spectrum, providing educational, spiritual and religious guidance, and offering welfare support.

Developing External Relationships   Reform Jewish chaplaincy aims to work with any other organisations, Jewish and non-Jewish, in pursuit of its core aims. Whilst primary emphasis is placed on the educational and pastoral functions, establishing positive working relationships over time with UJS, the United Synagogue chaplains and relevant university authorities is part of the Reform chaplain's role. This is an on-going process which needs to be regularly nurtured.

Developing Rabbinic Support   Given the limited numbers of Reform chaplains at present, it is essential the Reform rabbis assist the official chaplains and work with Reform students in their area. Reform chaplains will work with other rabbis to ensure that pastoral and educational support will be provided wherever possible for Reform students'.

(Written by Jonathan Boyd in December 1997)

Notes

---

1   This is the motto of the National Jewish Chaplaincy. The emphasis on the word *'all'* is original.

2   She is also a member of the national advisory committee for the Hillel Foundation, as is one of the regional National Jewish Chaplaincy Board Rabbis.

References

Abramson, H. 1979, 'Migrants and Cultural Diversity: on Ethnicity and Religion in Society', *Social Compass*, 26 (1):5-29

Acland, T. and Azmi, W. 1998, 'Expectation and Reality: Ethnic Minorities in Higher Education', in Acland T. and Modood, T. (eds.), *Race and Higher Education*, London: Policy Studies Institute, pp.74-86

Acland, T. and Modood, T. (eds.) 1998, *Race and Higher Education*, London: Policy Studies Institute

Adia, E., Roberts, D. and Allen, A. 1996, *Higher Education: the Ethnic Minority Student Experience*, Leeds: Heist

al-Azmeh, A. 1993, *Islams and Modernities*, London: Verso

Aldridge, A. 1993, 'Negotiating Status: Social Scientists and Anglican Clergy', *Journal of Contemporary Ethnography*, 22 (1):97-112

Allen, P. M. 1998, 'Towards a Black Construct of Accessibility', in Acland T. and Modood, T. (eds.), *Race and Higher Education*, London: Policy Studies Institute, pp.86-95

Ally, M. 1979, 'The Growth and Organisation of the Muslim Community in Britain', *Research Papers*, Centre for the Study of Islam and Christian Muslim Relations, Selly Oak Colleges, Birmingham, no.1

Anthais, F. and Yuval-Davis, N. 1992, *Racialized Boundaries: ethnic, gender, colour and class divisions and the anti-racist struggle*, London: Routledge

Anwar, M. 1994, *Young Muslims in Britain: Attitudes, Educational Needs and Policy Implications*, Leicester: Islamic Foundation

Arthur, J. and Shapiro A. 1995, *Campus Wars: Multiculturalism and the Politics of Difference*, Oxford: Westview Press

Ballard, R. (ed.) 1994, *Desh Pardesh: the South Asian Presence in Britain*, London: Hurst & Company

Barot, R. (ed.) 1993, *Religion and Ethnicity: Minorities and Social Change in the Metropolis*, Kampen, The Netherlands: Kok Pharos Publishing House

———— 1993, 'Religion, Ethnicity and Social Change: An Introduction', in Barot, R. (ed.) *Religion and Ethnicity: Minorities and Social Change in the Metropolis*, Kampen, The Netherlands: Kok Pharos Publishing House, pp.1-17

Barry, N. 1996, 'Liberalism' entry in *The Social Science Encyclopaedia*, London: Routledge, pp.468-470

Bauböck, R. and Rundell, J. (eds.) 1998, *Blurred Boundaries: Migration, Ethnicity, Citizenship*, Aldershot: Ashgate

Bauman, Z. 1997, 'Universities: Old, New and Different', in Smith, A. and Webster, F. (eds.) *The Postmodern University: Contested Visions of Higher Education in Society*, Buckingham: Society for Research into Higher Education and Open University Press, pp.17-27

Baumann, G. 1996, *Contesting Culture: Discourses of Identity in Multi-Ethnic London*, Cambridge: Cambridge University Press

———— 1999, *The Multicultural Riddle: Rethinking National, Ethnic, and Religious Identities*, London: Routledge

Baumann, M. 1999, 'Multiculturalism and the Ambiguity of Recognising Religion' http://www.uni-marburg.de/fb11/religionswissenschaft/journal/diskus/baumann.html, *Diskus (Internet journal of religion)*

Bebbington, D. 1992, 'The Secularization of British Universities since the Mid-Nineteenth Century', in Longfield, B.J., and Marsden, G.M. (eds.) *The Secularization of the Academy*, Oxford: Oxford University Press, pp.259-277

Beckford, J. 1989, *Religion and Advanced Industrial Society*, London: Unwin Hyman

Beckford J. and Gilliat S. 1996a, *The Church of England and Other Faiths in a Multi-Faith Society*. Unpublished report to the Leverhulme Trust and the Church of England

———— 1996b, *The Church of England and Other Faiths in a Multi-Faith Society*, University of Warwick: Warwick Working Papers in Sociology, 21

———— 1998, *Religion in Prison: Equal Rites in a Multi-Faith Society*, Cambridge: Cambridge University Press

Benhabib, S. 1991, 'Models of Public Space: Hannah Arendt, the Liberal Tradition and Jürgen Habermas', in Calhoun, C. (ed.), *Habermas and the Public Sphere*, Cambridge, Mass.: MIT Press

Berger, P. 1969, *The Sacred Canopy*, New York: Anchor Books

Bhatt, C. 1997, *Liberation and Purity: Race, New Religious Movements and the Ethics of Postmodernity*, London: UCL Press

Blundell, P. 1999, 'Under One Roof: University Chaplaincy and Multi-Faith Dialogue', *Australian Religion Studies Review*, 12 (2):149-154

Bodi, F. 1999, 'All Eyes on New Muslim Prison Adviser', *Q News*, September, no.311:12-15

Bora, F. 1994, 'SOAS Student Union Attempts to Overturn Ban on HT at Campus', *Q News*, no.3:33

Braham P., Rattansi, A. and Skellington, R. (eds.) 1992, *Racism and Antiracism*, London: Sage/Open University

Brierley, P. (ed.) 1997, *UK Christian Handbook – Religious Trends 1998/9*, no.1, London: Christian Research

Brighton, T. (ed.) 1989, *The Church Colleges in Higher Education – 150 Years*, Chichester: West Sussex Institute of Higher Education

British Muslims Monthly Survey, December 1995, 3 (11), Selly Oak College, Birmingham: CSIC

Brothers, J. 1971, *Religious Institutions*, Essex: Longman

Brown, D.W. (ed.) 1994, *Higher Education Exchange*, Dayton, OH: Kettering Foundation

Bruce, S. 1995, *Religion in Modern Britain*, Oxford: Oxford University Press

Brummett, B. 1990, *The Spirited Campus: the Chaplain and the College Community*, New York: Pilgrim Press

Calhoun, C. (ed.) 1991, *Habermas and the Public Sphere*, Cambridge, Mass.:MIT Press.

Caplan, R., Zea, M., Reisen, C., and Beil, C. 1997, 'Predicting Intention to Remain in College Among Ethnic Minority and Nonminority Students', *The Journal of Social Psychology*, 137 (2): pp.149-160.

Carmichael D., Hubert J., Reeves, B. and Schanche A. (eds.) 1994, *Sacred Sites, Sacred Places*, London: Routledge

Casanova, J. 1994, *Public Religions in the Modern World*, Chicago: University of Chicago Press

Chauhan, K. 1997, 'Hindu Students Forum and the quest for roots', *Asian Age*, 27th November

Chemers, M. *et al* (eds.) 1995, *Diversity in Organisations: New Perspectives for a Changing Workplace*, London: Sage

Church of Scotland 1998, *A Policy for the Church of Scotland in relation to University Chaplaincy*, General Assembly of the Church of Scotland

Cockburn, C. 1991, *In the Way of Women: Men's Resistance of Sex Equality in Organisations*, London: Macmillan

Cohen, P. (ed.) 1995, *For a Multicultural University*, New Ethnicities Unit: University of East London, working paper no.3

———— 1995, 'The Crisis of the Western University' in Cohen, P. (ed.), *For a Multicultural University*, New Ethnicities Unit: University of East London, working paper no.3, pp.1-7

Cohn-Sherbok, D. and Lamb, C. (eds.) 1999, *The Future of Religion: Postmodern Perspectives*, Middlesex: Middlesex University Press

Committee for Higher Education of the Roman Catholic Bishops' Conference of England and Wales, 1997, *The Presence of the Church in the University Culture of England and Wales*, London: Bishops' Conference of England and Wales

Committee of Vice-Chancellors and Principals, 1998, *Extremism and Intolerance on Campus*, London: CVCP

Cortés, C. 1991, 'Pluribus & Unum: the Quest for Community Amid Diversity', *Change*, 23 (5):8-13

Davie, G. 1994, *Religion in Britain since 1945: Believing Without Belonging*, Oxford: Blackwell

———— 2000, *Religion in Modern Europe: a Memory Mutates*, Oxford: Oxford University Press

Davis, C. 1994, *Religion and the Making of Society: Essays in Social Theology*, Cambridge: Cambridge University Press

Demerath, J. *et al* (eds.) 1998, *Sacred Companies: Organisational Aspects of Religion and Religious Aspects of Organisations*, Oxford: Oxford University Press

Department for Culture, Media and Sport (with the Lambeth Consultation Group on the Millennium in association with the Inter Faith Network for the UK) 1998, *Marking the Millennium in a Multi-Faith Context*, DCMSSJO263NJ.3M

Dobbelaere, K. 1998, essay on 'Secularization' in Swatos, W. Jr (ed.), *Encyclopaedia of Religion and Society*, London: SAGE/AltaMira Press

Eade, J. 1993, 'The Political Articulation of Community and the Islamisation of Space in London', in Barot, R. (ed.), *Religion and Ethnicity: Minorities and Social Change in the Metropolis*, Kampen, The Netherlands: Kok Pharos Publishing House, pp.29-42

———— 1994, 'Identity, Nation and Religion: Educated Young Bangladeshi Muslims in London's "East End"', *International Sociology*, 9 (3):377-394

Earwaker, J. 1994, 'Cultured Chaplains', letter to *The Guardian*, 5th July

Fay, P. 1994, 'Increase in hospital chaplains', *Church Times*, 23rd December

Fern, R. 1997, 'Fathers say their prayers', *Guardian Higher*, 25th November

Filmer, P. 1997, 'Distinterestedness and the Modern University', in Smith A. and Webster, F., *The Postmodern University: Contested Visions of Higher Education in Society*, Buckingham: Society for Research into Higher Education and Open University Press, pp.48-59

Fineman, S. and Gabriel, Y. 1996, *Experiencing Organisations*, London: Sage

Forest Health Newsletter 1993, 18 (November)

Frankel B.G. and Hewitt W.E. 1994, 'Religion and Well-being Among Canadian University Students: the Role of Faith Groups on Campus', *Journal for the Scientific Study of Religion*, 33 (1):62-73

Frosh, S. 1991, *Identity Crisis: Modernity, Psychoanalysis and the Self*, London: Macmillan

Furlong, M. 2000, *C of E: The State It's In*, London: Hodder & Stoughton

Furniss, G. 1995, 'Religious Counselling and the Pluralistic American Context: the case of Hospital Pastoral Care'. Unpublished paper given at the annual meeting of the Religious Research Association (RRA), St Louis, MO, USA, 28th October

Galeotti, A.E. 1998, 'Toleration as the Public Acceptance of Difference', in Bauböck, R. & Rundell, J. (eds.), *Blurred Boundaries: Migration, Ethnicity, Citizenship*, Aldershot: Ashgate, pp.259-280

Garland, M. 1996, 'Newman in His Own Day', in Turner, F. (ed.), *John Henry Newman: The Idea of a University*, London: Yale University Press, pp.265-281

Gay, J. 1981, 'Religious Bias', in Warren-Piper D. (ed.), *Is Higher Education Fair?*, Guildford: Society for Research into Higher Education, pp.140-159

General Synod Board of Mission 1992, *Multi-Faith Worship: Questions and Suggestions from the Inter-faith Consultative Group*, London: Church House Publishing

Gibbon, P. 1992, 'Equal Opportunities Policies and Race Equality', in Braham P., Rattansi, A. and Skellington, R., *Racism and Antiracism*, London: Sage/Open University, pp.235-252

Gutman, A. (ed.) 1994, *Multiculturalism*, New Jersey: Princeton University Press

Habgood, J. 2000, *Varieties of Unbelief*, London: Darton, Longman and Todd

Hamilton, M. 1998, 'Secularisation: now you see it, now you don't', *Sociology Review*, 7 (4): 7-30

Hammond, P. 1965, 'Segmentation of Radicalism: the case of the Protestant Campus Minister', *The American Journal of Sociology*, LXXI (2):133-143

————— 1966, *The Campus Clergyman*, New York: Basic Books, Inc.

Harries, R. and Brichto, S. (eds.) 1998, *Two Cheers for Secularism*, Northamptonshire: Pilkington Press

Herberg, W. 1960, *Protestant Catholic Jew*, New York: Anchor Books

Heward, C. and Taylor P. 1993, 'Effective and Ineffective Equal Opportunities Policies in Higher Education', *Critical Social Policy*, 37:75-94

Hey, J. 1989, 'The Anglican Connection', in Brighton, T. (ed.), *The Church Colleges in Higher Education – 150 Years*, Chichester: West Sussex Institute of Higher Education, pp.58-69

Higgins, R. 1996, 'Human Rights', in Kuper A. and Kuper J (eds.), *The Social Science Encyclopaedia*, London: Routledge, pp.385-387

Higher Education Funding Council for England 1994, '*Overview of Recent Developments in HE*', report no. M2/94, Bristol: HEFCE

————— 1997, *Profiles of Higher Education Institutions*, Bristol: HEFCE

Hilpern, K. 1999, 'The Worker Within', *The Independent*, 3rd June, p.11

Hoekema, D. 1997, 'Politics, Religion, and Other Crimes Against Humanity', *Bulletin of Science Technology and Society*, 17 (2-3):73-6

Hogarth, T. 1997, *The Participation of Non-traditional Students in Higher Education*, HEFCE Research Series

Inayatullah, S. 1998, 'Alternative Futures of the University', *Futures*, 30 (7):589-602

Inner Cities Religious Council 1996, *Challenging Religious Discrimination: a Guide for Faith Communities and their Advisers*, London: Department of the Environment on behalf of the Inner Cities Religious Council

Ipgrave, M. 1996, *University Chaplaincy: the Inter-Faith Challenge*, unpublished presentation given at a consultation for recently appointed chaplains, Launde Abbey, Leicestershire, January 1996

Jackson, R. 1997, *Religious Education: An Interpretive Approach*, London: Hodder & Stoughton

Jacobson, J. 1998, *Islam in Transition: Religion and Identity among British Pakistani Youth*, London: LSE/Routledge

Jamieson, L. 1994, 'Putting God on the Shopping-list', *Church Times*, 16th December

Jenkins, D. 1988, 'What is the Purpose of a University – and what light does Christian faith shed on this question?', *Studies in Higher Education*, 13 (3):239-247

Jenkins, R. 1996, *Social Identity*, London: Routledge

Jenkins, T. 1997, 'People To Think With', London, *Church Times*, 30th October

————— 1999, *Religion in English Everyday Life: An Ethnographic Approach*, Oxford: Berghahn Books

Jewson, N. and Mason, D. 1992, 'The Theory and Practice of Equal Opportunities Policies', in Braham P., Rattansi, A. and Skellington, R., *Racism and Antiracism*, London: Sage/Open University, pp.218-234

Jewson, N. and Mason, D., with Bowen, R., Mulvaney, K. and Parmar, S. 1991, 'Universities and Ethnic Minorities: the Public Face', *New Community*, 17 (2): 183-199

Joly, D. 1995, *Britannia's Crescent: Making a Place for Muslims in British Society*, Aldershot: Avebury

Kaye, R. 1993, 'The Politics of Religious Slaughter of Animals: Strategies for Ethno-Religious Political Action', *New Community*, 19 (2):235-250

Kelly, P. 1998, 'Internationalisation and a Post-development Vision', *Futures*, 30 (7):739-744

Kennedy, D. 1995, 'A Cultural Pluralist Case for Affirmative Action', in Arthur, J. and Shapiro, A. (eds.), *Campus Wars: Multiculturalism and the Politics of Difference*, Oxford: Westview Press, pp.153-176

King, U. (ed.) 1990, *Turning Points in Religious Studies*, Edinburgh: T&T Clark

Kingston, P. 1994, 'The Lord is My Shepherd', *Guardian Higher*, 28th June

————— 1998, 'Forum for Peace', *Guardian Higher*, 22nd September

Kumar, K. 1997, 'The Need for Place', in Smith, A. and Webster, F. (eds.), *The Postmodern University: Contested Visions of Higher Education in Society*, Buckingham: Society for Research into Higher Education and Open University Press, pp.27-36

Kunda, A. 1994, 'The Ayodhya Aftermath: Hindu vs Muslim Violence in Britain', *Immigrants and Minorities*, 13 (1):26-47

Kundnani, H. 1999, 'A Fair Question', *The Guardian*, 10th February

Kuper, A. and Kuper, J. (eds.) 1996, *The Social Science Encyclopaedia*, London: Routledge

Legood, G. (ed.) 1999, *Chaplaincy: The Church's Sector Ministries*, London: Cassell

————— Legood, G. 1999, 'Universities', in Legood, G. (ed.), *Chaplaincy: The Church's Sector Ministries*, London: Cassell, pp.132-143

Lewis, P. 1994, *Islamic Britain: Religion, Politics and Identity among British Muslims*, London: I.B. Tauris

Longfield, B.J. and Marsden, G.M. (eds.) 1992, *The Secularization of the Academy*, Oxford: Oxford University Press

McClelland, V. 1973, *English Roman Catholics and Higher Education 1830-1903*, Oxford: Clarendon Press

Malik, S. 1998, 'Lord Nazir of Rotherham', in *Q News*, no.295, September, pp.10-12

Marsden, G.M. 1992, 'Introduction', in Longfield, B.J. and Marsden, G.M. (eds.), *The Secularization of the Academy*, Oxford: Oxford University Press, pp.3-8

————— 1994, *The Soul of the American University: From Protestant Establishment to Established Nonbelief*, New York: Oxford University Press

————— 1996, 'Theology and the University: Newman's Idea and Current Realities', in Turner, F. (ed), *John Henry Newman: The Idea of a University*, London: Yale University Press, pp.302-317

Marshall, G. (ed.) 1998, *Oxford Dictionary of Sociology*, Oxford: Oxford University Press, second edition

May, J. 1989, 'A Case Study: Derbyshire College of Higher Education', in Brighton, T. (ed.), *The Church Colleges in Higher Education: 150 Years*, Chichester: West Sussex Institute of Higher Education: 69-84

Milojevic, I. 1998, 'Women's Higher Education in the 21st Century', *Futures*, 30 (7):693-703

Modood, T. 1990, 'Catching up with Jesse Jackson: Being Oppressed and Being Somebody', *New Community*, 17 (1):85-96

————— 1993, 'The Number of Ethnic Minority Students in British Higher Education: some grounds for optimism', *Oxford Review of Education*, 19 (2):167-181

————— 1994a, *Racial Equality: Colour, Culture and Justice*, London: Institute for Public Policy Research

————— 1994b, 'Establishment, Multiculturalism and British Citizenship', *Political Quarterly*, 64 (4): 53-73

————— 1997, 'Culture and Identity', in Modood, T. and Berthoud R., with Lakey, J., Nazroo, J., Smith, P., Virdee, S. and Beishon, S., (eds.), *Ethnic Minorities in Britain: Diversity and Disadvantage*, London: Policy Studies Institute, pp.290-338

————— 1998a, 'Anti-Essentialism, Multiculturalism and the "Recognition" of Religious Groups', *Journal of Political Philosophy*, 6 (4):378-399

————— 1998b, 'Multiculturalism, Secularism and the State', *Critical Review of International Social and Political Philosophy*, 1 (3):79-97

Modood, T. and Shiner, M. 1994, *Ethnic Minorities and Higher Education – Why Are There Differential Rates Of Entry?*, London: Policy Studies Institute

Modood, T. and Werbner, P. (eds.) 1997, *The Politics of Multiculturalism in the New Europe: Racism, Identity and Community*, London: Zed Books Ltd.

Modood, T. and Berthoud R., with Lakey, J., Nazroo, J., Smith, P., Virdee, S. and Beishon, S. (eds.) 1997, *Ethnic Minorities in Britain: Diversity and Disadvantage*, London: Policy Studies Institute

Moeller, C. 1964, 'Religion and the Importance of the Humanist Approach', in Ross, M. *et al, Religion and the University*, Canada: University of Toronto Press, pp. 65-111

Mueen, N.S. 1993, 'A Conversation with Mahmud al-Rashid', *Q News*, 2:22

Murchland, B. (ed.) 1991, *Higher Education and the Practice of Democratic Politics*, Dayton OH: Kettering Foundation

Nadhi, F., 1994, 'Editorial', *Q News*, 23rd October

Neal, S. 1998, *The Making of Equal Opportunities Policies in Universities*, Buckingham: Society for Research into Higher Education/Open University Press

Nesbitt, E. 1998, 'British, Asian and Hindu: identity, self-narration and the ethnographic interview', *Journal of Beliefs and Values*, 19 (2):189-199

Nesbitt, E. and Jackson, R. 1993, *Hindu Children in Britain*, Staffordshire: Trentham Books

Nicholls, D. 1967, *Church and State in Britain Since 1820*, London: Routledge and Kegan Paul

Nielsen, J. 1992, *Islam, Muslims, and British local and central government: structural fluidity*, Centre for the Study of Islam and Christian-Muslim Relations, Selly Oak Colleges, Birmingham. Research paper no.6

————— 1995, *Muslims in Western Europe*, Edinburgh: Edinburgh University Press

Nye, M. 1996, 'Hare Krishna and Sanatan Dharma in Britain: the Campaign for Bhaktivedanta Manor', *ISKCON Communications Journal*, 4 (1):5-23

Pakes, A. 1999, 'Complain Please', *Times Higher Education Supplement*, 16th July

Parekh, B. and Bhabha, H. 1989, 'Identities on Parade', *Marxism Today*, June: 24-29

Parsons, G. (ed.) 1993, *The Growth of Religious Diversity: Britain from 1945, Volume 1 – Traditions*, London: Routledge in association with The Open University

Powney, J. and Weiner, G. 1992, *Outside of the Norm: Equity and Management in Educational Institutions*, London: South Bank University

Ragins, B.R. 1995, 'Diversity, Power and Mentorship in Organisations: a Cultural, Structural and Behavioural Perspective', in Chemers, M. *et al* (eds.), *Diversity in Organisations: New Perspectives for a Changing Workplace*, London: Sage, pp.91-133

Raza, M. 1991, *Islam in Britain: Past, Present and the Future*, Leicester: Volcano Press Ltd

Reid, H. and Burlet, S. 1998, 'A Gendered Uprising: Political Representation and Minority Ethnic Communities', *Ethnic and Racial Studies*, 21 (2):270-287

Ridley, S. 1989, 'Theological Perspectives over 150 Years', in Brighton, T. (ed.), *The Church Colleges in Higher Education: 150 Years*, Chichester: West Sussex Institute of Higher Education, pp.34-49

Riem, R. 1998, *An Examination of Values in Higher Education*, University of Nottingham

Rosaldo, R. 1994, 'Cultural Citizenship and Educational Democracy', *Cultural Anthropology*, 9 (3):402-411

Ross, M. *et al* 1964, *Religion and the University*, Canada: University of Toronto Press (for York University

Rowe, M. 1990, 'Barriers to Equality: The Power of Subtle Discrimination to Maintain Unequal Opportunity', *Employee Responsibilities and Rights Journal*, 3 (2):153-163

Runnymede Trust 1997, *Islamophobia: a challenge for us all*, London: Runnymede Trust

Russell, A. 1980, *The Clerical Profession*, London: SPCK

———— 1998, 'The Rise of Secularization and the Persistence of Religion', in Harries, R. and Brichto, S. (eds.), *Two Cheers for Secularism*, Northamptonshire: Pilkington Press

Rutherford, J. (ed.) 1990, *Identity: Community, Culture and Difference*, London: Lawrence and Wishart

Saifullah-Khan, V. 1974, *Pakistani Villagers in a British City – the World of the Mirpuri Villager in Bradford and in his Village of Origin*, Ph.D. thesis, University of Bradford

Sampson, C. 1982, *The Neglected Ethic: Religious and Cultural Factors in the Care of Patients*, Maidenhead: McGraw-Hill

Schogger, D. 1998, 'Moderate Muslim Students: Militants Cannot Halt Dialogue', *Jewish Chronicle*, 6th November 1998

Scott, P. 1997, 'The Postmodern University?', in Smith, A. and Webster, F. (eds.), *The Postmodern University: Contested Visions of Higher Education in Society*, Buckingham: Society for Research into Higher Education and Open University Press, pp.36-48

Senior, B. 1997, *Organisational Change*, London: Pitman Publishing

Sessa, V. and Jackson, S. 1995, 'Diversity in Decision-Making Teams', in Chemers, M. *et al* (eds.), *Diversity in Organisations: New Perspectives for a Changing Workplace*, London: Sage, pp.133-156

Sharpe, E. 1999, '"Time-honour'd Lancaster": Some Reminiscences', in Cohn-Sherbok, D. and Lamb, C. (eds.), *The Future of Religion: Postmodern Perspectives*, Middlesex: Middlesex University Press, pp.225-234

Sharp, K. and Winch C. 1994, 'Equal Opportunities and the Use of Language: a Critique of the New Orthodoxy', *Studies in Higher Education*, 19 (2):163-175

Singh, R. 1990, 'Ethnic Minority Experience in Higher Education', *Higher Education Quarterly*, 44 (4):344-359

Smith, A. and Webster, F. (eds.) 1997, *The Postmodern University: Contested Visions of Higher Education in Society*, Buckingham: Society for Research into Higher Education and Open University Press

Smith, A. and Webster, F. 1997, 'Changing Ideas of the University', in Smith, A. and Webster, F. (eds.), *The Postmodern University: Contested Visions of Higher Education in Society*, Buckingham: Society for Research into Higher Education and Open University Press, pp.1-15

Smith, D. 1989, *The Challenge of Diversity: Involvement or Alienation in the Academy*, ASHE-ERIC Higher Education Report No.5, Washington DC: George Washington University

———— 1994, 'Community and Group Identity: Fostering Mattering', in Brown, D.W. (ed.), *Higher Education Exchange*, Dayton, OH: Kettering Foundation, pp.29-35

———— 1995, 'Organisational Implications of Diversity in Higher Education', in Chemers, M. *et al* (eds.), *Diversity in Organisations: New Perspectives for a Changing Workplace*, London: Sage, pp.220-244

Smith, G. 1998, 'Ethnicity, Religious Belonging and Inter Faith Encounter: Some Survey Findings from East London', *Journal of Contemporary Religion*, 13 (3):333-353

Spickard, J. 1999, 'Human Rights, Religious Conflict and Globalisation: Ultimate Values in a New World Order', *MOST Journal on Cultural Pluralism*, 1:1 http://www.unesco.org./most/vl1n1spi.htm

Swatos, W. Jr (ed.) 1998, *Encyclopaedia of Religion and Society*, London: SAGE/AltaMira Press

Tajfel, H. and Turner, J.C. 1986, 'The Social Identity Theory of Intergroup Behaviour', in Worchel, S. and Austin, W. (eds.), *Psychology of Intergroup Relations*, Chicago: Nelson-Hall, pp.7-24

Taylor, R. 1988, 'The Queen's University of Belfast: the Liberal University in a Divided Society', *Higher Education Review*, 20 (2), pp.27-45

Thom, K. 1987, Summary of B. Morgan *Anglican University Chaplains: an Appraisal of the Understanding of Mission and Ministry in the work of Anglican University Chaplains in England and Wales 1950-1982*, Ph.D. thesis, University of Wales, 1986, London: Church of England

Thorne, H. 1998, *Chaplaincies in Multicultural Universities: a summary of the survey of staffing levels, space allocations and multicultural activity in English University Chaplaincies*, Surrey: Kingston University

Thornton, K. 1990, 'Interfaith Worship on Campus', *Cross Currents*, 40 (Spring), pp.27-33

Tinto, V. 1993, *Leaving College: Rethinking the Causes and Cures of Student Attrition*, Chicago: Chicago University Press

Tsui, A., Egan, T. and Xin, K. 1995, 'Diversity in Organisations: Lessons From Demography Research', in Chemers, M. *et al* (eds.), *Diversity in Organisations: New Perspectives for a Changing Workplace*, London: Sage, pp.191-219

Turner, F. (ed) 1996a, *John Henry Newman: The Idea of a University*, London: Yale University Press

———— 1996b, 'Newman's University and Ours', in Turner, F. (ed), *John Henry Newman: The Idea of a University*, London: Yale University Press

Ucko, P. 1994, 'Foreword', in Carmichael D., Hubert J., Reeves, B. and Schanche A. (eds.), *Sacred Sites, Sacred Places*, London: Routledge

UK Action Committee on Islamic Affairs (UKACIA), 1993, *Muslims and the Law in Multi-Faith Britain: need for reform*, London: UKACIA

Vertovec, S. and Peach, C. (eds.) 1997, *Islam in Europe: the Politics of Religion and Community*, London: Macmillan/CRER

Walker, A. 1994, 'Holy expendable?', *Times Higher Education Supplement*, 18th April

Waqar, I.A. and Husband, C. 1993, 'Religious Identity, Citizenship, and Welfare: the case of Muslims in Britain', *The American Journal of Islamic Social Sciences*, 10 (2):217-33

Warren-Piper, D. (ed.) 1981, *Is Higher Education Fair?*, Guildford: Society for Research into Higher Education

Webber, A. 1993, *The B'nai B'rith Hillel Foundation 1953-1993*, London: Hillel Foundation

Weeks, J. 1990, 'The Value of Difference', in Rutherford, J. (ed.), *Identity: Community, Culture and Difference*, London: Lawrence and Wishart, pp.88-100

Weiner, G. 1998, '"Here a Little, There a Little": Equal Opportunities Policies in Higher Education in the UK', *Studies in Higher Education*, 23 (3):321-333

Weinstock, D. 1998, 'How Can Collective Rights and Liberalism Be Reconciled?', in Bauböck, R. and Rundell, J. (eds.), *Blurred Boundaries: Migration, Ethnicity, Citizenship*, Aldershot: Ashgate, pp.281-304

Weller, P. 1990, 'The Rushdie Affair, Plurality of Values and the Ideal of a Multi-Cultural Society', *Navet Papers*, 2 (October): 1-12

———— 1992a, 'A New Way Forward in Church and Higher Education?', *Collegium*, 1 (2):64-73

———— 1992b, 'Religion and Equal Opportunities in Higher Education', *Journal of International Education*, 3 (3):53-64

———— 1997, (ed.) *Religions in the UK: a Multi-Faith Directory*, Derby: Derby University and Inter Faith Network for the UK, second edition

Wheeler, C. and Schmalzbauer, J. 1996, 'Between Fundamentalism and Secularization: Secularizing and Sacralizing Currents in the Evangelical Debate on Campus Lifestyle Codes', *Sociology of Religion*, 57 (3):241-257

Wildman, P. 1998, 'From the Monophonic University to the Polyphonic Multiversities', *Futures*, 30 (7):625-633

Williams, E. 1999, 'Angels in dirty places', *Times Higher Education Supplement*, 2nd July

Williams, J., Cocking, J. and Davies, L. 1989, *Words or Deeds: a Review of Equal Opportunities Policies in Higher Education*, London: Commission for Racial Equality

Wilson, B. 1966, *Religion in Secular Society*, London: Watts

Wittenberg, A. 1964, 'The Relationship between Religion and the Educational Function of the University', in Ross, M. *et al*, *Religion and the University*, Canada: University of Toronto Press (for York University, UK), pp.111-128

Wolfe, J. 1998, 'Rabbi wins battle for kosher flats', *Jewish Chronicle*, 23rd October

Worrall, B.G. 1988, *The Making of the Modern Church: Christianity in England Since 1800*, London: SPCK

Wright, P. 1985, *Going Public*, report of the National Consultation of Polytechnic Chaplains

Yaqub, S. 1998, 'Universities dance to Zionist tune', *Q News*, August 1994, no.294

Young, I.M. 1995, 'Social Movements and the Politics of Difference' in Arthur, J. and Shapiro A., *Campus Wars: Multiculturalism and the Politics of Difference*, Oxford: Westview Press

Young, K. 1992, 'Approaches to Policy Development in the Field of Equal Opportunities', in Braham P., Rattansi, A. and Skellington, R., *Racism and Antiracism*, London: Sage/Open University, pp.252-270

Zald, M. and McCarthy, J. 1998, 'Religious Groups as Crucibles of Social Movements', in Demerath, J. *et al* (eds.), *Sacred Companies: Organisational Aspects of Religion and Religious Aspects of Organisations*, Oxford: Oxford University Press, pp.24-49

Index